THE FASCINATING DOMINICAN REPUBLIC

Julie!
Thank you for all you did for me in this new chapter in my life!
Steve

ESTEVE REDOLAD

The Fascinating Origin of the Dominican Republic
All Rights Reserved.
Copyright © 2022 Esteve Redolad
v3.0

The opinions expressed in this manuscript are solely the opinions of the author and do not represent the opinions or thoughts of the publisher. The author has represented and warranted full ownership and/or legal right to publish all the materials in this book.

This book may not be reproduced, transmitted, or stored in whole or in part by any means, including graphic, electronic, or mechanical without the express written consent of the publisher except in the case of brief quotations embodied in critical articles and reviews.

Outskirts Press, Inc.
http://www.outskirtspress.com

ISBN: 978-1-9772-4845-9

Cover Photo © 2022 www.gettyimages.com. All rights reserved - used with permission.

Outskirts Press and the "OP" logo are trademarks belonging to Outskirts Press, Inc.

PRINTED IN THE UNITED STATES OF AMERICA

[After] a foreign power's interference, a bloody revolution, a total victory, frequent bonds between the two peoples long separated, a community of ideas in the struggle, a unity of aspirations, signs of friendship, help and compassion amid the trials, must we revive old hates that should be extinguished, never to be reborn? Organization and outrage continued in the town, in the center of the island, and all across the territory. For how long will parties toy with the destiny of these two pueblos? When will these wicked idols fall from their pedestals?

       Newspaper *La Regeneración* September 1865[1]

Table of Contents

Acknowledgements i
Introduction iii

PART ONE. Colonization and exploitation of the island of
Hispaniola (1492-1606) 1
1. How, and Why, Columbus Found the Caribbean 3
2. Exploration and Exploitation of the Antilles 10
3. The Americas, Fair Game for European Powers 25
4. Colonial Expansion and Exploitation of the Island 28
5. Problems with the Native Slaves 35
6. African Slaves in Hispaniola 43
7. Loss of Influence of Hispaniola 50
8. Spain Tries to Protect Its Interests in the Indies 53
9. Osorio's "Devastaciones" (1606) 60

PART TWO. Saint Domingue, slavery, races, and revolutions
(1606 - 1821) 63
1. The Origin of Saint Domingue 65
2. One Island and Two Colonial Systems 72
3. Slavery in Santo Domingo and in Saint Domingue 77
4. The Slave Revolution in Saint Domingue 83
5. The Conflict Between France and Spain 96

6. The Treaty of Basel (1795) 102
7. Toussaint Louverture, A French General Against French Power 110
8. Napoleon Changes Toussaint's Plans 121
9. French Invasion of Santo Domingo 128
10. Slavery and Blackness in Santo Domingo 134
11. Santo Domingo Feels Spanish Again 136
12. La España Boba (Meek Spain) 141

PART THREE. Three declarations of independence in search
of an identity (1821-1865) 145
1. First Independence (1821) 147
2. Official Independence (1844) 163
3. The Annexation Period 186
4. Opposition to Annexation 208
5. The Restoration War 217
6. Third and Final Independence (1865) 221

Epilogue 238
Timeline 241
Bibliography 244
Notes 245

Acknowledgements

This is a free version of the book, originally written in Spanish, that I had the privilege to write in 2019.

While I did receive a lot of help and advice back then, writing in English was a significant new challenge for me - as English is my third language - a challenge that I could only face with the help of many. I want to acknowledge and thank all those who have helped me in writing this English version, especially Rev. Robert Fictum, Rev. Tom Suriano, Jackie Slana, Kathryn Lalonde and Rev. Steven Avella among others. While their generous and dedicated help has made this book a good read, they are in no way responsible for any inaccuracies, mistakes or errors which are solely and entirely my own.

Likewise, I would like to thank the World Mission Ministries Office of the Archdiocese of Milwaukee, especially its Director Dr. Antoinette Mensah, for encouraging and supporting this project.

This book is a summary of the work of many dedicated scholars. I am extremely thankful for their research that I have used to build this narrative. I have utilized mainly the works of Anne Eller (*We Dream Together*), Orlando Inoa (*Historia Dominicana*),

Frank Moya (*Manual de historia dominicana*), Graham Nessler (*An Islandwide Struggle for Freedom*) and Hugh Thomas (*La trata de Esclavos* and *El Imperio Español*).

Esteve Redolad, 2021

Introduction

Among the many thousands of islands that exist in the world, eighteen of them are split by political lines into two countries.[2] But in only one of these islands, neither of the two countries that make up the island possess any other territory outside of it. The island was called Haiti, then Hispaniola or Quisqueya, and now it belongs to two countries: the Dominican Republic and the Republic of Haiti. They share 29,398 sq. miles of land and many stories.

These two countries have different languages and different traditions. While the Dominican Republic has one of the highest economic growth rates in Latin America, Haiti is at the bottom of the development index. Ethnically, the population in the Dominican Republic is mostly mulatto, while in Haiti the population is primarily black. In the former, they speak Spanish; in the latter, Creole. These are important differences but somehow merely accidental. Some other disparities have more dangerous implications, such as stories and legends of old wounds, insults, and battles, which feed and perpetuate social prejudices in both directions.

When we see the disparities between the two countries, the question naturally pops up: What happened here? Why is Creole spoken in Haiti? Why was the Dominican Republic the only country in Latin America that did not become independent from Spain or Portugal?

As is often the case, there are no simple answers to these questions. The good news is that, although they are not simple, the answers are fascinating.

This book is not intended to be a treatise about Dominican history nor an exhaustive or academic work. From a primary bibliography, it will convey and review how fascinating the events that happened in the Dominican Republic were, and with it also in Haiti, since, as neighbors, their stories are often intertwined. These pages do not explain a tale of heroes and villains but stories of people who jumped on the bandwagon of history with their contradictions and doubts, as we all have. It is a story of fratricidal rivalries, cruel confrontations and battles, unexpected betrayals, unlikely alliances, tragic decisions, and shared ideals. A story that, like life itself, is fascinating.

PART ONE
COLONIZATION AND EXPLOITATION OF THE ISLAND OF HISPANIOLA (1492-1606)

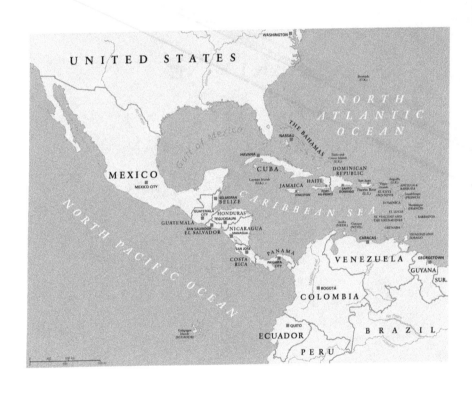

1.

How, and Why, Columbus Found the Caribbean

Constantinople and the price of pepper in 1453

Constantinople, today's Istanbul, is a beautiful city in Turkey located right between Europe and Asia. The city was founded around 700 BC, before even some books of the Old Testament were written. Due to its strategic location, Istanbul was crucial for trade, especially in spices such as ginger, cinnamon or cloves, transported from Asia to Europe via Istanbul. Europe's obsession with importing spices was not trivial, it was one of the few methods available to preserve food and, for some, it meant a very profitable enterprise. In 1511, you could buy a kilo (2.2 pounds) of pepper for a gram (0.04 ounces) of silver in the Far East and then sell it in Europe for thirty grams of silver,[3] a 3,000% profit.

In the first half of the 15th century, the major trade routes between South Asia and Europe were controlled by the Ottoman Empire, except for the city of Constantinople, still the capital of the Eastern Roman Empire under the rule of the Christian Emperor, Constantine XI. In 1453, after a siege that lasted for months, the emperor finally lost the city to the Ottomans. The new owners were Muslims, who did not fare well with Christian Europe. Thus, the last and most crucial direct trade route with Asia was shut down. Europe was forced to look for new routes to the East.

Looking for an alternate route to Asia

The Portuguese found a route around Africa. Not a simple undertaking, considering that they had to navigate more than 12,000 miles, anchoring, of course, at several ports on the African coast.

There was another way. It was somewhat uncertain since no one had ever tried it before. In 1492, Christopher Columbus, an expert Genoese (Italy) navigator, adventurous and ambitious, was looking for someone to finance his revolutionary project: to reach India by sailing West. Although by then, to the wise and knowledgeable, it was known that the earth was spherical; in the popular imagination, the Earth was as flat as it seems when you walk on it, until proven otherwise. At its edges, the oceans ended in impressive waterfalls where there were all kinds of monsters and dangers. Any person wanting to go in that direction could only be considered out of their mind. It could only be the measure of human stupidity and a guaranteed call for misfortune.

However, for the Spanish monarchs, it was a risk worth taking. To open a direct route to India was a priceless advantage, and they decided to sponsor Columbus' trip.

Understandably, the sailor's adventure did not instill much confidence among people. As the ships were leaving the port to the Indies, those present were not prone to much fanfare as for them the crew could be considered already dead.[4]

Nevertheless, under the Spanish flag, Christopher Columbus, named Admiral of the Ocean Sea by the Catholic Monarchs, dared to sail West, convinced that he would find the Indies. Columbus only made two miscalculations: one almost killed him, the second one, undoubtedly, saved him.

Columbus' first mistake

The admiral's first mistake was calculating the circumference of the Earth as one third smaller than it is. It's a bit like mistaking a baseball for a softball. According to his calculations, India was supposed to be 2,680 miles away from Spain, when in fact, the eastern coast of Japan is 12,240 miles away from the Iberian Peninsula. Proportionally, and using Dominican geography, it is as if someone traveling from *San Cristóbal* believes that has arrived to *Punta Cana* (133 miles) when in fact has only reached *Santo Domingo Este* (33 miles). Or for Midwesterners, imagine somebody is convinced that Minneapolis is somewhere in the Madison area. It was not an innocent mistake. He kind of asked for it. It turns out that two hundred years before Christ, in Greece, a certain Eratosthenes quite accurately calculated that Earth had a circumference of 25,000 miles. Unfortunately, for his contemporaries, a sphere of that size was too large to conceive. Due to this scientific bias, other astronomers took the task of repeating observations and calculations to determine a more "plausible" size. That is why they finally concluded, erroneously, that the Earth had a circumference of 18,000 miles. This one, for them was a more reasonable measure, and was therefore popularly accepted. Columbus opted for this second theory and based his calculations in preparation for the journey upon it.

Columbus's second mistake

The second error was not due to some biased miscalculation, but solely to lack of knowledge: he did not know, and therefore he did not expect, that on his journey he would stumble upon an entire continent. Not even on his deathbed was Columbus aware that he had reached a new continent. He always believed that the land he was settling in were islands in China, and that he had reached Asia from the Eastern side.

Crossing the Atlantic

In all fairness we should say that Columbus discovered America in the exact same way the natives -Taino, Caribs and other tribes- in turn, "discovered" him. Obviously, he was not the first person to reach the New World. If that had been case, he would have found nobody upon arrival. The natives arrived there some thousand years earlier, ironically, from Asia, by hiking, not sailing, over the ice near the North Pole.

Columbus had not even been the first European to arrive to the continent. There is evidence that by 1000AD, some Vikings from northern Europe reached present-day Canada, though they never intended to establish settlements. Rather, they went to stock up on fish and secure a supply of wood.[5]

We should, however, recognize Don Cristóbal Columbus's merits. On September 6, 1492, he and his crew headed West from the Canary Islands towards the unknown, sailing through the Atlantic Ocean, also bleakly known as the Sea of Darkness[6] (*Mare Tenebrosum*). The adventure was dangerous as both the destination and the duration of the journey were, in a very literal and scary way, uncharted territory. After sailing for 30 days, Asia was not yet in sight. At last, three days later, they saw land. We know they did not land in Asia, but we are not sure the exact spot of the Lesser Antilles where they first landed.

Columbus arrives at the Lesser Antilles (1492)

The expedition landed at dawn on October 12. With much solemnity and ceremonies -including flags and notaries- they took possession of the land in the name of the Spanish Crown. All this, under the astonished gaze of the natives,[7] who did not know if to laugh at the beards of those characters in ridiculous robes or to take refuge in fear. Incidentally, since the explorers were convinced that they had reached the Indies, the native tribes would be known as "Indians" not only in Spanish but also in English, perpetuating thus a fateful mistake for five hundred years and counting.

Just two days after arriving at the Lesser Antilles, Columbus and his men captured seven natives and "suggested" they travel back to Castile to learn Spanish and work as translators on future travels. We have no idea how he communicated all this, but what seems certain is that the Admiral was not wasting time! It is hard to imagine what could be going through the minds of those seven people as they were observing such an odd character. As events unfolded, two of the seven managed to escape, while the other five actually did go to Spain to learn Spanish.[8]

The *"conquistador"* was a man of character. Even before arriving on the island of Haiti (later on, Hispaniola), he was planning a way to take the entire population of natives to Castile, presumably as slaves. We do not know where the idea came from, or if he had any notion of how many people he was talking about, but he estimated that with 50 armed men he could dominate all the natives.[9]

At the same time, though, Columbus seemed to be somewhat confused. He had a letter from the king of Spain himself to be handed over to the Great Khan,[10] the highest authority in Asia, but even though Columbus was convinced that he was in Asia, he hesitated to deliver the letter to the "Indians." Who knows? Perhaps he considered that those people did not seem drawn to grand ceremonies and solemnities as the occasion would require. The letter was thus kept, for another, maybe more solemn, opportunity.

La Hispaniola at last

On December 5, 1492,[11] after almost a month wandering about the Caribbean islands, Columbus reached the island of Haiti, which means "land of mountains" in the Taíno language. The island is also known as Quisqueya. This name, initially used in 1865, is an indigenous name that allegedly refers only to the modern Spanish side of the island as opposed to the Haitian side. It was made famous by Emilio Prud'Homme's verses sung in the Dominican National Anthem.[12] Be that as it may, in 1492 its original native name was promptly changed to La Hispaniola.

On December 13, a week after their arrival, the expedition had already moved inland to inspect the territory. Just three days later, Columbus had an interview with the local chief, or *cacique*, Guacanagarix.[13] These two would be the central characters of the first business transaction between two worlds, completely unknown to each other a mere month and three days before. The *cacique* supplied the ship *La Niña* with cassava, yams, and peppers. In exchange for all that, he received one of Columbus' shirts.[14] It is, perhaps, the most expensive shirt in history. By the unbalanced nature of the transaction, we can grasp how things were going to be in the future.

The swapping of products and practices started quickly. In fact, only two weeks after Columbus' landing, the sailor Rodrigo de Jerez became the first Spaniard to see the natives smoking tobacco. Of course, he was the first European to imitate them only sixteen days after arriving at the New World.[15] Another interesting tradition the Spaniards noticed was the ornaments and jewelry made of pure gold that were used by the natives. That certainly gave them an extra incentive to be interested in that new place.

The Spanish explorers did not know exactly where they landed. They were sure it was Asia, although not the continent. But by then, they had enough information about the place and the exact location. It was time to go back to Spain and plan for a second trip. Then an incident happened that changed the history of Hispaniola.

Preparations to return to Spain and a change of plans

By New Year's Eve of 1492 as the Spanish expedition was ready to return home, the largest of Columbus' ships tragically struck a coral reef off the north coast of Hispaniola near to today's *Cap-Haïtien*. It was a bit like the Titanic: less dramatic, no ice, no victims, and no movie, but the consequences would be quite significant. The ship that ran aground could no longer be used.

With one less ship, there was no room for all the sailors to return to Spain. The incident forced Columbus to leave thirty-nine men behind. Using the remains of the grounded ship, they built a military garrison named *Fuerte Navidad* (Fort Christmas), because, well, it was Christmas time. He instructed those who remained to continue collecting gold samples and to wait for another Spanish expedition to arrive.[16] Once left alone, however, the men did not wait. Sure enough, one year later, by the time the Spaniards returned on their second trip, all of the men in *Fuerte Navidad* were found dead.

Shortly we will see what happened to them, but for now it's worth noting that the decision to build a fort on the island somehow changed the initial purpose of the Spanish presence in the New World. As you recall, the goal of the expedition was to look for a new passage to ensure a fluent trade with the Indies. However, what started as a journey to open new trade routes became a journey for conquest and settlement in the new land.

2.

Exploration and Exploitation of the Antilles

Columbus' second trip (1493-1496)

Once in Spain, Columbus met with the monarchs and made proper arrangements for a second trip. Since they already knew their destination, this time, he planned the journey resolutely. The plan was simple: to expand, exploit and conquer. The commercial needs of the first voyage seemed to be of secondary importance. Now it was about taking possession and exploiting the island's resources.

The travelers on the second trip

One year after his first voyage, Columbus returned to Hispaniola. The expedition this time was considerably larger: seventeen ships and 1,500 travelers with the intention of exploring and colonizing the territories that had been "discovered" the year before. The Spaniards brought with them -and introduced to the Americas- pigs, horses, cows and wheat. They also brought an essential product that settled quite easily on the new lands and would become crucial in Dominican history: sugar cane,[17] originally from New Guinea, 10,000 miles from Hispaniola.

Among the passengers on this second trip were nobles, masons and carpenters, some traveling with their wives and families. Most of them, however, were farmers who hoped to mine gold and earn easy money in the new promised land. Columbus, on the other hand, was hoping to establish a commercial colony.[18] There were also priests on board. They celebrated the first mass in the New World, presided by Fr. Pedro Arenas and joined by Fr. Bernardo Boyl, who would become one of Columbus' staunch enemies (as we will explain later). Do you recall those five natives who were supposed to go to Spain to learn the language? They did go and now were on board coming back home as translators.[19]

On a curious note, among those intrepid adventurers, we also find the first tourist to the New World. It was the rich and pious abbot of Lucerne. He crossed the ocean to the Caribbean, going through uncountable hardships, solely for the pleasure of seeing something new.[20] Little could he imagine that after 500 years, tourism would be one of the most important sources of income for the island. In 1984, 560,000 tourists visited the Dominican Republic. Thirty years later (2017) the visitors reached six million.[21]

Second arrival to Hispaniola

Before reaching Hispaniola for a second time, the fleet arrived at some of the Lesser Antilles' islands, where they took thirty natives,[22] most likely as slaves. When they finally disembarked at Hispaniola, they saw the disaster: *Fuerte Navidad* was totally destroyed. What was left of the *Fuerte* and the men was a rather unpleasant landscape. Some of the Spaniards were furious and wanted immediate and swift revenge. Others, more cautious, were hoping to know what happened.[23] It seems that the group of men who were left behind explored the area, as instructed, but not only to find gold but also to capture some women. The natives, of course, saw their uninvited guests as a threat and decided to finish them off. Little did they imagine that other bearded and odd men were going to return. And return they did on November 27, 1493. There was no immediate retaliation, but the seed of mistrust was already planted on both sides.

Eleven days after their second arrival, on December 7, 1493, perhaps realizing that the place was not safe, Columbus set sail along the coast, all seventeen ships searching for a better site to settle. They spent an entire month looking for *"posada."*[24]

The group was battered. They had been at sea for more than seventy days and that was no cruise line. To live in the ships was a source of great discomfort. They were crammed in and survived next to a wide variety of cargo needed to establish a colony, including working tools and all sorts of domestic and farm animals. Each ship carried an average of ninety people, but cattle used most of the space on deck.[25] The seeds, carried to plant new crops, were beginning to rot, many animals were ill, the ships were in very poor condition, and food was scarce. Let's keep in mind that the travelers were not just rough seamen as in the first expedition, so it is not surprising that at this point they were desperate and eager to set anchor anywhere to end the nightmare. At last, Columbus decided to disembark at the mouth of the Bajabonico River. The place could not have been worse. It was an unprotected area, highly unsanitary and the soil was barren. To make matters worse, they had no idea where the alleged gold mines could be.[26] Nonetheless, they disembarked and named the place La Isabela. The history of the first Spanish settlement in the New World was about to be very short: after six years it was abandoned entirely.

The foundation of La Isabela *(1494)*

On January 6, 1494, La Isabela (named in honor of the Spanish Queen, Isabel) was officially founded. It was the first European settlement in what is today the American continent.

La Isabela had about 200 huts and occupied about two hectares. That is the size of today's Quisqueya Juan Marichal stadium in the city of Santo Domingo (about two American football fields). The town included warehouses and a church where priests celebrated the first mass on the very same day of its foundation. Of course, of all the houses, the biggest was Admiral Columbus', an early sign that the European social structures were to be perpetuated in the New World.

Columbus' men promptly began to work on what they were most interested in: the search for gold. They did find some, with the help of native Taínos, but not as much gold as they were hoping to obtain. The systematic scarcity of gold over the years became a recurring challenge in the history of colonization. They did, however, keep finding enough of it to maintain their hopes alive and continue searching for more.

About a year after its foundation, in March 1495, Columbus left La Isabela with 200 men, twenty horses and twenty dogs to explore the interior of Hispaniola. He had the help of the local chief, Guacanagarix (the one who bought Columbus' shirt), who, very conveniently for Columbus, was a staunch enemy of chief Caonabo,[27] allegedly responsible for the *Fuerte Navidad* massacre.[28]

With all these new movements and allegiances, the natives, especially the Taínos, were probably puzzled about their peculiar and uninvited guests.

Taínos, Caribs and other native tribes

The life of the natives was by no means a bed of roses (not even of *Bayahíbe* roses which would later become the Dominican Republic's national flower). There were almost constant conflicts and wars between the different chiefdoms and between tribes. Some say that were it not for the Spanish invasion, the Taínos most probably would have obliterated the Siboney tribe, and the Caribs, in turn, would have annihilated the Taínos.[29]

However, the small population, compared to the enormous territory and the abundance of resources, allowed them to have a relatively peaceful life. They lived on fish and local fruits and produce. The Spaniards found pineapple so succulent that they called it *"the queen of all fruit."*[30]

Taíno society was highly organized. At the time of Columbus' arrival, they were organized in five great confederations, led by chiefs or *caciques*. Under them were other minor chieftains. The names of the five *caciques* were Guarionex, Caonabo, Bohechío, Guacanagarix and Cayacoa.[31] Some of them would become main characters of a story that, not even in their wildest dreams, could they have ever imagined.

What happened to the natives?

The fate of the natives on the island is often the subject of heated debate. Some believe the *conquistadores* were the direct and immediate cause of the natives' extinction. A more moderate opinion is that the ethnic agony of the Taíno people was spread out over several decades and could be attributed to several factors. The answer is probably somewhere in between. Two things we know for sure: one, the Taínos disappear soon after the arrival of the Spaniards, and two, in a very real way, they are still present on the island until today. And there is no contradiction in saying this.

Let us see number one: The Spaniards did not systematically exterminate the Taíno population; however, the natives' numbers were drastically reduced and they eventually became extinct a few decades after the conquistadors' arrival. That was basically due to lack of food, the hard-working conditions to which they were subjected, and to illnesses. From 1494 to 1508, a period of just fourteen years, the numbers of "Indians" declined from 377,500 to 59,000.[32] (85% of them died). That's an average of 24,000 people per year.

Number two: Although is not often mentioned, we know that miscegenation (some would say mixed marriages) was an early phenomenon in the island. As early as 1495, some men from Columbus' expedition settled inland with native women.[33] Many Spanish colonists partnered with Taíno women, because there were few European women, and because in their sexist mentality the conquerors probably would have not much regard towards native women's opinions. It is worth noting that by 1514, around half of the Spaniards in Hispaniola had indigenous wives.[34] That same year, the King of Spain issued a royal decree authorizing the marriage of Spanish men to Indian women.[35] As we can see, the theory of the Taíno decimation is true inasmuch as traditions, language and culture disappear but, in all probability, most Dominicans have indigenous DNA in their blood. Arguably, as far as the "amount" of native DNA is concerned, and considering the massive increase in population, there might be more native DNA overall now than before the Spaniards' arrival.

Besides the DNA, the Taíno culture has left a handful of words that have made it to the 21st century, and are embedded in Spanish (and English) vocabulary such as hammock (*hamaca*), hurricane (*huracán*), canoe (*canoa*), savanna (*sabana*) and tobacco (*tabaco*).[36]

About the conquistadores

Columbus was an accomplished navigator but not a very good ruler. He could not control the constant abuse of his men towards the natives and he lacked experience in civil administration and political skills.[37]

He did not have it easy. For conquerors and sailors, decorum and etiquette were not the most common attributes. They were even lacking among the noblemen. In fact, the primary motivation for most of the men who settled in La Isabela was ambition and power. And that, as we all know, can corrupt even the most well-intentioned person. Some witnesses complained about the men asserting that they *"had no idea of what to do, and the only thing they were expecting was to be paid."* Columbus was also the target of bitter complaints, namely that despite being an experienced sailor, his *"main goal was to mine gold in Hispaniola and assign local chiefs to collect it and deliver it to him as a tribute."*[38]

Another informative testimony explained this about the men and their mission:

> *They are the sort of men who have no intention of converting the Indians or colonizing and remaining in the land. They are only driven by the desire to find gold or any type of wealth. They subordinate honor, morality, and honesty to this end, and they commit all kinds of fraud and countless other crimes to achieve it.*[39]

At the same time, these critical voices had this to say about the natives: *"It was not that they were weak, in fact, they were far from being weak, they were basically kind."*

There were two other important facts that certainly did not help to ease the tension with the natives: one, the crude reality that the allegedly nearby gold mines were nowhere to be found, and two, the fact that after sailing for two solid months, the mariners had not yet been paid.

Columbus' first enemies

Under these circumstances, it is not surprising that the first conflicts the Spaniards encountered were not with the natives but among themselves. A certain Cuneo, an opponent of Columbus, recorded that several men tried to conspire against the Admiral during the journey. The conspiracy was revealed, and Columbus swiftly crushed the revolt. He ordered some of the traitors to be flogged, others had their ears or their noses cut off, and some were hanged.[40] It should not come as a surprise that, as the situation was getting so out of hand, many settlers were already eager to return to Spain.[41]

Their opportunity arrived soon enough.

In mid-February 1494, out of dire necessity, Columbus had to send the king's representative, Antonio de Torres, back to Spain with a letter asking the monarchs to please send the wages for the sailors and food. Torres set sail with as many as 12 ships, leaving only five behind. The exodus of Spaniards was substantial. Besides Columbus' letter asking for money and food, Torres traveled with 250 settlers, probably overwhelmed from too many adventures and calamities. He also carried some gold, cinnamon, pepper, firewood, and 27 natives, as a way to compensate for the small amount of gold.[42] He also took 60 parrots. That was, probably, the trip that introduced syphilis to Europe.[43]

The exchange of products was already unstoppable. Fernando Colón, Columbus' son, reported as early as 1494 of a promising harvest of chickpeas, wheat, sugar cane, melons, cucumbers, and grapes near La Isabela.[44]

Columbus remained in La Isabela in command of 900 men, five ships and a settlement loaded with pessimism, uncertainty, and despair. Hunger made them more prone to diseases: many men were suffering from yellow fever, and syphilis affected nearly a third of the explorers.[45]

Columbus continues to explore

After spending five months on the island of Hispaniola, Columbus decided to set sail and continue his exploration of what he still considered the Indies. Perhaps a good psychologist at that time would have already noticed that his strength was navigation and exploration, not governance. But the lack of psychologists and the relentless ambition that too often has ruined so many good plans, got the best of him. In the following months, the Admiral would explore Cuba and Jamaica.

Columbus wanted to accomplish his dream, to reach the Asian continent. That was his goal. He was convinced that Hispaniola was a minor island of East Asia. As they sailed westward, in an act of apparent despair, he had the notary on board write an astonishing statement to be signed, under oath, by sailors and passengers. They were to swear that the land they were sighting was the edge of the Mangi province in Southern China, or perhaps Malaysia. Alas, it was present-day Cuba. Impressively, they all swore that were they to continue that course, they would have inevitably seen China. They also vowed to remain resolute in that opinion or else have their tongues cut off and (not *or*), pay a fine of ten thousand maravedis. The efforts of the natives to convince the explorer that those lands were in fact an island were in vain. It is indeed a remarkable anecdote to make us ponder about the reliability of the Admiral's reports. Predictably, all aboard signed the document except one. The Abbot of Lucerne, the first intercontinental tourist, who also joined that extra cruise to Cuba and Jamaica, refused to sign. The Abbot was the only one to admit that he had no idea where he was.[46] Truth be told, of course, no one knew.

It will not be until 1519 (20 years later), that in a decree establishing King Charles' sovereignty in the new, western territories the expression "West Indies" will be used to differentiate them from the "East Indies" (the genuine ones). Columbus died thirteen years before that decree.

Problems in La Isabela in the absence of Columbus

In the small town of La Isabela things were not going well. While Columbus was on discovery mode, he left his son, Diego, in charge. It was a risky move since the man was from Italy and barely spoke any Spanish.[47] To help him, or to control him (or both), a governing board was created to govern La Isabela.

In 1494, three ships loaded with supplies finally arrived from Spain. Among the newcomers was Bartolomé Colón, Christopher's younger brother. As the situation developed, there were sharp disagreements between the Columbus brothers and the local governing board, on account of the authoritarian ways the siblings were conducting themselves. The tension ran so high that, as the three ships were going back to Spain, Father Bernardo Boyl (the one who attended the first mass) and Captain Pedro Margarit joined the departing crew with the specific mission of reporting the matter to the Spanish monarchs.[48]

The natives are enslaved

Meanwhile, in his journeys through the other islands of the Caribbean, Columbus was providing himself with slaves for his new colony as the search for gold and other minerals required the extraordinarily harsh, and forced, labor of the natives. Since the natives of La Hispaniola were not numerous enough, people from other islands had to be used.[49]

As mentioned earlier, the fleet that arrived at La Isabela with supplies, and with Bartolomé Colón, went back to Europe. The metropolis expected the New World to bring some benefit. For sure, the 60 parrots brought to Spain on the first trip would have been very entertaining, but they would not do the trick. The expectation was to get gold home. But alas, gold in La Hispaniola was scarce. Paradoxically, if they had found all the gold they craved, most likely it would have lost its value. Someone has taken the time to calculate the volume of all the gold that has ever been mined worldwide throughout history; properly melted it would cover a soccer field with a three feet high golden layer.[50]

Columbus was so desperate to gain back the monarchs' favor and to save his reputation that he decided to compensate for the absence of precious metals with slaves. In a single raid, up to 1,660 men and women were captured and around 400 were sent to Seville.[51] Half of them froze to death during the journey.

For the ones who made it, Columbus' friend, Juanotto Berardi, was to negotiate their price with none other than Amérigo Vespucci,[52] whose name today shines immortal and proud over an entire continent. Interestingly, when he died in Seville, Vespucci left as part of his inheritance some property, including five slaves, two of them black, one Guanche (a native of the Canary Islands) and two a mixture of Spanish and guanche. Rumor has it that the latter could have been his natural children.[53]

War between conquerors and Taínos (1495)

On February 1495 Alonso de Ojeda, one of Columbus's companions and future explorer of what would later become Venezuela and Colombia, deceived the native chief Caonabo, inviting him to an encounter to discuss a peace agreement. He did not negotiate peace. Instead, he made Caonabo a prisoner at the Admiral's house in La Isabela. In retaliation for his imprisonment, Monicaotex, Caonabo's brother, allied with the chiefs Guarionex and Bohechío to wage war against the Spaniards.

Guacanagarix informed Columbus about the plan, and the Admiral decided to set out inland on a punitive expedition together with Bartolomé, Ojeda, and several natives, guided by Guacanagarix himself, subduing all who did not obey him. The raid lasted ten months.

On May 24, 1495, one of the bloodiest massacres against the natives of Hispaniola, known as the Battle of Santo Cerro, took place in present-day Vega Real valley. The Spaniards were outnumbered 10 to 1, but the lack of men was widely compensated by their weapons, horses and their use of Alano dogs, particularly trained for hunting people. The natives themselves described these dogs as a *"diabolical invention."* Besides, the soldiers of the small but experienced Spanish army were clad with iron armor and trained to kill, while the natives were naked, shooting arrows and using *"macanas"* (wooden batons). This is how 220 Spaniards defeated more than two thousand natives. Many were killed, others made prisoners and taken as slaves according to the testimony 21-year-old Bartolomé de las Casas[54] who was a lawyer and a companion of Columbus on his second trip. He later became a future advisor to governors, a priest, a historian, and always a fervent defender of the native Indians.

Meanwhile, Caonabo, one of the most valuable prisoners, was sent to Spain. Unluckily he drowned under mysterious circumstances in a shipwreck.[55] Some say, however, that he died on the journey and was simply thrown into the ocean. We will never know.

Taxing the natives

The open conflict changed everything. On March 30, 1495, the Catholic monarchs declared the island part of Spanish territory. With such a declaration, traveling to the West Indies (the Americas) was only allowed with a proper license.[56] Spain recognized the natives as Spanish citizens, which would give them some rights while making them liable to pay taxes. Sure enough, all natives ranging from 17 to 70 years old, had to pay the Spanish Crown regularly with products from each locality, be it gold, pesos or bales of cotton.[57]

By then, the atmosphere in the colony was very hostile. The Columbus brothers no longer had the prestige nor the authority they once enjoyed among the natives and the Spaniards. The Spanish monarchs knew it, and Christopher knew that they knew it. In an attempt to prevent the situation from getting completely out of hand, on March 10, 1496, Don Cristóbal left for Spain to defend himself before the monarchs.

The foundation of Santo Domingo

As Columbus was making the necessary arrangements for the journey, a young man from the Spanish province of Aragon named Miguel Díaz, approached him with an exciting story. He told him that, a few days before, he wounded a servant of Don Bartolomé Colón. Terrified by the consequences of the incident, the young man with five or six companions ran off from the settlement. Wandering the island, he arrived at the southern coast, near the mouth of the Ozama River, where some natives received them and gave them shelter and food for a time. The natives were ruled by a chief, a woman known as Catalina, who somehow felt attracted to the *Aragonés*. Fearful that the Spaniard would abandon her, she tried hard to find ways to persuade him to remain in that part of the island. To that effect, she informed him about rich gold mines in the vicinity. Díaz made inquiries about the wealth of the mines, observed the beauty of the countryside, the excellence of the Ozama River, and the safety of the natural harbor where it flowed.[58] Her plan worked. We do not know exactly what the Admiral's reaction to the story was. As he left for Spain, he left behind a very delicate situation at La Isabela and a beautiful tale of a promising place.[59] In his absence, this idyllic enclave would become the city of Santo Domingo.

The city of Santo Domingo was founded in 1496, only four years after the first arrival of the *conquistadores*, with the authorization of the monarchs and backed with a letter from Columbus himself. The new settlement was to be the new administrative center and capital instead of La Isabela. Two more cities, Santiago and Bonao would be founded the year after that. Still, most of the Spaniards in La Isabela moved to the new capital, which was constructed in a traditional grid shape.[60] By 1500 La Isabela was abandoned entirely. From then on, the name Santo Domingo would apply to the city and the entire island.

In that same year, on September 21, 1496, Fray Ramón Pané baptized the first native of the Americas.

Moving from La Isabela to Santo Domingo did not sit well with everyone. Francisco Roldán, who was the mayor, did not like it at all. He was enraged and accused Bartolomé of being *"stubborn, cruel, and greedy."*[61] Roldán, along with around 70 rebels, defying the authorities, left and settled in Xaragua (near present-day Léogane, in Haiti).[62]

Columbus' third trip (1498-1500)

By the time of Columbus' third voyage, recruiting sailors in Spain to cross the Atlantic was becoming a problem. The hardships and perils of life on the island were already known.[63] Ironically that was particularly true about the third journey that included an epidemic among the sailors. The crossing ended on July 31, 1498, as they reached the shores of the island of Trinidad. The expedition continued to the mouth of the Orinoco River, in present-day Venezuela, where for the first time the Spaniards touched continental land. It could have been a significant event, but it went uncelebrated since they were still oblivious of such an accomplishment. Had they been aware, they would have celebrated it most probably with pulque (or chichi), a local alcoholic beverage prepared with corn. Columbus had earlier introduced it to Spain and it was already abundant in Castile,[64] only six years since the arrival to the New World.

After one month exploring the Caribbean Sea, Columbus arrived at Hispaniola on August 30, 1498 and entered the new city of Santo Domingo. He soon realized that many settlers had died, about 160 were sick, and most alarmingly, many men had joined Roldán and his rebellion. Columbus' return could have turned the rivalry between the two leaders into an open struggle for power, but the Admiral ended the conflict in a surprising yet logical way. In an open confrontation, Roldán had the best chance to win, since he had the weapons from La Isabela. So, Columbus appointed Roldán as the Mayor of the island (the second most important judicial office), gave houses and land to the rebels, and granted permission to 15 of them to return to Spain.

Most of the rebels ended up settling in the central area of the island, while Roldán himself remained in Xaragua where according to his own words, *"the land was fertile, and you could find the most beautiful and well-fed women in the whole country."* These were the robust criteria of the *conquistadores*.

The natives of the Caribbean sail to Spain as slaves (1499)

The rebels returned to Spain in a fleet of two ships with some Spanish *hidalgos* and 330 native slaves, including women and children. As the vessels reached the port of Cádiz and the slaves were being disembarked, an exceptional person witnessed the episode. Luckily for the slaves and unfortunately for the traders, it was none other than Her Majesty *Isabel La Católica*. The Queen was upset, as she considered slavery an immoral practice. She was outraged to learn that slaves were handed over to people who were not among the nobility. So, without hesitation on July 20, 1500, by a royal decree, she ordered that all the Indians kidnapped by the *conquistadores* were to be returned to Hispaniola [65]

In addition to being direct witnesses to the slave trade, the Spanish royals were very much aware of the conflicts and complaints regarding the Columbus family. To settle the matter, they sent a judge and investigator, Don Francisco de Bobadilla. He arrived at Santo Domingo on August 23, 1500 as the new governor. One of his first gubernatorial acts was to arrest Christopher, Bartolomé and Diego Colón, and shipped them to Spain in chains where they arrived a month later.[66]

3.

The Americas, Fair Game for European Powers

Columbus' expeditions opened the door to a whole new world for Europe, a door that turned out to be much more extensive than anyone could have imagined. As much as the Spanish Crown tried to maintain control of the new territories, it was impossible to keep over 16 million square miles of land hidden or protected.

Columbus' navigational mistake in 1492 was logically a major setback in the plan to open a new commercial route to the Indies, but it offered a whole new market, new lands, and new resources not only for Spain but also for the rest of Europe. The new continent was so vast that Spain would not be able to claim it all for itself. There was just too much world to be "discovered" and too many people keen to pursue it. They did not know it back then, but to the West of Europe 25,000 miles of coastline were about to be opened for new dreams, adventures, and businesses.

The English and Portuguese

Five years after Columbus arrived in America, in 1497, Giovanni Caboto arrived at present-day Labrador in search of a commercial route to China. Labrador is on the East coast of present-day Canada. Caboto, like Columbus, was Italian, but his journey was sponsored by the English Crown. Accordingly, and following Eurocentric practice at the time, he claimed those lands for England.

Portugal also had its own "discoverer": Pedro Álvarez Cabral. Don Alvarez was heading towards the Cape of Good Hope, the southernmost tip of Africa, to surround the entire continent and move north following the East coast of Africa. From there, he was to continue the journey to India. But alas, as he was sailing south, he diverted the route and took a considerable detour of 1,400 miles and reached present-day Brazil. It is still debated among historians if Cabral reached Brazil purposely or by mistake.[67] Either way, his arrival to the Brazilian coasts, turned several thousand square kilometers of land into Portuguese soil by virtue of the Treaty of Tordesillas (1494), that divided the continent, still to be fully discovered, into Spain and Portugal. The Treaty was signed only, and very conveniently, by Castilians and Portuguese.

The legacy of Amerigo Vespucci

Another famous discoverer was Amerigo Vespucci, the man we found earlier in Spain, trading with Caribbean slaves. Vespucci not only had skills as a navigator, but he apparently was also a decent writer. Six texts attributed to him, though maybe written by a ghostwriter, narrate his (real or embellished) adventures. In his writings, he describes with great fervor the women he encountered during his travels.[68] Some of these stories were so fascinating that they became best sellers. His letter *Mundus Novus*, written in 1504, relates a Castilian expedition of 1497 and was translated into several languages.[69]

Vespucci is known, along with Ojeda (the one who captured Caonabo), for sailing along the coasts of present-day Colombia and Venezuela. On his trip along the coasts of Aruba he observed many natives living in houses *"planted at sea, as the city of Venice."* That's

THE AMERICAS, FAIR GAME FOR EUROPEAN POWERS

why they called those lands "Little Venice" or "Venezuela."[70]

But sure enough, what our friend Amerigo (which is Italian for Emery) is best known for is giving his name to an entire continent (and eventually a country). He was the first person of certain influence to realize that the lands being traveled by Europeans for several years were not part of the Indies, but a full-fledged new continent. To honor this "realization," it was later determined to call said continent "America."[71] The last "o" was changed to an "a" (a feminine termination in Latin), to be consistent with the other continents (Africa, Asia, Australia and Europa).[72]

The name of Columbus was not used for the continent, not out of contempt, but most probably because the cartographers genuinely believed that Vespucci was the first European to reach the continent.[73]

The first world map that included "America" was published in 1507. The map became quite popular, and around 1,000 copies were printed and distributed in Germany and other parts of Europe. What is intriguing is that it already included the Pacific Ocean. A surprising fact indeed if we consider that Vasco Núñez de Balboa was the first European who gazed at the Pacific…six years later! We do not know if the cartographer had some unknown information or new insights; or perhaps there were secret expeditions with unreported information.[74] The fact remains that there was an entire ocean appearing on a map before its existence was (officially) known.

Another remarkable fact about this map is that it is probably the most expensive map in history. In 2003 the United States Library of Congress paid $10,000,000 for it.[75]

We will soon return to the interests of international colonial powers in the New World, since it will be a determining factor for the future of the island. But for now, let us return to the events in Hispaniola.

4.

Colonial Expansion and Exploitation of the Island

In 1501 Br. Nicolás de Ovando became the governor of the island. His name is well known in the Colonial Zone of the City of Santo Domingo, as today, his Palace is a five-star hotel that bears his name. He was 52 years old when he succeeded Bobadilla, a controversial governor who lasted only one year. Ovando arrived at the island with 2,500 people in 26 ships, an impressive number, considering the Spanish population in Hispaniola was about three hundred inhabitants![76] Most of them lived in the city of Santo Domingo and in the urban centers of Concepción de la Vega, Bonao, Xaragua, and Santiago de los Caballeros (St. James of the Knights), named to honor the knights who moved from La Isabela to the new town.[77] Many of the settlers to these new towns were men who started families with native women.[78]

Ovando arrived not only with a good number of people but also with enough mulberry sprouts to start the production of silk and sugar cane. This crop was to become of enormous importance for the island's economy and history.

On September 3, 1501, the same day that Ovando was appointed governor, it was ordered by royal decree that any journey to the New

World required the authorization of the monarchs. Keep this fact in mind, because it will be of importance for the future of the island. The goal of the decree was to collect tariffs and to control the population in the new empire.[79]

Columbus' fourth voyage

The arrival of Ovando, however, did not end Columbus' story. Not at all. The Spanish courts punished the Admiral for his mismanagement in the affairs of Hispaniola, and he was prohibited, by the monarchs themselves, from disembarking at the island to avoid riots. He was allowed, however, to make a stopover for technical reasons. His holdings and property were taken from him, and he no longer had the exclusivity of the journeys to the New World. Others could sail to "discover" more land for Spain.

But Columbus was allowed to sail. On May 9, 1502, we find him leaving Spain yet again, sailing to the Lesser Antilles. As fate would have it, arriving at his destination, a storm left his ship in a sorry state, and he had no choice but to go to nearby Santo Domingo to repair the vessel. When the sailor asked permission to enter the port, Ovando, untrustingly, denied him entry.[80]

Ovando and a lesson about resentment

As it turns out, Columbus reached Santo Domingo when the 26 ships that had arrived with Ovando were about to return to Spain. The Admiral was probably, and understandably, upset for being banned from what he considered his island, but still had the good sense to advise Ovando to delay the departure of the fleet as a hurricane was advancing. Columbus preached by example and took refuge at the Azua de Compostela Bay. The storm found him there.[81] Ovando, on the contrary, did not listen to Columbus's recommendation and allowed the fleet to depart. You should blame resentment for this one. It was a total disaster. Out of 26 ships that left Santo Domingo, three managed to return to the damaged port of the city and only one made it to Spain. The rest disappeared in the storm that took, among many others, the former governor Bobadilla, the rebel Roldán and chief Guarionex.[82]

After the storm, Columbus was able to continue his journey to Jamaica and Cuba, and from there went southbound towards present-day Honduras. On August 1st, the first interaction between Europeans and Mayans took place. From there, he returned to Spain, where he died on May 20, 1506, oblivious to the fact that he had discovered a new continent for the Europeans, and convinced that he almost reached continental Asia.

It was not until 1521 that the Portuguese Fernando de Magallanes crossed the Pacific and arrived at the Philippines, being the first European to reach Asia traveling west, 29 years after Columbus' first journey.

Ovando and the 1503 massacre

Meanwhile, in Hispaniola Ovando seemed to be better at governing than Columbus and had a clearer idea of what the colony was supposed to look like. By use of force and violence, he managed to "pacify" the entire island of any indigenous insurrection. One of the best-known episodes is the cruel murder of Anacaona, the widow of the late Caonabo. Anacaona invited almost a hundred of her notables and other fellow Taínos to a party she gave in Ovando's honor. There was entertainment and dancing amidst a friendly atmosphere and a celebration that went on for three days. Suddenly a rumor began to circulate among the Spaniards that their hosts were planning a conspiracy. That kind of unconfirmed, and suspiciously convenient, rumor would play a special role in the Spanish conquest of the Americas.

Perhaps the rumors were justified, since the natives vastly outnumbered the Spaniards, who feared a possible attack in the middle of the night. Ovando then treacherously suggested a display of weapons from both sides. The natives loved the idea. But at Ovando's agreed signal, (laying his hand on the golden cross of the Order of Alcántara), his men opened fire. The cavalry surrounded the *caciques* and prevented anyone from escaping. Then they set the place on fire. Anacaona was arrested and hanged in the Plaza de Santo Domingo, for rebellion. From then on, no one threatened the authority of the Governor of the island. All the *caciques* that Columbus knew between 1492 and 1494 had died.[83]

New towns in Hispaniola

During Ovando's era there was an expansion of new settlements. By 1508 seventeen cities were already created. The oldest were: La Vega, Santiago, Bonao and Santo Domingo. Other cities founded during Ovando's time were: Buenaventura, Salvaleón de Higüey (Higüey), Santa Cruz de Haniguayana (or Icayagua), El Seibo, Cotuí, San Juan de la Maguana, Azua de Compostela, Puerto Real, Lares de Guahaba, Santa María de la Vera Paz, Villanueva de Yaquimao and Salvatierra de la Sabana.[84] The last five were located in present-day Haiti. Ovando also built a port in Puerto Plata (Silver Port) on the island's north coast. Its name comes from Columbus' first journey, when, as he was sailing off its coast, he saw the mountains glittering like silver.[85]

Ovando's policy to create new towns in Hispaniola was motivated by the need to have better control of the population, so he could carry out any policy directed by the monarchs.

The new Santo Domingo

The 1502 hurricane that destroyed Ovando's ships also devastated the city of Santo Domingo. The governor had to carry out its re-foundation on the other bank of the Ozama River which is the current Zona Colonial (Colonial Zone).

Besides his own palace, Ovando planned to build a cathedral to replace the thatched roof church. The project was delayed for twenty years, and the first stone was laid in January 1521. The building was consecrated in 1541. He also built the Remedios chapel and would start the works of the San Francisco convent[86] and the hospital of San Nicolás de Bari. These buildings were among the first Spanish architectural works in the New World.[87] Ovando's strategy marked the beginning of a great tradition in the enormous Spanish territory: the sturdy, solid buildings that have endured as silent witnesses to the history of the conquest, exploitation, revolution, and liberation of many American societies.[88]

Santo Domingo became the steppingstone of the Spanish conquest and exploration of Puerto Rico, Jamaica, Cuba, Darien (Panama) and Yucatan (Mexico), organized by important Spanish figures such as Diego Velázquez, Hernán Cortés, Alonso de Ojeda or Rodrigo de Bastidas.

Santo Domingo is also historically significant for being the seat of the first political, judicial, and economic European-like organizations in the New World. In 1503, in Spain, the *Casa de Contratación de Indias* (House of Trade) was created for warehousing imported and exported goods from and to America. Likewise, it was in Santo Domingo that the first university in America was founded in 1538.[89]

Ovando will be remembered for spearheading the Spanish growth of Santo Domingo, but he was discreetly instrumental in promoting an unknown, 19-year-old notary from Medellín (Spain), and distant cousin as the scribe of the new town of Azua, in October 1506. His name was Hernán Cortés.[90]

Cortés arrived at Santo Domingo, registered as a citizen, and obtained a plot of land to cultivate. That same year, he took part in the conquest of Hispaniola and Cuba, receiving a large amount of land and native slaves for his efforts. Ovando assigned him a *repartimiento* (a number of natives to work on his fields as payment of tributes) and appointed him notary of the city of Azua. During the next five years, he settled in the colony. Cortés then moved to Cuba, and from there, he sailed to undertake his famous conquest of México.[91]

Sugarcane: blessing and curse of Hispaniola

Around the time of the colonial boom at the beginning of the 16th century, a faithful, crucial and polemical companion of Hispaniola's history was introduced: sugarcane.

There is evidence that the first sugarcane mill was installed near La Concepción de la Vega in 1504. Sugar production began to develop as an industry from 1505 to 1506. The first mill that produced sugar on a commercial scale operated in Nigua, San Cristóbal. By 1517 enough sugar was produced to be exported to the motherland.

In 1520, three sugar mills were operating, and only seven years later, nineteen hydraulic mills (*ingenios*) and six animal-powered mills (*trapiches*) were fully working. Another twelve were under construction and became fully operational by 1548. Most of these mills were owned by prominent colonists. Among others, the Treasurer, the Court's Secretary, and some council members of Santo Domingo.[92] Slowly and steadily, sugar was becoming the new "sweet gold" for the colony.

Sugar became popular also in Europe. It was so easily accessible that people would often develop black teeth due to cavities. Amazingly enough, black teeth became a sign of wealth, so much so, that some would artificially blacken their teeth to pretend they had enough wealth to afford such excesses.[93]

There was, however, one issue that needed to be resolved: sugarcane plantations required a lot of labor, strong and at the same time cheap. Slaves were needed. Here is an informative comparison: A coffee plantation employed dozens of workers; a sugar plantation required hundreds.[94]

5.

Problems with the Native Slaves

By 1508, sixteen years after the Spaniards arrived at the island, the native population had declined drastically from 400,000 to about 60,000. The diseases brought by the newcomers,[95] the abuse and mistreatment of the conquerors towards the natives, and the wars being waged against them turned out to be, unsurprisingly, a lethal combination.[96] Some argued that the drastic decrease in population was due mainly to a smallpox outbreak, but the disease did not affect the area until 1518, and by that time the indigenous population was about 25,000.[97]

Some remnants of the Taino culture survive until today, like a few words imported into the Spanish language, cave paintings, and artifacts of the time.[98] However, by and large, the indigenous traditions, language, and culture quickly disappeared. The diseases, excess of work, the collapse of traditional agriculture, and the massive introduction of livestock, contributed to the natives' decimation and their hope in their future. The dramatic drop in births and the number of suicides (by drinking an easy-to-make bitter cassava juice) are signs of this hopelessness. Their political organization also fell apart. Moving the Taínos from their traditional family villages to new towns was one of the causes that put an end to their cultural identity. They were banned from fishing and hunting and were left to eat, almost exclusively, their traditional cassava bread.[99] The *conquistadores* were extremely successful in dismantling the natives' past which seemed necessary for the Spanish to control them.[100]

Some may suggest a wise historical caution not to judge the issue of slavery and the mistreatment of natives out of its proper historical context. But such a "caution" looks at the events only through one point of view, and secondly, in this case, does not apply, since critical voices and open protests were heard very clearly from the Spaniards' side.

Montesinos' sermon (1511)

In 1510, fifteen Dominican friars arrived at Hispaniola, and it took them only a year to figure out what was going on in the colonies. One of them, Fray Antonio de Montesinos, on the fourth Sunday of Advent of 1511, with the church full, in the presence of colonists, the wealthy and noblemen, was ready to address the congregation: "Ahem ahem ..." the sermon began:

> *I have come up here to make known to you our sins against the Indians. I am the voice of Christ in the desert of this island. Therefore, it is convenient that, with attention, with all your heart and with all your senses, you listen carefully. I will be the voice that you never heard, the harshest and hardest and most frightening and dangerous, a voice that you never thought you would ever hear ...*
>
> *This voice,* he said, *is that you are all in mortal sin, and you will live and die in it, because of the cruelty and tyranny that you use with these innocent people. Tell me, with what right, with what justice do you have in such cruel and horrible servitude those Indians? With what authority have you made such detestable wars to these people who were in their meek and peaceful lands? ... How do you have them so oppressed and*

fatigued without giving them food or curing them in their illnesses, that from the excessive work you give them, they incur and die, or rather, you kill them, to extract and acquire gold every day?

And what care do you have to teach them, to know God the creator and be baptized, hear Mass, keep the feasts and Sundays? Are those not men? Don't they have rational souls? Are you not compelled to love them as yourself? Don't you understand that? Don't you feel this? How can you be so oblivious and naïve? Be assured that in the state you are in, you cannot save yourself more than the Moors or Turks ...[101]

Uncomfortable silence prevailed in the church as if the avid colonists had never pondered the rights of the Indians. After all this time conveniently ignoring the issue, we could hope that the sermon was finally a wake-up call that filled them with remorse. But no luck there. Even if it was true remorse, it was short-lived. After that Sunday, the owners visited the governor at his palace and demanded a proper punishment for the preacher. They also visited the monastery to speak with the friar's superior. He dismissed them and explained that Montesinos had spoken on behalf of all the community of Dominicans.[102] The colonists were not the only ones protesting about Montesinos' insult. The Franciscan priests were equally offended, as they too were slave owners.[103] The abuses suffered by the Indians by some clerics seemed to become so widespread that many years later, in 1578, the King of Spain himself had to order the bishops in the Americas to punish those clergymen who mistreated the natives.[104]

As per Montesinos' affair, he was given an ultimatum: to withdraw his allegations or else be punished accordingly. The superior simply replied that the cleric would preach the following Sunday. The affronted were satisfied, convinced that Montesinos would indeed retract his harsh words.

The following Sunday came, and the friar spoke again: "*I will repeat what I said last week.*" And he repeated it and added that he would refuse to confess any colonists and conquerors just as he would refuse confession to a bandit. Now that was a serious issue, since he was ready to deny God's forgiveness. Defiantly, he dared them to write to the authorities in Spain or whoever they deemed appropriate if they had any complaints. The church was crowded with angry settlers who managed to refrain from taking any further action. And though the episode seemed to die down, the Spanish empire would no longer be the same.[105]

The King intervenes

The matter was reported to the king himself and to the superior of the Dominicans. They made their move against Montesinos. When the friar had his chance to inform the monarch about what was really happening, a formal discussion about the issue ensued. They concluded that the natives were to be treated as free souls and instructed in the Catholic faith. They could, however, be subjected to coercion to be indoctrinated in Christianity. To be forced to learn about Christianity seems an obvious oxymoron. It was agreed that the natives should work for their own benefit and not only for the colonists. In addition, they should be paid enough to buy clothes and other items.[106] There was an exception: the members of the Caniba tribe could be enslaved[107] because they practiced cannibalism (that's where the word comes from), and that was considered a preposterous custom. This exception, in a somehow twisted way, became the rule.

Enslavement continues

The Spanish owners soon found a way to have slaves and remain within the new laws. When they would find natives in other islands of the Antilles, no matter to what tribe they belonged, they would be registered as Caniba Indians, since there were no visible physical characteristics that would distinguish the different tribes. In that way, following the "Caniba exception," all the natives captured could be made slaves.[108] The other exception to force natives into slavery, as mentioned before, was directed to those resisting being indoctrinated in the Catholic faith. This provision, of course, would give plenty of leeway for use in a wide range of situations.

Eventually, despite the royal proclamations against slavery, the capture of Indians from other islands to work in Santo Domingo continued. In 1514, two hundred of them were captured from Curaçao. In the following months, between two and five thousand were sent to Hispaniola, but two-thirds of them died at sea. Those who reached Santo Domingo were auctioned and marked by the buyers with letters on their faces,[109] a tradition that went unchecked until 1532, when the King of Spain signed a royal decree forbidding marking the Indians with red hot irons.[110]

There was another problem that made slaves even more necessary: the Spanish population in the island was decreasing. The situation was so desperate that in 1514, the Crown offered 250 free passages to travel from Spain to Santo Domingo, including the expenses needed to settle in the colony.[111]

The arrival of Hieronymites friars

In 1516, Cardinal Cisneros took the reins of Spain, as King Ferdinand died and the future King Charles I was only 16 years old. Cisneros was determined to bring about justice in the Indies. He decided to ask the prior of the religious order of the Hieronymites to rule those lands. The Order had a reputation for good stewardship and was neutral in the rivalry between Franciscans and Dominicans.[112]

The friars' arrival was a cause of concern for many who depended on forced labor in their properties. As the religious brothers were assessing the situation, they noted that the island was almost depopulated. In 1516, the households in all towns and cities of Hispaniola barely reached 715, which meant around 4,000 people,[113] an average of 0.13 people for every square mile. To give you an idea, today, the density of the Dominican Republic is 581 inhabitants per square mile.

In 1517, Cisneros received a letter from Judge Zuazo, in Santo Domingo, in which he explained how he found the island:

> *It was a great shame to consider how the whole island, being very populated and full of people before these judges arrived, and now it seems just shepherds' huts. Outside of Santo Domingo city, the places more populated had at most 30 or 40 [households]. San Juan would not have more than 25, Azua 37, Salvatierra de la Sabana only 15 ..., and Santa María del Puerto de la Laguna and Concepción de la Vega had 40. Lares de Guahaba had completely disappeared.*[114]

The natives, in turn, were a mere 11,000, and a year later, the smallpox epidemic reduced them to 3,000.[115]

A brief history of chief Enriquillo

The few natives that still survived were not about to sit idly by waiting for their demise. One of their best-known leaders and rebels against the Spaniards was chief Guarocuya or Enriquillo. Enriquillo belonged to the high aristocracy of the Xaragua chiefdom and was Anacaona's nephew, who, in turn, was Bohechío's sister, the chief of Xaragua. Enriquillo's father died in a Spanish raid during a peaceful indigenous protest; he was raised in a monastery in Santo Domingo; one of his mentors was Bartolomé de las Casas. Guarocuya was baptized with the name of Enrique (Henry) and later nicknamed Enriquillo. He was a brilliant and able man, learned Spanish, and assimilated the customs of the colonists. He also learned about Western legislation and the rights granted to the colony's subjects and was recognized and respected as a chief by the people.

Enriquillo was married to the mestiza Mencía, Anacaona's granddaughter; (that is, his wife was also his first cousin once removed). Both were part of Francisco de Valenzuela's *repartimiento* (colonial forced labor system), at his *encomienda* (the land that the natives would toil for the landowner), in San Juan de la Maguana. Despite working under a system of semi-slavery, Enriquillo's *ecomendero* treated him and his family well. It all changed when Francisco de Valenzuela died and his son Andrés succeeded him. Andrés treated the Indians with contempt and had no regard or respect for them, subjecting them to cruel exploitation. The situation became even worse when Andrés Valenzuela abused and mistreated Mencía. Enriquillo complained, but the Spaniard, instead of admitting his wrongdoing, insulted and beat him. Valenzuela harshened the repression, and tension between the natives and the Spaniards became unbearable. Enriquillo could no longer tolerate such humiliation; he was going to fight for his rights, and he wouldn't do it alone. The rebel cacique began an extensive tour of the different indigenous settlements in order to win the support of caciques such as Villagrán, Matayco, Incaqueca, Gascón, Vasa, Maybona and Tamayo. During 1519-1520 the Indians began a night walk that would take them to the Bahoruco mountains, lands that belonged to Enriquillo's father. There they started a revolt that would last for several years. The Spaniards, who used all kinds of weapons and tactics of war, could not defeat the local guerrillas.

Enriquillo had learned military tactics with the Spaniards. He based his strategy on three basic rules. First: take advantage of ambushes, attack, and steal all the weapons possible. Second: attack from the top of the mountains with stones and other solid materials and avoid direct frontal combat. And third: place the most expert caciques in the steepest places in the mountains, and take women, the elderly and children to safety. This guerrilla strategy would be repeated, by several rebels, many years later, in future conflicts within the island.

The battles between Indians and Spaniards lasted for several years, until finally, with the peace of Barrionuevo, a treaty signed in 1533 by the cacique and the Spanish Barrionuevo, the bloody war of Bahoruco, came to an end.

Enriquillo died on September 27, 1535, in the city of Azua, losing a month-long last battle against tuberculosis.[116] In his will he indicated that he wanted to be buried in the church of Azua, in present-day Pueblo Viejo of Azua, because, as he said, this town gave him plenty of proof of loving him.[117]

The Hieronymites reach a puzzling conclusion

But we should return to 1516, as the Hieronymites friars saw the deplorable state of the natives and the island in general. They were overwhelmed by the situation. Understanding how the Indians could eventually become extinct, they tried to concentrate them in villages of 400-500 inhabitants, with the ability to produce their own crops, raise their own livestock and hunt and fish with legal permission.[118]

The friars wanted to protect the Indians and at the same time ensure production on the island, so the brothers eventually wrote to Cisneros with their rather noteworthy conclusion:

> *After six months on the island, and after having verified the shortage of labor and the harsh climate that demand from the Indians an excessive effort, it would be necessary to have African slaves because, as we know from experience, they will bring a great benefit.*[119]

6.

African Slaves in Hispaniola

As a result of Friar Antonio Montesinos' protests, a complex and a forty-year long controversy began about how, and what, the natives were to be considered. The main issue was whether the Indians were people, and if so, whether they could be enslaved. According to some, the fact that such a debate even took place was a credit to Spain, because no other empire would even consider entering in such discussions that could easily conclude that the benefits in the colonies, based on forced labor, should cease. The debate was perhaps commendable, but quite suspiciously, nobody mentioned the African slaves. A questionable omission indeed, as the plantation owners would know, sadly enough, that African slaves were skilled in agriculture and had higher resistance.[120] It became a very convenient exclusion, since the solution to the "Indian problem" would be, coincidentally, African slaves.

One of the Hieronymites friars, Fray Manzanedo, was sure that sooner or later the indigenous population would become extinct and believed that the lack of workers could only be compensated by introducing slaves from Africa or naborías (indigenous) from other islands.[121]

Eventually, the Hieronymites agreed with the colonists about the need to obtain permission from the Crown to import Africans to work in the sugarcane plantations, with the possibility to be remunerated as business expanded. The business would become a success and, little by little, the southern region of the island would be populated with slaves from Africa.[122]

Fray Manzanedo wrote to King Charles I explaining that all citizens of Hispaniola were asking His Majesty to grant them a license to import Africans, because the Indians were not enough for the colonists to support themselves. He requested to send as many women as men. Since blacks raised in Castile could become rebellious, he also asked to send *"bozales,"* from southern Senegal, the best territory in Africa for slaves, to avoid *"Muslim corruption"* as much as possible.[123]

Judge Zuazo, the priors, and Father Las Casas, believed that the only way to solve the labor shortage was to import Africans. He stated that *"Hispaniola was the best land in the world for blacks."*[124]

Yes, Fray Bartolomé de las Casas supported the new strategy. In his desire to defend the interests of the indigenous population and protect them from ill-treatment, Las Casas spent years proposing to send African slaves. In 1535, he wrote a letter to the king claiming that the remedy for Christians was to send five or six hundred Africans or as many as needed, to each island. A few years later, in 1550, he would explain, remorsefully, that he realized it was not the right thing to want to substitute one form of slavery for another.[125]

The exploitation of African slaves was, sadly enough, not a new business. Christopher Columbus knew about slavery before his journey to America. In Cape Verde, Seville, and the Canary Islands there were African slaves. He himself had a black servant, and some theories suggest that on his second voyage, most likely, there were African slaves on board.[126] But now, however, there was talk of importing black slaves to work on the plantations of Hispaniola.

On September 18, 1505 (only 13 years after Columbus arrived to America), after receiving favorable reports about the possibility of mining copper in Hispaniola, King Ferdinand ordered three caravels to depart from Seville, with all the necessary equipment for the job, including 100 African slaves.[127]

Possibly some of them, along with some native slaves, were the ones who built the Ozama fortress in 1508 and the new buildings in the colonial zone.

The king authorizes sending African slaves to Hispaniola (1510)

On February 10, 1510, five years after the first shipment of 100 slaves, the king granted permission to send two hundred more.[128] At long last, the importation of gold from Hispaniola to Spain grew substantially during the first ten years of the century.[129]

At the beginning, the slaves did not come directly from Africa but were residents in Europe. In this way, Spain would benefit from the trade. The Hieronymites were so perplexed and overwhelmed by the situation that they decided to return to Spain. They realized the abuse that was being committed against the slaves, but they did not see how the island could prosper without them. Once in Spain, they met with Cisneros himself to let him know their inability to carry out their mission.[130]

The slave trade from Africa to Santo Domingo

The demand for slaves increased as the gold mines were becoming more productive, and the sugarcane industry was growing. So much so that an official from the House of Commerce of Seville calculated that 4,000 African slaves would be needed to work at Hispaniola,

Jamaica, Cuba, and Puerto Rico, the biggest islands of the empire. Without hesitation, the shipment was authorized to be brought directly from Africa without going through Spain. Las Casas still agreed.[131]

There was a logistical problem in that Spain had no territories in Africa and could not directly obtain slaves. The solution was to give *licencias* (authorizations) to private traders. The *licencias*, of course, were bought from the Crown. Once granted, sellers and buyers conducted the deal privately. Between 1529 and 1537, the Crown gave as many as 360 licenses to transport slaves from Africa to Peru.[132]

Until 1640, to supply slaves to its American empire, Spain resorted to Portuguese merchants and later on to the Dutch, French and British.

There were already experts on the subject. Alonso de la Parada, a well-known lawyer from Seville, proposed to buy all the slaves that the Spanish empire needed from the monarch of Portugal, who did have territories in Africa. According to De La Parada, four thousand slaves were required, of which half had to be women so that men would feel more comfortable and procreate in the New World.[133] In the long run, also private Spanish companies signed up for the deal. A contract was given to a Catalan company, the Barcelona Company, to supply slaves to Puerto Rico, Santo Domingo and Margarita. In 1758, the Catalan Pearl became the first Spanish ship to arrive at San Juan, Puerto Rico, directly from Africa.[134]

But let us see how the whole system worked.

How the slave trade worked[135]

The first move for the colonial powers was to hire specialized European trading companies, such as the Dutch West Indies Company. These companies were the intermediaries, supervising private European merchants while regulating their interaction with Africans.

European traders went to the African coasts loaded with goods to be exchanged for slaves. These goods were very diverse, mostly textiles, but also alcohol, firearms, tools, and manufactured utensils.

The business, of course, had suppliers in Africa. Europeans seldom ventured inland in search of slaves. They reached the coast and would remain there as instructed by African rulers and to protect themselves from diseases. The area chiefs controlled the captives' destiny and demanded from the Europeans the payment of high taxes for their purchase and export. They were also responsible for capturing and transporting them to shore. Most slaves were prisoners of war, but some were accused of murder, witchcraft, debt, or theft; others had simply fallen out of favor. Once the transaction was done, the European traders only had to ship these captives.

The supply of slaves to the New World became a well-rounded business for European and African traffickers, for the Crown and for the landowners in the Americas. Slaves could be bought in Europe or Africa for 45 or 50 pesos and sold in America for at least twice as much.[136] And this is how over 350 years, some 12 million people from Africa embarked for the American Continent. An estimated 2 million did not reach their destination.[137]

Of all the Spanish Monarch's businesses in his Kingdoms, by 1630, the slave trade became the most profitable and secure.[138]

The Africanization of the New World

The first and obvious consequence of the slave trade was the change in demographics in Hispaniola and throughout the New World. As early as 1530, a contemporary chronicler, Fernández de Oviedo, wrote that Hispaniola seemed a New Guinea because more people had African blood in their veins than Spanish.[139]

The relationship between blacks and whites varied depending on the areas. In Puerto Rico, there was a kind of understanding between them as they had to face the fierce attacks of the Caribs from the Lesser Antilles and the incursions of the French pirates. In both Cuba and Santo Domingo, there was a reasonably peaceful rapport between masters and slaves.[140]

In other parts, there was an alliance between blacks and natives. As early as 1533, a group of Indians, led by a certain Henríquez (possibly the same Enriquillo we spoke of earlier), started a rebellion against the Spaniards and were joined by many Africans. As these uprisings were mercilessly put down, some Africans managed to flee to the forests and ended up mixing with and fighting alongside the natives.[141]

In other parts of the Caribbean, the Indians themselves owned black slaves. It did not happen in the big islands of the Caribbean, but in the Lesser Antilles. When Indians attacked Spanish settlements, they often kidnapped black slaves and employed them in their communities. It is estimated that in 1612 as many as 2,000 African slaves were in the hands of the Carib Indians.[142]

Import of slaves to the Americas

The introduction of slaves to Santo Domingo was constant and uninterrupted for 300 years and ended in 1822 during the Haitian occupation, as we will explain later. This continued import of approximately one million Africans would mark the character of Hispaniola inevitably and permanently.

In 1640 in all Spanish America, there were around 340,000 African slaves. About half were in Peru and the Andes region, 80,000 in New Spain (México), 45,000 in present-day Colombia, more than 25,000 in Central America, and 16,000 in the Antilles.[143]

AFRICAN SLAVES IN HISPANIOLA

Between 1650 and 1675, another 370,000 slaves were brought from Africa, an average of 15,000 per year (300 per week for 25 years!). In the following 25 years, it was even worse; the number increased to 600,000, that is, an annual average of 24,000. By then, the destination of most of the slaves was the Caribbean islands.[144] Martinique would receive about 40,000, Guadalupe 8,000, and what would become the illegal French settlement of Saint Domingue, 7,000.[145] And that was only the beginning.

From the beginning of the slave trade to its abolition 300 years later, it is estimated that some 10 million slaves from Africa reached the shores of the American continent (remember that about two million died on the journey).[146] Of these, only 6% disembarked in the United States. Most went to Brazil and the Caribbean. The French colony of Saint Domingue (of which we will talk at length in the second part of the book) imported more slaves than the United States, even though it was much smaller, and slavery was abolished 60 years earlier than in the United States. That reflects not only the prosperity of the French colony but also the cruelty to which they subjected the slaves.[147]

7.

Loss of Influence of Hispaniola

Shortly after Ovando's colonial boom, the influence of Hispaniola began to decline. The Spanish expansionists' thirst was not quenched in the island, and soon it became a springboard to venture and settle in new lands such as Cuba, Mexico, or Peru. Havana was becoming more valuable for the interests of the colonies in the new Spanish territories. Santo Domingo was a port of entry to the Americas but lost its commercial and strategic value.

By 1515 most of the gold exported to Spain still came from Hispaniola, but Cuba and Puerto Rico's mining was already significant. Only a few years later, Cuba produced half the gold, and Puerto Rico as much as Hispaniola.[148]

The population was in rapid decline. When Rodrigo de Figueroa, the island's governor from 1519-1520, replaced the Hieronymites friars, there were only a thousand settlers as many were leaving for Cuba.[149] The exodus of Spaniards was unstoppable. Hispaniola had not much to offer and was profitable only for a few sugar plantation owners.

Thus, as the African slaves arrived on the island to work in the sugar mills, the colonists continued emigrating to other parts like Mexico, where, as the rumors asserted, there was an overabundance of gold.

This early emigration was so severe that by 1528 five towns in Hispaniola disappeared. Without counting slaves, the city of Santo Domingo had three thousand people, and only one thousand lived in the rest of the island.[150]

Think about this: while in 1530 the island had 4,000 inhabitants, almost half of this number (1,600) arrived on Columbus' second voyage three decades earlier.

First slave rebellions

After 20 years of the continued importation of slaves, the first rebellions were starting to break up. Imagine a 20-year-old boy born to a slave couple knowing only about forced labor, abuse, and violence. Already in 1543, some slaves had escaped and lived in the mountains as fugitives. They were the first maroons (which means savages), escaped or freed slaves. They were the first to begin to revolt against the colonists.[151] One of the most prominent maroon leaders was Diego de Guzmán, from San Juan de la Maguana. That was not his original name, of course. We have to remember that slaves were given the family names of their masters, of their place of origin or of the profession they practiced. These rebel groups were small and dispersed and attacked the haciendas by surprise, using guerrilla warfare tactics that would be so crucial in subsequent Dominican history.

Increase of the black population

With the constant arrival of slaves, the black population increased much faster than the white settlers. In 1546 there were about twelve thousand people of color, while the colonizers would not reach 5,000.[152] By 1568, the number of slaves increased to 20,000. Following precise instructions, a third of these slaves were women, so that they would *"mate with the men."*[153]

Interestingly, the increase of African people on the island became a cause of concern, not only for the Spaniards. Enriquillo himself in 1533 agreed with the *conquistadores* that there were too many blacks in the Bahoruco area, and, in a curious and sad twist of history, Enriquillo, who was persecuted by the Spaniards ten years earlier, provided them with Indian guides to persecute black *cimarrones*.[154]

8.

Spain Tries to Protect Its Interests in the Indies

We noted earlier, and we repeat it now: the effort by Spain to control the colonies for its exploitation for the sole benefit of the metropolis, shaped, significantly, the history of Spanish America in general and the future Dominican Republic in particular. Maybe it could not have been any other way; who knows? What we do know is that Spain did not want to lose any of the New World's businesses to foreign powers in Europe, as other countries began to show too much interest in the Americas.

In 1503, only 11 years after Columbus arrived in America, Spain regulated all commerce with the Indies, whereby any business in the Americas was to be conducted only by Spain and to and from Cádiz or Seville.[155]

When Columbus' son, Diego, arrived at Hispaniola in 1506 as its sixth governor, he had precise instructions about controlling the arrival of new residents to the island. The list of those forbidden to set foot on the island was long. It included foreigners, Muslims, Jews, heretics punished by the Inquisition, and the descendants of those condemned at the stake. Likewise, the newly converted could not travel to the Indies unless they were black slaves and others born into the bosom of Christianity, and obtained a proper license (paying, of course) On top of all this, no one was allow to survey the island without the Crown's permission.[156]

In 1526 Spain banned all private travels to the Indies. All ships wishing to cross the Atlantic had to obtain a permit and then travel in official fleets. Business on the island could only be carried out from the port of Santo Domingo and by registered Spaniards. These restrictive rules permitted only two trips per year through the Atlantic.[157] This tight control could not last long. In Hispaniola alone, Spain had to control and protect 1,900 miles of coastline. That's a lot of miles, as many as the length of the border between the USA and México. In fact, the island of Hispaniola occupies 41st place of the 213 countries with the most miles of coastline.[158]

If you wonder whether Spain could carry out so much control on an almost uninhabited island, the answer is simple. It could not. It was a lot of land, hardly inhabited, and it could not be defended as if it were just my backyard. Trying too hard to control the arrivals to the island resulted in a total disaster. It was a failure that would lead, 50 years later, to the political division of the island.

Foreign incursions and contraband

Controlling Hispaniola and all the continental coastline that was gradually "discovered" was an impossible undertaking, since there were other colonial countries with an appetite for gold and a desire to conquer, among them France, England, Portugal, the Netherlands, and even Denmark.

The first international visitors in the area were pirates. The shipping of gold across the Atlantic through unpopulated islands encouraged the arrival of the first pirates in the Caribbean Sea. One of the earliest was a French pirate, Jean Fleury, who in 1522 managed to seize part of the Moctezuma treasure that Hernán Cortés had sent from Mexico.[159]

In 1528, again, French pirates had already reached the island of Hispaniola along secluded and deserted beaches.[160] A year before that, an English ship docked at the port of Santo Domingo and local authorities and the population received them in a friendly manner because they thought they were passing by on their way to North America. However, the visit was short-lived since they were, in fact, trading with the settlers right under their noses. They were bid farewell with cannonballs.[161]

What happened in 1538 was more significant. A French privateer, taking advantage of the hostilities between the kings Charles I of Spain and Francis I of France, attacked the town of Azua, assaulted and burned some houses and sugar mills, and stole sugar and hides. On his way out, he passed through Ocoa and did exactly the same thing.[162]

It was as if the word was spreading in global gossiping circles that Hispaniola was an open door for illegal markets and looting. So much so that in 1563, Lord Hawkins, an English merchant, bypassing the Spanish monopoly law, arrived at Puerto Plata with 300 slaves from Sierra Leone and other "products." He docked at the abandoned port of La Isabela, and then he just had to wait. Soon the villagers, including the priest, were seen rowing their boat towards the ship to exchange merchandise. News of the unusual event arrived at Santo Domingo, from where they sent a patrol and confiscated all the goods.[163] We just wonder how long it took for the news to arrive at the capital city (about 140 miles away), how long it took the patrol to reach La Isabela and how many business transactions were already complete by the time this happened.

The English pirate Sir William Drake sacks the city of Santo Domingo ... during a month (1586)

One of the most appalling episodes of foreign intrusion occurred in 1586. The main character of the story was Francis William Drake, one of Hawkins' sailors. For the Spaniards, he was a pirate at the British Crown's service. For the English, he is known with the honorary title of "Sir." You find him on Google as Sir Francis William Drake. The title "Sir" is an acknowledgment of the Crown to relevant English characters. Sir Drake and his men landed in Haina, 14 miles south of the Colonial Zone of Santo Domingo, and walked to the city that he captured without encountering much resistance. Amazingly enough, the pirates spent an entire month in the city looting and stealing as much as they could. During all that time, they set up camp inside the Cathedral. According to the story Francis Drake settled in the first chapel at the right side of the altar where he hung his hammock and, unfortunately, with a saber's strike, cut off the nose of a saint's image.[164]

After lengthy negotiations, Drake agreed to vacate the place. He received 25,000 ducats compensation, which was the value of all the city's jewels, silver, and gold. Besides, Drake managed to take with him the artillery, hides, sugars and sugarcane fistula (also known as *cañafistula, cañafistolo, cañadonga, chácara, guayaba cimarrona* or *casia purgante* although its scientific name is *Cassia Fistula*).[165] Sir Drake even took the church bells with him.[166]

According to the historian Emilio Rodríguez Demorizi, Drake's looting produced more misfortune for the island than the casualties caused by wars, hurricanes, and earthquakes.[167]

SPAIN TRIES TO PROTECT ITS INTERESTS IN THE INDIES

Holland, a new power in the Caribbean

In the early 1600s, another player appeared on the international piracy scene: the Dutch. The first Dutch pirates appeared in Africa in the late 1500s, and soon were also seen in America. Holland was creating what would become the world's largest merchant marine. And that was news. Amsterdam was becoming the world's largest center for finances and insurance, a profitable venture already in existence back then. Most of those engaged in the business were Sephardic Jews, that is, Jews of Spanish origin who were able to find in Holland a refuge from the Spanish and Portuguese Inquisition. They knew the volume and nature of the Spanish and Brazilian markets well. The wealth of the country soon allowed the Dutch to have the only army in Europe that could compete with that of Spain.[168]

Good times for the smuggling business

One hundred years after the Spaniards' arrival on the island, Hispaniola had quickly shifted from being a small and flourishing colony to becoming a semi-abandoned island at the mercy of foreign explorers and smugglers. As we saw before, the new cherished places were in Cuba and on the continent, where the great source of wealth was found.[169]

The only ones who could afford a lucrative and legal business were those few who had a sugar mill; the rest labored in ranching and subsistence agriculture. Due to the many restrictions imposed by Spain prohibiting any trade with foreign powers, the only option for the average family was to engage in contraband, which soon became a thriving business. The preferred area for this illegal trade was the northwestern part of the island, the ports of Puerto Plata, Monte Cristi, Bayajá, and La Yaguana in the south. It was an area far from Santo Domingo with a concentration of fairly big towns. Illegal trade became frequent with the consent and complicity of the local authorities and of course, included black slaves. Even the owners of cattle herds in other parts of the island preferred to take their livestock to the northern area and sell their hides to the smugglers since they paid them better than the legal Spanish traders.[170]

To have an idea about how big the smuggling business was, here are some impressive figures: Annually, the Dutch would send 20 ships of two hundred tons each to Hispaniola and Cuba.[171] Not bad for being illegal. Four thousand tons of merchandise per year or 8.9 million pounds is the equivalent 140 semitrailers' cargo. All these semis in a single lane would form a line of about two miles (In Dominican distance that would cover the entire *Avenida 27 de Febrero*, from *Pinturas* to *Núñez de Cáceres*, in present-day Santo Domingo). To import such a quantity of products, the Dutch had illegal hires throughout the Caribbean Sea and the collaboration of almost everyone. And do not think that they brought only essential goods. Contraband was not only an economic activity but also a cultural phenomenon. Through this contraband in the northern cities, they came in touch with Renaissance paintings, Lutheran Bibles, and various literary and artistic works. This cultural and religious influence in the area even led to the baptism of several converts to Protestantism, who had to choose foreign godparents as the official religion of the island was strictly Catholic.

The area where contraband was most prominent was known as the *Banda del Norte* (the Northern Band) and included Puerto Plata and Bayajá, among others. While the southern cities were a door opened only to Spain and controlled by the Spanish Crown, la *Banda del Norte* was a door to the world.

Smuggling in Hispaniola was so extensive that in the early 1600s, the French, English, Dutch, and even Portuguese traded most of its goods. They all docked their ships as far as possible from the city of Santo Domingo, where the Spanish royal bureaucracy was based. This economic independence was becoming a serious threat to Spanish interests.

Such was the turmoil on the northern shores that in January 1603, someone suggested a radical measure to end smuggling. It was a bold idea that, in the long run, would drastically and forever change the island's economic, social, and cultural structure.

9.

Osorio's "Devastaciones" (1606)

The idea of the *Devastaciones* (literally devastations or more loosely, annihilation or total destruction), was as simple as it was risky and ultimately useless. It would follow this logic: Since 1) There is a lot of contraband in the Northern Band, and since 2) we cannot control either trade or the people in that area; therefore, 3) let us vacate, empty, and depopulate the entire region. Get the people out of the place, smuggling ends, and there is nothing left to be controlled. As the saying goes, "to kill the snake cut off the head." But in this case, the saying did not apply, because another "head" would appear instead.

Osorio's plan did not seem ill-advised to anyone, and in 1606, it was implemented. Spanish authorities preferred a mass exile, moving people from their homes, houses, and lands rather than tolerating the growth of a cosmopolitan colony both in its peculiar form of commerce and in the multiplicity of elements in its culture.

It was called "Osorio's devastations," referring to the governor of the island Don Antonio Osorio. The towns of the Northern Band were destroyed: Puerto Plata, Montecristi, Bayajá, San Juan de la Maguana, and La Yaguana (present day Léogâne in Haiti). In the process, more than a hundred people who resisted leaving their homes were hanged.

The devastations were so total that there was no trace of the Spanish occupation in the area that today occupies Haiti.[172]

Osorio depopulated the western part of the island to maintain control over it, but by doing so, he lost it. The devastations caused a gradual but constant incursion of French settlers in the western portion of the island.

Some say that the colony of Hispaniola never recovered from that blow.[173] But history, like life, takes advantage of mistakes and misfortunes to open endless new possibilities. We don't know what would have happened if Osorio had had another idea for dealing with the problem. What we do know is that after his devastations, the island was to become a unique racial, social, and cultural meeting ground. Osorio did not realize that his plan was going to change Hispaniola dramatically.

These were the immediate effects of Osorio's plan:[174]

Only less than 10% (about 8,000) head of cattle could be moved to the designated places, which meant the abandonment of more than one hundred thousand cows (100,000!) and some fourteen thousand horses (14,000!). As a result, the number of wild animals in the depopulated area increased exponentially.

The destruction of the sugar mills in the area accelerated the decline of the sugar industry on the whole island; that combined with the loss of cattle and ginger plantations, increased poverty throughout the colony and decreased the commercial importance of Santo Domingo.

One of the positive consequences of Osorio's policy was that it favored the uprising of many slaves, since they now had vast depopulated areas in which to settle.

Many inhabitants of the *Banda del Norte*, which accounted for more than half of the island's population, emigrated to Cuba and Puerto Rico; this aggravated, even more so, the depopulation of Hispaniola. Vast territories of the Northern Band were left to the mercy of foreigners.

What happened after the implementation of Osorio's initiative was that people from other nations could not only do business in Santo Domingo, but they could settle along the depopulated area.[175] The Spaniards defended the territory from periodic incursions into the interior, but since they were not interested in repopulating the area, they would be incapable of protecting it forever.

And well, Osorio's Devastations did not prevent smuggling.

PART TWO
Saint Domingue,
slavery, races, and revolutions
(1606 - 1821)

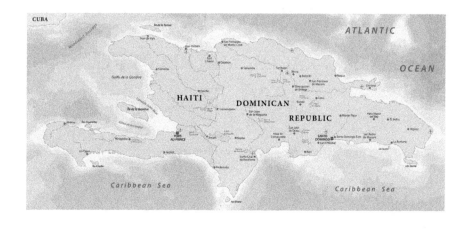

1.

The Origin of Saint Domingue

One of the consequences of Osorio's devastations of 1606 was the widespread poverty that affected the entire colony. Poverty and emigration to other countries caused a drastic reduction of tax revenues for the colonial administration to the point that the reserves were not enough to cover the expenses of public officials and the maintenance of the soldiers posted at Santo Domingo. The Spanish government had to reduce the number of soldiers by half. In 1608, Spain allocated an annual sum from Mexico, known as *El Situado*, to cover the colony's public expenses.[176] This subsidy lasted for the rest of the century. To make matters even worse, in 1617 there was an earthquake in the city of Santo Domingo with aftershocks that lasted for forty terrifying days.[177]

We know from the 1606 census that the population of the entire island was 1,616 households, approximately 8,000 people. Three thousand of them lived in the City of Santo Domingo. Those numbers do not include around 7,500 slaves working in sugar and ginger plantations (888 and 6,790, respectively). There were almost as many slaves as there were citizens.[178]

It was this state of poverty and defenselessness that enabled the move of foreign powers into the vicinity of the island.

Pirates of the Caribbean

The population in the Eastern part of the island was decreasing, but the Western territories were, effectively, depopulated. So, predictably, it was on those parts that new visitors began to appear. The first ones were English and Frenchmen who were expelled by the Spaniards in 1629 from the islets of Saint Kitts and Nevis in the Lesser Antilles. They settled on *Tortuga* Island, five miles from the northern west coast of Hispaniola. The Spanish army managed to drive away the invaders on three occasions (1630, 1635, and 1654), but there were few troops and no permanent settlements; consequently, the international visitors were always hanging around.

Tortuga Island became a pass-through place and somehow an anarchic location. The French adventurer Olivier Levasseur took control of it, and eventually it became a refuge of interesting characters such as filibusters and groups of international travelers dedicated to piracy. The word filibuster means pirate in Dutch. Intriguingly, and without any apparent connection between pirates and politicians, in the United States the term became popular during the 1850s when it was applied to efforts to hold the Senate floor in order to prevent action on a bill.[179]

The sea was their life, and Tortuga was their hideout. There were also buccaneers, who reached the unpopulated areas of Hispaniola hunting cattle and wild pigs. They fed on smoked meat, which they prepared in grills called *boucan*, hence their name.[180] In times of crisis, buccaneers would venture into the sea in search of easy booty from passing ships. The islet soon became famous for being a pirate's abode. It is named several times in the movie "Pirates of the Caribbean," and is also the setting for the graphic adventure novel "The Black Corsair" by the Italian writer Emilio Salgari.

But as famous as the Pirates of the Caribbean might be, the most powerful and successful pirate in history is said to have been a Chinese woman named Cheng I Sao. Ms. Cheng married a pirate, and upon his death, she very successfully took over her husband's trade from 1801 to 1810. Cheng had under her control a fleet of 1,500 ships and more than 80,000 sailors. She died in 1844 as a 69-year-old grandma.[181]

But let's go back to *Tortuga*. The little island was not only a good sanctuary for adventurers and pirates but an important strategic location, one that could be used by the English or French as a hub to advance their influence towards Hispaniola. In 1640 the little island was about to become an official English possession, but in a final attack, France defeated the British. From there on, the French started a systematic colonization of *Tortuga*, and with it, the incursion to Hispaniola's western part.[182]

The French strategy was clear. *Tortuga* turned into a center for maritime, military, and commercial operations and eventually a strategic position to expand the French influence to the big island. To that end, they planned to conspire against Spanish controls and interests and, above all, to take over the depopulated area of *"Tierra Grande"* (Big Land) as they called Hispaniola.[183] They would be extremely successful.

Gradually, the French explorers began to settle in Hispaniola. Unopposed and unchecked, they began to grow tobacco and hunt the cattle descended from those that could not be transported during Osorio's devastations. As time passed, France's presence in the West became slowly but surely a reality.[184]

The English plan in the Americas

The French were not the only ones interested in the *"Big Land."* The English defeat in *Tortuga* was a small stumbling block but they kept their interests on the American continent intact. In 1606 three ships departed from England with the settlers who would found Jamestown

(Virginia), one of the thirteen colonies that were to become the United States.[185]

England was also interested in the Caribbean and hoped to gain control of it, not only for strategic reasons but also to force out the Spaniards and with them, the Catholic faith. It was, in part, a religious mission.

On April 23, 1655, an English fleet of 346 warships with 13,000 men (7,000 sailors and 6,000 soldiers) commanded by Admiral William Penn and General Robert Venables, arrived at the city of Santo Domingo. The fleet's men were more numerous than all the island's inhabitants! This was not a smuggling mission, or a raid to loot the capital. This was an expedition to conquer Hispaniola, and with it, the rest of the Spanish possessions in America.[186] The Spanish colony was weak and underpopulated; it appeared to be a direct and definitive mission. But the English army was in for a big surprise.

As it turned out, the English troops were not well prepared and poorly equipped. According to contemporary chronicles, thirst became one of their worst enemies as they did not carry an adequate supply of water. The Spanish knew the terrain, and they received advance notice of the intruders' arrival. This proved crucial to the Spaniards' success. It took around 1,500 casualties for the English to retreat in humiliation and defeat.[187] Despite the might of the English forces, the Spanish managed to expel the invaders.

The survivors of the disaster moved on and attacked the island of Jamaica, also Spanish territory but even less populated and more poorly defended. They were victorious there. That is how, thanks to a British vendetta with Spain, Jamaica was declared English territory and remained part of the British empire until 1962. Up to today, Jamaica and Canada remain the only monarchies in the Americas, with Her Majesty Queen Elizabeth II of England as their monarch.

THE ORIGIN OF SAINT DOMINGUE

The French occupation of the West of the island (1656)

As the Spaniards had to deal with the English navy, the French, already firmly established in Tortuga by 1656, intensified the campaign to venture into Hispaniola's western "wasteland," to eventually take over the entire island. In 1659, the dwellers of Tortuga advanced and sacked the city of Santiago.[188] And thus began a story, at first brilliant, but ultimately dramatic, of what would become the French colony of *Saint Domingue*. The French did not bother to seek a different name for their new territory. They were comfortable enough to translate *Santo Domingo* into French. From then on, the western area of the island was named Saint Domingue. Followed by various and often violent border modifications, in 1804, Saint Domingue will become Haiti, while Santo Domingo, the eastern part, will be known as the *República Dominicana* (Dominican Republic) in 1844. But for now, when we mention *Santo Domingo*, we will be referring to the Spanish (and Eastern) part of the island and when we shall refer only to the city of Santo Domingo, we will specify so.

By 1667, nine hundred Frenchmen moved to Hispaniola and tripled the settlers in *Tortuga*.[189] It may not seem like much, but Santiago de los Caballeros, the second town of the colony, had a little over a thousand people.[190] In the following year, the French settled around Yaguana, the old city destroyed in Osorio's devastations, present-day Léogânne in Haiti. A few years later, in 1670, they were already in the Cape, renamed in 1711 as Cap-Français and later Cap-Haïtien. The first Frenchmen in Hispaniola engaged mainly in the production of tobacco to be exported to France[191] and livestock.

Spanish recognition of Saint Domingue (1678 and 1697)

Of course, the French presence on the island did not sit well with the Spanish authorities, and on several occasions, they sent troops to regain the places occupied by the French, who, in turn, kept strengthening their defenses. The situation was tense.

Everything began to change in 1678, with the Peace Treaty of Nijmegen. This treaty ended a series of territorial disputes between various European countries, including Spain and France. The two colonial powers additionally had to reach an agreement about the borderlines in Hispaniola. Spain was implicitly recognizing the French presence on the island.

Despite the tension between the two parties, their respective needs favored an active trade in horses, salted meat, and cowhide. Of course, such businesses were prohibited by the Spanish government.[192]

Three years after the Nijmegen Peace Treaty, in 1681, a census counted 7,848 people in the western part of the island (Saint Domingue), and half of them had weapons. The Spanish population, on the other side, had hardly 1,500 families clustered in small defenseless towns (except the city of Santo Domingo), scattered throughout the land.[193]

The Spaniards tried to withstand the French pressure at the border territories. In 1684, one hundred families from the Canary Islands settled to repopulate the area. Another hundred families arrived three years later. They settled in the border town of Bánica with the idea that the new settlers would protect their new homes and in doing so would also defend the strategic region.[194]

The arrival of Canarian families to the island has had a long-lasting influence on Dominican terminology. Seemingly typical Dominican words such as *"guagua"* (bus), *"añugado"* (choked) or *"harto"* (fed up), were in fact, imported from the Canary Islands.[195]

By the end of the 17th century, on three occasions (1690, 1691, and 1694) Spain battled unsuccessfully to expel the French army from the island. But by 1697, the hostility declined thanks to a peace treaty signed in Ryswick (The Netherlands) by Holland, England, Germany, and by the two colonial and European neighbors, Spain and France. The deal put an end to the Nine-Year War in Europe and, while it did not make any reference to the colonies in Hispaniola, fostered a new effort to coexist in relative peace. The governors of Santo Domingo and Saint Domingue felt the pressure to end the conflict regarding the border's limits. It was another implicit recognition by Spain of the French presence on the island.

The rapprochement between the two countries and, therefore, between the two colonies was further consolidated in 1701, when the King of France's grandson, Philip V, by way of intricate family alliances, took to the Spanish throne. That is how, overnight, after one hundred years of conflicts and skirmishes since Osorio's devastations, Spain and France became allied nations. It would still take 70 more years for the two countries to agree on the limits of the borders, recognized under the Treaty of Aranjuez in 1777: the northern border would follow the Dajabón River and in the south, the Pedernales River. Undoubtedly the political union of the two countries in Europe gave some political stability to the colonies of Hispaniola, but their economic and social development could not have been more different.

2.

One Island and Two Colonial Systems

During the 17th and 18th centuries, the colonies in Hispaniola developed two very different economic and social systems that would effectively define their future forever.

Santo Domingo: a subsistence economy

A key factor that explains the two economic routes of the colonies is their respective timelines. The French started their new colonial adventure in Saint Domingue around the turn of the 18th century. Santo Domingo, on the other hand, was by then, a 200-year-old colony. Let us put this simple fact into some perspective: More years passed from Columbus' arrival to Hispaniola (1492) up to the rise to the throne of King Phillip V (1701) than between the Dominican Republic's declaration of independence (1844) up to today.

So, in a very real way, by the beginning of the 18th century, for most families in Santo Domingo, the colony was not a foreign territory to be exploited for the benefit of the motherland, but the only home they and their ancestors ever knew.

And it was a lonely home indeed. Apart from the cities of Santo Domingo and Santiago de los Caballeros, the rest of the Spanish territory was unpopulated.

Santo Domingo, neglected by Spain, became one of its weakest possessions in America. What was once a prosperous land of sugar plantations gradually became a forsaken, nearly barren land with ranches, tobacco plantations, and plots worked by peasants, far from state control.[196] The economy was based on family subsistence agriculture and cattle ranches.

By 1688 the situation in Santo Domingo seemed so precarious that the French colony considered the possibility of occupying the Spanish side and gaining full control of the entire island.[197] But by then relations between France and Spain were becoming friendlier as both countries were about to share a king.

Saint Domingue: the prosperity (for the few) of a plantation economy

The impoverished situation of Santo Domingo contrasted sharply with that of Saint Domingue. Since the beginning, the French had very clear ideas of what to do with their colony. It was not about trade routes, or about evangelizing for the greater glory of God, nor about creating French settlements. Their piece of island had to function as a factory at the service of France. The plan was very successful, at the expense, of course, of importing vast numbers of slaves over two hundred years.

The general idea was that the colony was to be economically dependent and entirely subordinate to the motherland. It would not produce anything that the French government would not authorize, and, in general, to survive, the colonists would depend on the merchandise provided by the metropolis. The system was called "exclusive," since the French colonies would trade exclusively with France and only with French ships.[198]

The formal organization of Saint Domingue began in the early 1700s. The French divided the territory into three provinces: North, South, and West, each led by a governor and a quartermaster-general appointed by the King of France. In these lands, the French developed an intensive plantation system designed to produce coffee, cocoa, cotton, and indigo on a large scale. But it was sugar that made Saint Domingue the richest colony in the world.

The backbone of this prosperous economy was the forced and intense labor of African slaves. They were brought from the countries surrounding the Gulf of Guinea: present-day Senegal, Gambia, Ivory Coast, Ghana (Gold Coast), Nigeria, Togo and Benin (Slave Coast), Cameroon, Gabon, Republic of Congo, the Democratic Republic of the Congo and Angola. Other slaves were imported from Africa's East Coast, namely Mozambique and Madagascar.[199] Some estimated that, due to the working conditions, on average, the useful life of a slave was seven years.[200] The combination of technological developments for plantations, the constant importation of slaves, access to numerous trade routes (many of them illegal), and the rich and varied terrain of the colony made Saint Domingue an extremely productive plantation system.[201]

By 1789, three-quarters of the world's sugar was produced in Saint Domingue, and with it much of the wealth and glory of France.[202]

Marital problems in Saint Domingue

Despite the economic success of Saint Domingue, certain social problems were solved in questionable ways. One of them was the lack of European women as there were no significant migrations of French families to the island. Not surprisingly, as early as 1684 and as described in the chronicles of the time, the most apparent needs among the inhabitants of Saint Domingue were *"women and blacks."*[203]

The colony had so few women that when available, husbands could not afford to be too demanding about their prospective wives' reputations. As soon as a ship with women would arrive from France, the men who could afford it would purchase a bride. As the story goes, due to the extraordinary circumstances, some would change the wedding vows. Thus, the classical "yes I do" would be altered to a more nuanced: "I take you without knowing, or caring to know, who you are. Give me your word for the future. I acquit you of what is past." The tolerant tone wouldn't last long. Shotgun in hand, the groom, would add: "If you prove to be unfaithful, this (pointing at the shotgun) will certainly be faithful to my aim." Even by the 1780s, when the colony's financial success began to attract wealthier citizens, Saint Domingue continued to harbor a colorful mix of Parisian prostitutes, descendants of pirates, unwanted elements of French society, priests expelled by their national clergy and prisoners of war from Africa.[204]

Transformation and recovery of Santo Domingo (1700s)

From 1701 on, the authorities and inhabitants of Santo Domingo and Saint Domingue, pressured by their respective metropolises, maintained a peaceful alliance and collaborated with the efforts to defend their territories and possessions from a possible English threat.[205]

This period of stability caused a relative recovery in Santo Domingo, thanks, first of all, to the prosperity of Saint Domingue that was about to become the center of France's Atlantic economy,[206] and, secondly, to the negligence to which Spain had subjected it. Yes indeed: since Santo Domingo was no longer a priority for Spain, there was more freedom for trade between neighbors. The fact that Santo Domingo was one of the least valued enclaves in the Spanish Empire[207] saved it from its own misfortune. Santo Domingo was transformed. From being a colonial power for the benefit of Spain, it became an autarchic society based on subsistence agriculture, ranching, and illegal trade with foreign merchants, especially from Saint Domingue. In theory, Spain had to regulate commerce within the island, to be able to profit. But the people of Santo Domingo obtained better and cheaper products dealing with the English, French or Dutch, than through the official channels of the Spanish government. These foreign powers would trade meat and leather in exchange for textile products, weapons, or ceramics.[208] It was a profitable trade that went on under the radar of all the regulations which the Crown and the authorities attempted to establish in Santo Domingo.[209]

Spain had to tolerate the fact that Santo Domingo was a mere accessory to the prosperity of Saint Domingue, because this subordination was the price to pay to maintain Spanish sovereignty in that region.[210] After all, the prosperity of Saint Domingue also meant the relative prosperity of Santo Domingo.

Proof of this success was the re-foundation of several villas. In 1733, the town of San Juan de la Maguana became part of lands desired by the French. In 1735, Neiba was founded and in 1740 Dajabón; Montecristi was founded in 1751, Samaná in 1756 and in 1761 San Rafael. By 1738, the population in the Spanish colony had increased to 30,058. In thirty years, it was going to double, reaching 73,319.[211] At the end of the century, the population tripled, mainly because of the immigrants from the Canary Islands and the arrivals of slaves escaped from Saint Domingue. There were signs of investment and economic growth too, such as the establishment of cotton, cocoa, and indigo plantations around the city of Santo Domingo.[212]

3.

Slavery in Santo Domingo and in Saint Domingue

The different modes of production in the two colonies meant a sharp contrast in the number of slaves each imported and a difference between the slaves' working and living conditions on both sides of the island.

The life of slaves in impoverished Santo Domingo

Despite its population growth, Spain showed no intention of making Santo Domingo a productive land. It still was a rural colony with large semi-depopulated areas, its inhabitants widely dispersed, mainly dedicated to livestock and subsistence agriculture. In this context, the slaves were mostly domestic servants who helped around the house or the fields. There was not much control, and although there was poverty, they had some autonomy.

In 1715, 18,410 people lived in the Spanish colony, most of them colored.[213] By 1725 the French colony had 30,000 free people living there, and as many as 100,000 black or mulatto slaves.[214] Three slaves for every free person.

Santo Domingo did not have a great demand for slaves and, comparatively, laws and practices were more permissive, which allowed many slaves to obtain freedom. These conditions in Santo Domingo made it possible that already 150 years before the abolition of slavery, most of the population of the Spanish colony were free peasants, ex-slaves or descendants of slaves.[215] In fact, most of the ancestors of today's Dominicans were freed slaves long before the Haitian Revolution.[216]

Santo Domingo's population was mostly made up of descendants of African slaves, mainly ranchers and farmers, in a sparsely inhabited region. There were slaves working on some plantations, but in absolute and relative numbers, they were a minority compared with the French part of the island.[217]

A crucial point: Over the years, Santo Domingo had a mulatto majority, so much so that miscegenation was normalized and made it possible for many free non-white men to access important positions in the military, church, government and other institutions, defying the laws that prohibited it. This situation did not automatically eliminate racism, but the distance between blacks and whites was reduced significantly, as the color of a significant number of people of African descent became irrelevant in the eyes of local authorities.[218]

Slaves in Saint Domingue: the Pearl of the Caribbean

Things were quite different in Saint Domingue. The slave labor there produced half the world's coffee and as much sugar as several of the colony's leading competitors combined.[219]

Saint Domingue's business was so successful that it is considered *"one of the most profitable slave systems for exploiting plantations in all history."*[220]

Of course, it was so because of the use of massive, forced labor without any compensation or rights. The working conditions for the slaves were incredibly harsh. Think only of the oppressive heat, hurricanes, and lethal diseases. Both malaria and yellow fever killed about 50% of the new slaves in their first year on the island. As a result, their owners tended to neglect the weakest, in an effort to maximize their investment.[221]

In 1760, diseases, extreme working conditions, cruel punishments for petty infractions and poor nutrition killed half of the Africans who had arrived in the eight previous years.[222]

As early as 1685, the French King Louis XIV, in consideration of the cruelty to which the slaves were subjected, the refusal of the plantation owners to recognize their forced labor as humans, and the risk posed by the overwhelming majority of slaves compared to the colonists, passed a decree known as Code Noir (Black Code). It was an attempt by France to control the abuse of slaves by the colonizers of Saint Domingue. The Code did not question the institution of slavery nor try to reduce or monitor the massive importation of slaves into the colonies,[223] which did not stop growing until 1822. But considering that in France, the king could torture his free citizens or imprison them for life without trial, the Code Noir was a particularly advanced piece of legislation for its time.[224]

Slaves escape from Saint Domingue to Santo Domingo

The difference between the slave's living conditions between the two parts of the island was so relevant that many would flee from Saint Domingue to Santo Domingo. In 1677 twelve slaves ran away from French estates and were received as refugees in Santo Domingo, where the acting governor, Juan de Padilla Guardiola, welcomed them and allowed them to live there as free men. This plan had a political motivation: granting freedom to escaped slaves from Saint

Domingue, would encourage others to do the same, creating instability in the French colony. The Spaniards had only one, and one very telling, condition for accepting slaves from the west: they could not have been slaves of any Spaniard.[225] We can only assume that Spanish authorities would return the slaves to their former Spanish master, if such were the case. It seems clear that the welcoming of slaves had to do more with destabilizing the French than with making a statement against slavery.

The plan of welcoming Saint Dominguean slaves appeared to be working, so much so that the Spanish authorities created a special patrol with the sole mission of searching for slaves in Saint Domingue and taking them to a settlement near the city of Santo Domingo. The first to be relocated were a group from Angola known as Los Mina (or the Mines). We still have evidence of this camp's location. It is a neighborhood in the municipality of Santo Domingo Este called, unsurprisingly, Los Mina.[226] We have this account of a French inspector describing the settlement in 1871:

> *San Lorenzo de los Minas contains three hundred inhabitants, all free blacks. These blacks are descendants of blacks, taken from the northern part of the French colony... and of other fugitive French blacks who had been assembled in Santo Domingo in 1719, according to the orders of the King of Spain. The Spaniards with armed force refused to return the escaped slaves* [to Saint Domingue] *and they established that town, which took the name of Minas, because the main group among these blacks were from the kingdom of Minas, on the coast of Africa.*[227]

It is notable that the first insubordination of slaves in Saint Domingue had the support of another slave colony: Spain.

Number of slaves in Saint Domingue vs. Santo Domingo

The different socioeconomic situation on each side of the island, described above, produced a different set of revealing demographics regarding the number of imported slaves in the two colonies.

By 1687, Saint Domingue had 4,411 free whites and 3,358 slaves.[228] Things were about to be quite different a few decades later. Between 1721 and 1730, the French transported at least 85,000 slaves to Saint Domingue. This was an average of 25 slaves arriving each day in an uninterrupted fashion for nine consecutive years.

During a 15-year span (1730-1745), 180 ships from Nantes' port in France transported a total of 25,000 slaves. That is an average of 300 people per vessel. Three-quarters of these slaves would work for the new rich plantation owners in Saint Domingue.[229] It is estimated that in the last 25 years of the 18th century, In 6: the number of new slaves reached 100,000.[230]

By 1750, Saint Domingue had 150,000 slaves, ten times more than the number of white people.[231]

Fifteen years later, the slaves numbered more than 200,000.[232]

And the need for slaves kept growing. Some contemporaries considered that to maintain production levels on the plantations, 15,000 new slaves were needed per year.[233] It was a major and tragic miscalculation. The arrival of new slaves annually reached 40,000.[234] In 1789, there were as many as 520,000 slaves in Saint Domingue,[235] 90% of the total population.[236] In 100 years, France had imported approximately 800,000 slaves to the colony.

The numbers in Santo Domingo were noticeably different. In 1606 out of the 16,000 people living in Santo Domingo, about 9,500 were slaves. Almost two hundred years later, in 1789, the number of slaves was 15,000, just 15% of the total population.[237]

As we can see, in Saint Domingue the economic and social organization depended directly on forced labor. The slaves had no rights and no property. They only had one thing to their advantage: their sheer superiority in numbers. And they were about to use it.

4.

The Slave Revolution in Saint Domingue

Yes, there was a slave revolution in Saint Domingue. Strictly speaking, the episode is not part of Dominican History. Still, we can't understand what happened in Santo Domingo without knowing the events that ensued in the French colony during the first quarter of the 19th century. In turn, to understand the events that lead to the first and only successful slave revolution, we have to explore, even if briefly, the events that occurred in Europe, especially in France, at the end of the 18th century.

The French Revolution (1789)

For centuries, Western Europe had been organized into kingdoms and territorial powers progressively becoming national units, most of them governed by absolute monarchies with kings who had unlimited power. The monarch's authority, often in collusion with the Church, was declared to be of divine origin, thus not subject to his contemporaries' scrutiny or under any control. The monarchies were for life and hereditary in nature.

The kings' power passed on to their heirs without considering their abilities or merits. These monarchical systems were characterized by great social, political, and economic inequality. On the one hand, a few enjoyed numerous privileges, especially the aristocracy and the nobility, those in the monarch's family tree, and rich landowners or feudal lords with lands and army. This privileged class also included the ecclesiastical hierarchy made up of archbishops, bishops, and superiors of religious orders. On the other hand, a vast majority of peasants, small merchants, and workers had practically no fundamental rights or freedoms. The different kingdoms were entangled in endless battles and disputes among themselves to keep accumulating land and power.

Still today, there are 43 monarchies in the world, with a king and/or a queen. European monarchies are constitutional in nature; that is, they respect the constitution and the will of the people expressed in democratic elections. However, in the very center of Europe, the small country of Liechtenstein (it is three hundred times smaller than the Dominican Republic), its prince, Hans Adam II, can veto laws and dissolve parliament as he wishes. In general, though, kings and queens do not have executive power; at most, they retain some moral authority. They often act as ambassadors for their countries or try to rise beyond internal national political disputes. In other areas of the world, kings still hold real and absolute power in their countries, especially in the Arab countries and Asia. The Sultan of Brunei, Muda Hassanal Bolkiah, appointed all the country's legislative body members and those of the Supreme Court. His palace, coincidentally, has 1,788 rooms and is the largest residential house in the world.[238]

The monarchies' constant abuse of power triggered, first in France and later in most European countries, a social movement to establish democracy and a republican political system.

In 1789, the French Revolution broke out, upholding the ideals of liberty, equality, fraternity, popular sovereignty, and citizens' fundamental rights. It is not surprising that, in such an environment, there was an aversion to any privilege, whether civil or ecclesiastical.

At the forefront of the revolution was an emerging social class of traders and merchants. They were the new bourgeoisie: people without aristocratic roots or blue blood in their veins, people who had, nonetheless, a significant economic and social weight.

As we shall see, however legitimate these ideals were, in many instances the revolution ended up betraying its own values. After all, being a monarch, or a monarchist, is not the only path to despotism. In France, the cradle of revolution, Napoleon Bonaparte proclaimed himself Emperor in 1799. So much for democratic values! The revolutionary illusion only lasted for ten years. However, since then, democratic ideals would be the political goal in most of Europe and, eventually, in the colonies. In Saint Domingue, the echoes of the revolution's ideals would arrive soon and with surprising consequences. The notions of freedom, human rights, justice, equality, and fraternity (*fraternité* in the original French) resonated in a unique way in a population where 90% of its inhabitants were slaves.

The French Revolution was a violent episode: kings, queens, aristocrats, nobles, ecclesiastical hierarchy, nuns and priests were murdered, and their property was confiscated. This was done in an unhinged attempt to carry out the legitimate ideals of the revolution. Further proof that no ideology is worth embracing fanatically. In 1793, the King of France, Louis XVI, was executed on the guillotine. The name of this killing device, designed to carry out capital punishment, comes from a surgeon, Joseph Ignace Guillotin, who introduced this more "humane" way of slicing somebody's head off quickly and efficiently. The last execution by guillotine took place in France in 1977.[239]

The French Revolution reaches Hispaniola

Out of 194 countries, 125 have in their official name the term "republic."[240] Among them, of course, the Republic of Haiti and the Dominican Republic. The mere title "Republic" is in itself a declaration of intent to uphold democratic values. Born in Europe and the United States, ideals of Liberty, Equality, and Fraternity would soon spread to the colonies, and new social movements demanded that their governments adhere to them. But, as it will become apparent, all groups would understand the revolutionary principles in the way that best suited them.

The French Revolution's ideals arrived in Hispaniola in the form of a slave uprising in Saint Domingue and in the liberal spirit of many leaders of the future Dominican Republic such as José Núñez de Cáceres, Juan Pablo Duarte or Gaspar Polanco, as we shall see in due course. Other politicians and military figures in Dominican history aligned with more traditional monarchical sentiments. Among them, we find Pedro Santana, Buenaventura Báez, José Antonio Salcedo or Juan Sánchez Ramírez.

Many of the internal conflicts in what will become the Dominican Republic, before and after independence, stem from these two conflicting positions that arose from the French Revolution. But let us not get ahead of ourselves; first, we shall look at what happened with the slaves in Saint Domingue.

The slave revolution that whites and mulattoes started

As we said before, not everyone understood the French Revolution's ideals in the same way. In Saint Domingue, the first people to claim these ideals for their own were not the slaves but the plantation owners, both whites and free mulattoes. Among the white owners, there was a spirit of real disaffection towards the French colonial system.

For them, the Revolution meant having the same rights as the French and eventually political emancipation from France in the same way the United States gained independence from the British in 1776.

Another sector of Dominguean society that understood the revolutionary ideals in their own particular way was the free mulattoes. This group controlled as much as a third of the colony's properties. By 1700, the number of free mulattoes was around 12,000 and reached 28,000 by the end of the century. These mulattoes were the descendants of freeborn sons and daughters of the white masters' slave concubines. They could acquire the right of inheritance through the paternal line and owned property, often including black slaves.[241] They enjoyed a comfortable life, and many were educated in France. For this group, equality had to do with being equal to the white owners; freedom meant to have the same rights, to be able to vote, and to not be discriminated against.

In France, the mulattoes organized a society called the "Society of the Friends of the Negroes" to defend their rights. They were respected by the more liberal bourgeois groups in France. They requested the French National Assembly (the governing body of France established after the Revolution) to recognize them as French citizens with exactly the same rights as their white continental Frenchmen (rights of women were still not considered back then).[242]

The Assembly hesitated, as if the values of freedom, equality, and fraternity applied only to white French. The whites of Saint Domingue took advantage of this vacillation and began a repression campaign against the mulattoes, while asking for more rights for themselves and the ability to govern the colony with greater autonomy.

And then the Vincent Ogé's tragedy happened.

The life and death (1791) of Vincent Ogé

Vincent Ogé was one of those rich mulattoes, three-quarters French and a quarter African (his father was white, and his mother was mixed). His family was wealthy and owned a coffee plantation in Saint Domingue. After his education in France, Vincent returned to Saint Domingue to resume the family businesses. When the French Revolution broke out in 1789, he was in Paris and the experience awakened in him a vindictive spirit and a zeal to fight for the mulattoes' rights. He organized a movement demanding the right to vote for rich mulattoes, both in France and in Saint Domingue. Like other people of his social class, he owned slaves and did not question or challenge slavery. In 1790, he returned home and lobbied among the mulattoes for their rights in the upcoming colonial elections. He demanded that the authorities allow free mulattoes to vote and to hold public and government positions.

Ogé warned the French authorities:

> *I shall not call the plantations to rise... When I solicited from the National Assembly a decree* [granting full legislative powers to the Colonial Assembly, giving the colony almost complete autonomy in which free men and owners could participate], *which I obtained in favor of the American colonists, formerly known under the injurious epithet of 'men of mixed blood,' I did not include in my claims the condition of the negroes who live in servitude. You and our adversaries have misrepresented my steps in order to bring me into discredit* [by claiming he wanted abolition of slavery] *with honorable men. No, no, gentlemen! we have put forth a claim only on behalf of a class of freemen, who, for two centuries, have been under the yoke of oppression. We require the execution of the decree of the 8th of March. We insist on its promulgation... Before employing my means, I make use of mildness; but if, contrary to my expectation, you do not satisfy my demand, I*

am not answerable for the disorder into which my just vengeance may carry me.[243]

The governor refused these demands. Ogé gathered between 250 to 300 men, all free mulattoes, who started a protest. They achieved some victory over militia groups in the colony, but they were no match for the professional soldiers. The group took refuge in Santo Domingo, where they expected to be welcomed by the Spanish authorities. Big mistake. Santo Domingo returned the dissidents to Saint Domingue, and they were brutally tortured. Ogé and some others were murdered. It was 1791.[244] Ogé, a rich man and owner of slaves, would become a martyr and the symbol of the fight against injustices in a slave society.

The slaves react

The Ogé episode and the cause for the mulatto liberation soon became known to the black slaves who also rose up for their own freedom.

Two factors proved crucial for what was about to take place.

One: over decades of enslavement, and despite coming from different parts of West Africa, the slaves developed a common language blending French and native African languages: Haitian Creole.

Two: The slaves did not form a uniform mass of workers. The plantations' workforce was organized hierarchically. Among the slaves, some were foremen in charge of supervising other slaves. [245] These foremen, or managers, were leaders who had authority and had the respect of their peers. Their position as community leaders, paired with a new common cause for which to fight, created the perfect formula for the emergence of small slave armies scattered throughout the colony.

The revolt begins (1791)

Legend has it that it all started with a secret voodoo rite known as the *Bois Caiman Ceremony* in Morne-Rouge. In that ceremony, some two hundred slaves promised to organize and lead the revolt, establishing a network and a coordinated plan. These leaders held positions of rank in their plantations and had the authority to persuade other slaves to follow.[246]

From Bois Caiman, one by one, from one plantation to the next, they burned crops, properties and their owners along with them. The rebellion spread rapidly as more slaves joined, ready for total destruction. Soon things seemed to be out of control.

The revolt broke out in 1791 in the northern plantations of Saint Domingue, and it would not end until 1804. Whites and mulattoes were pressed to forget their disputes and face a situation that threatened to ruin them all equally.[247]

Incomprehensibly, for about two hundred years, the Haitian landowners and the elite failed to recognize the immense number of people they subjugated.

The governor of Santo Domingo, Joaquín García, who would have a key role in the following confusing years, informed his superiors in Spain that a slave army had begun an uprising in the neighboring colony: some black slaves, some free mulattos and even some whites, had launched a campaign to burn plantations and assassinate their owners.[248]

The slaves' surprising first claims

The French Revolution sought equality and freedom, and so did whites and mulattoes in Saint Domingue, each group in their own way. But what did the slaves want? Shocking as it may seem, they did not claim for either of these two rights...for now.

As it turned out, there were certain rumors, of course false, of the king in France granting the slaves three days off per week, softening their living and working conditions, and prohibiting whipping the slaves. The latter should come as a surprise since the Black Code of 1685 (100 years before!) already banned that particular practice. An excellent example to illustrate how irrelevant the laws coming from the motherland were.

As none of these measures were implemented, the slaves had a very specific cause for which to fight. No one mentioned equal rights; no one shouted freedom or emancipation. They merely wanted better living conditions. No one listened to their claims, and slowly but surely, these claims became more radical.[249] It is a very good example of how contingent history can be. The black slave leaders, who enjoyed some privileges in the plantations before the uprising, submitted a series of conditions to the Colonial Assembly, the French government's body in Saint Domingue. If the Assembly were to accept these conditions, they pledged to end the conflict.

Their demands were these: the release of the arrested, amnesty for those who took part in the revolt and, again, the prohibition from using the whip. It seems as if the rebels themselves were not sure about the revolution's success and were ready to go back to their everyday lives as long as there were no reprisals. For now, no one talked about abolishing slavery. Think of this: if the slaves' requests had been considered, the uprising would have ended. Now, do you suppose the French colonial authorities ever listened to the slaves' claims? They did not. They failed to see how weak their position was and refused to negotiate. Over the months, the insurgents' demands would become more and more radical.[250]

Santo Domingo supports the rebellion

The rebels did not fight alone. They had an unlikely ally: Santo Domingo. Make no mistake, Spain was not engaging in this dispute out of concern for the slaves. But by supporting the rebels, Spain had an opportunity to weaken France's power on the island and to regain some of the territories lost almost 200 years earlier.[251]

There were also some ideological factors to justify Spanish support of the slaves. Santo Domingo was still a monarchy, while France was a new republic that threatened to establish a different social and political order. The confrontation between the two colonies was part of a larger conflict between both systems -so much so that Spanish authorities in Santo Domingo were more afraid of a Republican threat than of a slave uprising.

The response of Santo Domingo's Governor, Joaquín García, to Saint Domingue's internal conflict was, by political necessity, deceitful. While, officially, he adopted a neutral position, he secretly helped the rebellious slaves. For example, the insurgents once in Santo Domingo could exchange their loot taken from the Dominguean plantations for weapons and food. A French general complained of the *"infernal Machiavellianism of the Spanish."*[252] Some French soldiers reported that many Dominicans did not stop trading with the rebels. *"These Dominicans,"* they said, *"continue to encourage the rebellious slaves in their crime; they give them provisions, weapons, and ammunition and allow them to export furniture from burned plantations and products that the slaves have stolen."* Insurgents and Spaniards even traded with French prisoners.[253]

The former slaves become pro-Spanish and monarchists

The support the former slaves received from Santo Domingo made them firm supporters of the Spanish monarchy. Some, imprisoned by the French, claimed that they were fighting for the King of Spain, who promised them total freedom, and asserted that they would die fighting. It should come as no surprise to learn that some of the main rebel leaders took refuge in Santo Domingo.[254]

We can appreciate the irony: former slaves fighting for their freedom as envisioned in the new republican values were siding with the monarchical, authoritarian, and pro-slavery authorities in Santo Domingo.

But, of course, it was not out of ignorance. For the rebellious slaves of Saint Domingue, Santo Domingo was a welcoming place that offered the possibility for trading and a place where even slaves would enjoy greater autonomy from the colonial state and the plantations.[255]

Another factor that explains the slaves' support for the monarchy was their knowledge of French monarchical signs and symbols. Their fight for freedom was not primarily a fight against the king but against the plantation owners. After all, the French king issued decrees and laws prohibiting extreme cruelty and promoting other measures to protect the slaves, such as providing enough food and clothing for them.[256]

The Catholic Church also supports the slaves' cause

The Catholic Church's interest in the conflict emanated mainly from the fact that the Church was one of the fiercest enemies of the French Revolution's ideals. Besides, most slaves professed the Catholic faith, in compliance with the Black Code of 1685. Consequently, many viewed the Spanish confessional state with sympathy as opposed to the new atheist, anti-monarchical, and anti-clerical French system. For the clerics of Santo Domingo, the slave revolution was a sort of divine punishment against the French.[257]

Some believers could boast that both Saint Domingue and Santo Domingo had a special devotion to Our Lady of Altagracia.[258] Still today, it is a very popular devotion both in the Dominican Republic and in Haiti. [259] To this day, in continuing a long historical tradition, the faithful from the Western part travel all the way to Higüey (the far eastern corner of the island) for the annual pilgrimage to Altagracia.[260]

France's uncomfortable response to the rebellion in Saint Domingue

France needed to act, but it was in an awkward position. On the one hand, in Europe, there was a struggle for freedom and equality, while, on the other hand, the colonies still kept slave-system laws. What to do with the rebellion in Saint Domingue? At first, the landowners sought help from England, a country with a robust monarchical tradition,[261] but the move only added more tension to the situation.

On April 4, 1792, the Constitutive National Assembly, the new French governing body, in an attempt to appease the situation, decided to grant citizenship to free mulattoes and gave them the same rights as the whites.[262] Such a measure, understandably, did not sit well with white owners, and even less so with black slaves who were not even mentioned in this new agreement. The situation was already so tense that mulattoes and white owners ended up joining forces against the slaves who, by then, were ready to fight any oppressive group regardless of color or race.[263]

In that same year, anticipating the difficulties in implementing the new law in Saint Domingue, the National Assembly sent 6,000 soldiers[264] led by Commissars Léger-Félicité Sonthonax and Étienne Polverel. Their main objective was to maintain and protect the rights of the new mulatto citizens and, at the same time, to end the slave revolution.

The commissioners encountered strong opposition from the French authorities in Saint Domingue, who would not accept and tolerate sharing equal rights with free mulattoes. The situation was so tense that only three days after the commissioners' arrival, they deported the Dominguean governor himself, Mr. Blanchelande, back to France. He was the Monsieur who executed Vincent Ogé. Blanchelande would be guillotined in Paris alongside his assistant, who also happened to be his son.[265]

Sonthonax's mission, again, was not to free the slaves, but quite the opposite, to suppress the slave rebellion and to enforce the decree giving equal rights to free mulattoes and white owners.[266] The plan would be a total failure because he was not ready to follow through.

The French Commissioner realized that it was too late to fix the situation; the only viable move to keep control of Saint Domingue was to abolish slavery. But his radical idea, in his effort to maintain stability in the colony, would face an unsurmountable problem when Europe declared war against France.

5.

The Conflict Between France and Spain

France's war against Spain, England, Holland, Austria and Prussia (1793)

The situation was as unstable on the island as it was in Europe itself. France experimented with a new political system, challenging the traditional European monarchies, thereby becoming a direct threat to several neighboring countries. The events in France questioned and threatened the authority of the kings in a very real way. In the name of democratic and modern ideals, the revolutionaries invaded Holland, and in 1793 they executed the French King, Louis XVI. That was the last straw. That same year, a coalition of conservative monarchies -England, Austria, Holland, Prussia, and Spain- declared war on France.[267]

Almost one hundred years (1701-1793) of relative stability between France and Spain were about to end, and in Hispaniola everything was going to change.

The declaration of war in Europe opened an opportunity for the English to launch a military campaign for control of Saint Domingue. As part of their army, they enlisted slaves from the island in return for their freedom.[268] An awkward promise, if we consider that in the neighboring British colony of Jamaica, many blacks were still slaves. In Santo Domingo, there was an interest in advancing on the French part of the island, and the two new allies, Spain and England, eventually invaded part of Saint Domingue.[269] It was open war.

By April 1793, Santo Domingo's governor, Joaquín García, announced a program that *"would admit under the king's sovereign protection all the* [Saint Domingue] *Blacks who have sustained the war against the diabolical tenets of the whites."*[270] Let us be clear: For García, the *"diabolical tenets"* were the liberal ideals of the French Revolution, and the "whites" were the French now at war against Spain. He was conveniently ignoring the obvious fact that he was as white as the French. García cleverly promised that *"all good French people, without distinction of state or condition,* [thus including also the slaves], *would receive the king's* [of Spain] *protection should they join the Spanish side."*[271] As you can imagine, the slaves' liberation was not the governors' concern. Two years later, in an exchange with the Spanish prime minister, García himself wrote: *"slavery is the most useful and beneficial asset on the island."*[272]

However, for the Spaniards, it was an opportunity to organize raids into Saint Domingue's territory and to mobilize five military companies (two of them made of *moreno* soldiers) in preparation for the invasion and control of Saint Domingue.[273]

The rise of Toussaint Louverture

Among the ex-slaves who fought with Spain against France was a certain Toussaint Louverture. Louverture did not win his freedom in the revolution, but 20 years earlier, in 1770.[274] He was a coachman on the Bréda plantation. He was a slave but did not work on the plantation. He received some education, and ten years before the revolution was freed by his master. Louverture got a few acres of land, was able to buy his own slaves, and start a new life as a planter.

Seemingly, when the revolt broke out in 1791, Louverture's first move was to take his former master to safety and only then joined the rebellion. Louverture, as was common among freed people of color at the time, had a rather French-style cultural and social outlook. He spent the rest of his life concealing the fact that he too had exploited slaves on his plantations.[275]

At any rate, in due time, Toussaint Louverture and his army would thwart the Spanish, English and French plans in Saint Domingue. He would become the leader for whom the slave cause had been waiting, and he was building a large army behind him. Toussaint joined the Spanish cause, and as early as August 1793, in a public letter addressed to the French representatives, he denounced *"the criminality of the French Republicans, who have executed King Louis XVI as if he were a villain."* And he added: *"As long as God gives us the force and means, we will acquire another Liberty, different from that which you tyrants pretend to impose on us."*[276] Thus, a liberator of slaves opposed those who fought against slavery (the French Republicans) while backing a monarchical system that would support slavery.

From slaves in Saint Domingue to soldiers of the Spanish army

The alliance between the Spaniards and the rebels of Saint Domingue mobilized some 10,000 men on the Spanish side. With that kind of military power, by the end of 1793 most of the north of Saint Domingue fell into Spanish hands.[277]

An astonishing transformation was thus taking place. The slave rebels were no longer seen as feared insurgents but as valuable assets for military recruitment to expand the Spanish troops.[278]

Think about this: The slaves who started a revolution only two years before became coveted recruits for the English and the Spanish armies.

THE CONFLICT BETWEEN FRANCE AND SPAIN

But events were about to take an unexpected turn.

Abolition of slavery in France, August 29, 1793

Sonthonax and Polverel, the commissioners sent by France to bring order to the colony, understood that the only way to resolve the conflict was to abolish slavery. They might have seen the apparent contradiction of upholding the revolution's values while keeping in place a slave system of production. So, in an extraordinarily bold move, they unilaterally declared, on behalf of the French government, the end of slavery in Saint Domingue.

Now, to save the colony, the French owners in Saint Domingue had to free their slaves, who were in turn the basis of its prosperity.[279] The alternative was to face a force made up of former slaves and the Spanish army, which ironically represented a monarchical power that still practiced slavery. How about that?

At any rate, Sonthonax's decision was risky but proved to be successful. The movement for emancipation was growing strong in France. A mixed commission from Saint Domingue attended the National Convention in Paris, and, persuaded by Sonthonax, agreed to take abolitionist measures. By February 4 of 1794, France promulgated a universal emancipation law for all French territories.[280] It was the first declaration of its kind in all the Americas. Now, that changed the whole picture.

The rebels switch sides: from the Spanish to the French army

The liberation of slaves became a handy tool for the French Republic to recruit troops for its own army, following the practice of the Spanish military. In fact, emancipation turned out to be a crucial weapon of war that helped Saint Domingue, cornered by a coalition of English, Spanish and former slaves' armies, to gain the upper hand.[281]

As soon as the end of slavery came into effect in Saint Domingue, many blacks fighting for Spain moved to the French side. One of the most influential leaders to defect was none other than Toussaint Louverture, after only one year serving in the Spanish army. In 1794, he joined the French forces with his 4,000 men.[282]

The exodus of soldiers from the Spanish to the French side was so sudden and numerous that the French army had soldiers still wearing Spanish symbols and uniforms.[283]

This shifting of alliances should not come as a surprise. The recruitment of former slaves by the Spanish and the English armies had a fundamental flaw: the former slaves were supposed to fight for freedom when in fact, slavery was still prevalent in these two countries and their territories, and plantation owners had no interest in ending it.

The French regain ground in Santo Domingo

With their regenerated troops, the French recovered much of the territory lost to Spain not long before (Hincha, Las Caobas, Bánica, San Miguel de la Atalaya, and San Rafael), and its residents had to move to San Juan de la Maguana and Azua on Santo Domingo's side.[284] It is entirely plausible that the same ex-slaves who some years back conquered those lands for Spain would now be fighting to take them back for France.

Emigration of ex-slaves to Santo Domingo

But not all former slaves became soldiers. Some in Saint Domingue left the fight and took over small plots and began small-scale subsistence farming. Others made a more drastic choice.

After 1794, many people who were formally declared free in Saint Domingue moved to Santo Domingo. It is easy to explain why: Many preferred to move from an emancipatory but severe regime to a country where slavery was still practiced, but living conditions were more tolerable.[285]

You could think, and rightly so, that once France declared universal emancipation, the slaves' revolution was no longer required, even more so as the former slaves were now fighting together with the French army against the Spanish and the English. Why would these former slaves continue to fight? Be patient; lots of things happened that need to be explained.

One of these occurred 4,600 miles away from the island, and it changed the whole political scenery spectacularly.

6.

The Treaty of Basel (1795)

By the end of the 18th century, Europe was mired in an institutional crisis. Six years after the beginning of the French Revolution, things got out of hand, and war broke out between European powers. The monarchies of Spain, England and Holland fought against the Republic of France. It was, above all, a turf war. In one of these territorial skirmishes, France occupied part of northern Spain. On July 22, 1795, Spain, to recover this occupied land, signed the Treaty of Basel with France. According to this treaty, France would give back to Spain the regions taken in the Peninsula, and Spain, in return, would give away all their territory in Hispaniola to France. After several centuries of settlers, pirates, conflicts, encounters and trades, for hundreds of families who had had those lands as their home for generations, everything was to end at the stroke of a pen on treaty parchment.

The Treaty of Basel had 17 articles that directly affected border issues between France and Spain. But number 9, only three lines, read like this:

> IX. *In exchange for the restitution referred to in article IV* [the northern Spanish territories bordering France], *the King of Spain, and his successors cede and relinquish all the Spanish part of the island of Santo Domingo to the French Republic.*

THE TREATY OF BASEL (1795)

And the treaty gives precise instructions about how to proceed with the transition:

> *A month after the ratification of the present treaty is known on that island [of Hispaniola], the Spanish troops will be ready to evacuate the places, posts and establishments that they occupy, and hand them over to the French troops for the French Republic. That includes cannons, munitions of war and any items available necessary for their defense. The inhabitants of the Spanish part of Santo Domingo, who for their interests or other reasons prefer to leave to other possessions of His Catholic Majesty [of Spain], can take their belongings and do so within one year from the date of this treaty. The respective generals and commanders of the two nations shall agree on the measures to be taken to implement this article.*[286]

It is hard to imagine the reaction of the residents of Santo Domingo as they received the news. The treaty might have been a positive accomplishment for the historical chronicles in the Peninsula and for the coexistence of the two neighboring nations in Europe. For Santo Domingo, however, the treaty was devastating and unsettled the lives of thousands of Dominicans.

No one, neither in Spain nor in France, seemed to realize a major flaw with the plan. As it turns out, Saint Domingue was no longer controlled by the French but by the former slave turned military leader, Toussaint Louverture. Toussaint fought with the Spanish army and then alongside France, but at that point, he had his own army and did not have to respond to any colonial power.

Santo Domingo is in limbo (neither Spanish nor entirely French)

Following the Treaty of Basel, Santo Domingo administratively assumed the laws that applied to Saint Domingue. So overnight, Santo Domingo became an emancipated colony, and slavery became illegal.[287] Although, as you know, easier said than done.

In August, a month after the Treaty, France approved a new constitution establishing the principle of legal integration, whereby the same laws would apply to France and to all its colonies, unlike in the past, where different territories had different laws. That, of course, meant that everyone had the same rights, including the right not to be enslaved or relegated to a different legal status based on race, color, or ancestry.[288]

Santo Domingo was left in a puzzling situation. On the one hand, there was an operational Spanish colonial administration, including Governor García, but, on the other hand, few French officers arrived at their new posts. The residents, in turn, were unsure who their legitimate authorities were or to which country they belonged.[289]

In truth, no one knew. While the region was officially France, the Spanish authorities still managed to maintain partial power in Santo Domingo until 1801, in part because the French authorities had other military priorities in Europe.

Only a few French officials and military personnel arrived at the colony. Revealingly, much of the French correspondence during those years still referred to Santo Domingo as "the Spanish part." It was not inaccurate since Governor García and other Spanish officials maintained a large part of their local civil and military authority.[290] French authorities entrusted the colony's plantations and the central government to Spanish officials; consequently, for a time, there was no radical social change.[291]

1795: Is Dominican sentiment being born?

Regardless of the level of confusion provoked by the radical social and economic changes, what seemed predictable was the Dominicans' frustration and anger towards the Spanish metropolis. Considering that there was an ongoing war between ex-slaves and the French against the Spanish, the negotiated surrender that completely ignored the island's fragile situation was nothing short of a stab in the back. It is worth it to read the article again to grasp the gravity of the treaty: *"The King of Spain and his successors cede and abandon the entire Spanish part of the island of Santo Domingo to the French Republic in all property."* Since Osorio's devastations in 1606, about 200 years earlier, the island had learned to live as part of two nations, in a tense relationship, a prosperous trade, with border conflicts, and a cultural and racial mixture. The struggle against the French had fashioned a true feeling of nationhood among the inhabitants of Santo Domingo, defined in terms of the most refined Hispanic identity (*Hispanidad*)[292] But these three lines of the Treaty would cast doubt on how much the Spanish authorities cared about Santo Domingo and the Dominicans. One can only wonder, given these circumstances, how "Spanish" would Dominicans feel, knowing that the motherland had relinquished control of Santo Domingo to the French.

People in Santo Domingo would never identify with France, but after the Treaty of Basel, probably many people in Santo Domingo did not feel very "Spanish" either.

The tortuous and difficult handover of Santo Domingo to the French

The person in charge of dealing with the political chaos during those years was Captain Joaquín García, governor of Santo Domingo. He had to deliver the colony to France. It took him as long as five years and several failed attempts to accomplish his mission and, even then, as we will see, he was not entirely successful.

There was confusion, to be sure, but the Spanish colony's handover to the French was very real and already happening. French authorities took concrete administrative measures for Santo Domingo to become irreversibly French.

The handover of Santo Domingo meant a change of identity for its inhabitants, from Spanish subjects to French citizens.[293]

The inhabitants of Saint Domingue emigrate to Santo Domingo

There was another aspect regarding the unification of the island: on the French side, the plantation system could no longer be based on the massive exploitation of slaves, and the French authorities had to limit their citizens' freedom. Only by controlling the labor force could the French regime establish economically profitable plantations.[294] But in principle, as no one was bound to one particular side of the island, the plan had some surprising consequences.

As you remember, some years earlier, when the slaves of Saint Domingue would flee to Santo Domingo searching for a better life, they did so illegally. After the island's unification, nothing could prevent its citizens from moving West to East. This free movement, of course, would apply to all citizens, including freed slaves.

Despite the successful emancipation process, in Saint Domingue, Toussaint Louverture, our slave hero, implemented an oppressive labor regime and harsh military obligations. Like so many people with too much power, Toussaint proved exceptionally cruel with whoever would dare to oppose him. When his own nephew, Moïse backed an uprising of cultivators protesting forced plantation labor in 1801, Toussaint had him executed along with 5,000 of his followers.[295]

The strict conditions of labor prompted many free workers to emigrate to Santo Domingo, triggering a swift response from the French authorities. An order was issued to prevent *"a formal invasion of the territory* [Santo Domingo] *belonging to the* [French] *Republic."* [296] Of course, there was no "invasion." There was no foreign army, no pirates. French citizens were moving to another part of their own country. It was not only the French who were scared by this "leakage" of labor. Toussaint himself wrote in 1799: *"a great number of our cultivators take refuge in the Spanish part, which weakened Saint-Domingue's labor force and therefore constituted an abuse that must be suppressed."*[297]

The choice for the recently freed was clear. In Saint Domingue, they had two main alternatives to make a living: working on the plantations or joining the military. In Santo Domingo, the majority were mulatto descendants of slaves, and some where still slaves. In general, through generations, the mulatto population had forged spaces with greater personal and economic autonomy, for instance as ranchers or peasants. They were poor but free.

Naively, the French military man Antoine Chanlatte wrote in 1800: *"What is surprising but nonetheless true, is that the slaves even in the Spanish part have preferred their state* [of bondage] *to the facility that they had to go to the French part where liberty awaited them."*[298]

Mr. Chanlatte failed to comprehend that freedom *"à la French"* was harsher than life *"à la Dominican,"* where for centuries the peasants formed and preserved their own version of freedom in the mountains and in the field.

The rural autonomous peasantry, spread throughout the country, was a constant element in the social and economic landscape of Santo

Domingo; it persisted despite several attempts by Spanish, French and later Haitian powers, *"to subordinate it to their own political agendas."* Not even Toussaint, with all his military might, having won the war against slavery and becoming the most powerful man on the island, was able to turn Santo Domingo's economy into a plantation system.[299]

New racial conflicts

The Treaty of Basel generated an unexpected reaction on the Spanish side. As the colony was technically France, the slave owners in Santo Domingo were worried that they could lose their slaves. To avoid such a fate, they organized a massive emigration to other Spanish territories, taking their slaves with them. As the situation unfolded, some French agents in the colony encouraged these slaves to rebel against the practice.[300]

It was a new and, in turn, sad legal problem. According to the treaty, those citizens of Santo Domingo who were willing and able had one year to leave the island and were allowed to take their property with them. But, and here is the rub, for those unwilling to be part of the French colony, slave laws would still be in effect, and thus, Spanish authorities claimed that slaves were to be considered property and therefore had to leave with their owners.[301] The French maintained that this was not a valid argument, since the right to be free (universal right) is more important than the right to property (civil law).[302]

According to Toussaint himself, some 3,000 slaves emigrated with their masters from Santo Domingo. That represented a fifth of those who lived in the colony at the time. It was one more obstacle to Toussaint's hopes of turning Santo Domingo into an economy based on large plantations and, therefore, he tried to stop this practice.[303]

Santo Domingo, a slave state, pro monarchical and... pro-British

The situation was confusing and not only from a social and legal point of view. There were some political conundrums too. The inhabitants of Santo Domingo were traditionally Hispanic and monarchists and they viewed becoming, overnight, part of a Republic with skepticism. Not only that, as lax as the slave situation could be, slavery in Santo Domingo was still legal when the new emancipationist rulers took power. Some slave owners even presented a petition to the Spanish king to invalidate the Treaty to recover their property, including their slaves.[304]

Thus, among Dominican plantation owners there was a growing anti-republican and anti-abolitionist sentiment. Unsurprisingly they felt closer to the English who defended monarchy and slavery than to their new French rulers, and, predictably, they ignored Toussaint's call to swear allegiance to France. In fact, many Dominicans would welcome English ships into Santo Domingo's ports, and they would swear allegiance to them in exchange for protection against the French. Many even joined the English forces.[305]

The hostility against the French was born out of fear but also included a degree of racism. A French colonist explained his view when the residents of Bánica cheered the English army:

> *If White Republicans came to take possession* [of Santo Domingo], *then we would be able to count on the fidelity of the majority of* [Santo Domingo's] *inhabitants, but if blacks come, and above all only blacks, then the Republic's support among Dominicans would quickly evaporate.*[306]

7.

Toussaint Louverture, A French General Against French Power

How Toussaint became the island's leader (1798)

In 1795, Toussaint recovered for the French the territory of Saint Domingue that had been occupied by the Spanish army.[307] His next goal was to halt the English incursions. This campaign would make Toussaint, by then one of many military leaders on the west side, the island's undisputed leader.[308]

The English had occupied important areas in Saint Domingue and launched raids in Santo Domingo's territory. They hoped to control the sites of Laschaobas, Bánica, Neiba, San Juan de la Maguana, and Azua before the French did.

The Spanish governor García, in theory, had to keep his troops in Neiba, San Juan, and Azua to stop the English advance. But in reality, those regions were technically France, so García as the Spanish governor of a relinquished territory, remain neutral. Thus, the English took Neiba and San Juan without resistance[309] and appointed Lord John Simcoe as the governor of the conquered territories. The English enclaves were defended with 14,800 men. About half of them were former slaves who fought for England in exchange for freedom and goods. A somewhat contradictory policy since the nearby British colonies had as many as 70,000 slaves.[310]

The war's prospective outcome looked favorable for Toussaint, since he faced the English army with some 15,000-20,000 men,[311] and they had the home-field advantage. The English did not know the territory, and probably many did not know the war's ultimate goal. The outcome was unsurprising.

In July of 1797, the English, by then the most important maritime power in the area, bombarded Puerto Plata for three hours and looted the city.[312] But six months later, Toussaint began a decisive attack and sent an army of 11,000 men from Fort Liberté, north of Saint Domingue, to Laschaobas. After a 160-mile march (about 54 hours walking), they still managed to defeat the Spanish and English soldiers, including also *"black troops"* at the service of England.[313]

By March of 1798, Toussaint was already celebrating his victories in Neiba, San Juan, and Laschaobas, condemning the traitors of the French Republic and those who served the *"projet liberticide"* (freedom killer project) of the English.[314]

That same year, the English left the island for good.[315]

Toussaint: the unwanted French hero

Toussaint was in total control of the situation. His commitment to France seemed real, but it was fragile. The French authorities became progressively more suspicious of their unwanted hero as he kept accumulating moral, military, and political power.

Amid this unstable situation, there was still some business to be completed: Santo Domingo's transfer to France. General Rochambeau had to take control of the new French territory, but he refused to do so *"with an army of blacks."*: Toussaint's army. Thus, the French entry to the Spanish side was postponed.[316]

The next attempt to take possession of Santo Domingo took place in 1798. This time, to García's dismay, General Hedouville, governor of Saint Domingue, did not want to discuss the issue. The problem, again, was Toussaint. Hedouville wanted to move to Saint Domingue and, at the same time, try to snatch Toussaint's political and military control. He failed and was forced to leave the island. Toussaint's power was no match for the French authorities.

Toussaint's plans in Saint Domingue

Before Toussaint entered Santo Domingo, he became involved in Saint Domingue's affairs. In May 1796, French authorities coming all the way from France met with the colony's Governor Monsieur Laveaux and the civil commissioners to discuss the island's future. The situation was extraordinarily uncertain as their authority was weakening rapidly. That became obvious as Toussaint also showed up for the meeting. Together they began to work for the reconstruction and reorganization of the country, mainly Saint Domingue, since Santo Domingo did not yet have a strong French military and administrative presence.

Toussaint intended to maintain the plantation system. He returned the properties to their rightful owners seeking to reach a balance between white, black, and mulatto. Surprisingly, he forced former slaves back to their usual jobs, albeit as wage earners, to *"suppress vagrancy."* The workers would share a quarter of the production, half would go to the public treasury, and the other quarter would be for the owners.[317] He established dealings with the United States to supply him with arms, food, and other merchandise in exchange for colonial products.[318]

TOUSSAINT LOUVERTURE, A FRENCH GENERAL AGAINST FRENCH POWER

Toussaint followed some democratic and participatory principles of the French Revolution, but he also wanted Saint Domingue to become the productive colony of yesteryear.

Civil war in Saint Domingue and total power for Toussaint

But Toussaint had an internal problem: Saint Domingue was divided into the Northern and the Southern Province. He controlled the northern part, but General André Rigaud ruled the south. This general belonged to the French army, was a mulatto, and fought for the mulattos. His prejudice against blacks was such that he wore a brown wig with straight hair.[319] Rigaud did not accept being ruled by a black man who only a few years before was a coachman on a plantation in the north. The civil war in future Haiti broke out in 1799. In one year, Toussaint defeated his opponent. His power seemed to be unstoppable. In 1800 he became Governor and Commander-in-Chief of the French Army at Saint Domingue, and his main goal was to restore the colony to its former glory.[320]

Several factors explain Toussaint's rise to power. His mastery of the art of war, his unscrupulous use of brute force, an inexhaustible intensity (they said he only slept a few hours at night), and a charisma fueled by popular proclamations about the ideals of liberty and equality. We will find these same qualities in a contemporary character, Napoleon Bonaparte.[321] We will talk about him in the next chapter.

Anxiety and uncertainty about Toussaint's entrance into Santo Domingo

Meanwhile, in Santo Domingo, Governor García was gradually preparing to hand over the colony and gather the Spanish soldiers in the capital city. The plan was for the Spanish troops to depart as soon as the French army would arrive at the capital.[322] But García was no longer sure that he could control the city until the French would officially take over. It became apparent that Toussaint would take matters into his own hands and would capture it before them.

The Spanish Crown pressured him not to organize more evacuations, as the citizens were facing a highly uncertain future. Still, García tried to extend the deadline for leaving the country one more year.[323] The uneasiness, uncertainty, the feeling of isolation must have been asphyxiating.

In 1799, Toussaint was making plans to occupy the Spanish part despite opposition from the French government. The outcome was inevitable, and the owners in Santo Domingo were already afraid of losing their slaves.[324] They made desperate requests to Spanish officials to postpone the colony's transfer.[325] The Spanish Governor, however, was making the necessary arrangements to leave the island.

That same year, several ships arrived at Santo Domingo with *"El Situado"* (a periodic amount of funds sent to defray the public expenses of Santo Domingo). On those same ships, the members of the Royal Court (the judges) left the island. Only García remained with the last troops of the Santo Domingo garrison, some 1,200 men.[326]

Toussaint wants French authorization to take Santo Domingo

By 1800, Santo Domingo was poorly defended, and Toussaint had an army of 10,000 men next door. He could have taken the Spanish colony effortlessly. But the general had other plans, since he was not ready to take Santo Domingo as an ex-slave and be second-guessed by the French. Santo Domingo had to be taken officially and on behalf of France. So, in a bold and defiant move, Toussaint pressed the French governor, Phillipe Roume, to sanction his entry to Santo Domingo on France's behalf. Under threat, the permission was granted.

The French general Kerverseau contended that for the inhabitants of Santo Domingo, the problem was not the French army's arrival but becoming Toussaint's subjects, as the King of Spain did not cede the territories to Toussaint, but to the French Republic.[327] On June 26, Roume issued a new decree canceling the previous authorization to Toussaint. It was already too late.[328]

As the French authorities were complaining, *"Toussaint sent the white general Pierre Agé on a diplomatic mission to meet with Governor García, with whom he was to arrange for the long-delayed effective transfer of authority over Santo Domingo to the French Republic, represented by Toussaint."*[329]

What was Toussaint's interest in invading Santo Domingo?

But why was Toussaint interested in Santo Domingo? He was already the maximum authority in Saint Domingue where he could fulfill his political vision; taking Santo Domingo only meant further conflict with France and Spain...Why?

On the one hand, to control Santo Domingo meant a drastic increase in production, which would ensure its political survival. And on the other hand, it would guarantee the eradication of slavery on the Spanish side, which -though already illegal- was still commonly practiced.[330]

According to Toussaint himself, in 1800, auctions of French black citizens were still being made in Azua and elsewhere. Many Spaniards were engaged in this traffic. Consequently, he concluded, very conveniently for his interests, it was necessary to save the *"Frenchmen"* of Santo Domingo and preserve black citizens from slavery. To do so, he had to take that Spanish part of the island, especially Azua.[331] According to some estimates, by June 1800, there were ten to twelve thousand slaves in Santo Domingo, of a total population of 150,000.[332]

Another reason to occupy Santo Domingo was to improve the defensive position from a French attack since it was the island's most vulnerable part.³³³ Toussaint's fear of a French retaliation was well-founded. In France, an ambitious young General seized power and wanted his country to dominate in America. His name was Napoleon Bonaparte.³³⁴ But for now let's continue to follow Toussaint's steps.

Toussaint's dealings with the United States

While France and Spain allied against Toussaint, the latter started trading with the United States. Interesting choice. With the power and influence which he had, Toussaint could have campaigned and struggled for slave emancipation in other countries as well, for instance the slaves in Jamaica and the United States itself. Still, he preferred to sign secret non-aggression and trade treaties with those two countries in 1799. A more aggressive decision would have helped the slave's cause beyond Saint Domingue, but the colony's financial recovery and his own political survival proved to be more important.³³⁵

Toussaint's business with the United States enabled him to obtain weapons and supplies for his troops. In September 1800, he received 20,000 rifles, 10,000 pairs of pistols, and 60,000 pounds of gunpowder from the United States.³³⁶ It proved to be a valuable resource for the step he was about to take the following year. Toussaint benefited from the trade with by the US, while Dominicans were denied the benefits of legal trade with North Americans.³³⁷

Toussaint finally enters Santo Domingo

On January 26, 1801, Toussaint, vindicated by the Treaty of Basel and by the French "approval," and conveniently ignoring Roume's counter-orders, entered the city of Santo Domingo with 10,000 men without much resistance from the 1,500 troops defending it.³³⁸ The

French officials, already established in Santo Domingo, did not receive their "countryman" with much glee. On the contrary, most of them embarked for Venezuela and other parts of the Antilles.[339] That was the level of trust that the French felt for the revolutionary rebel.

But most of the residents did not leave the island and were first-hand witnesses of an astonishing scene:

> *I remember the confusion, the terror, and surprise of those observing the black troops with their military and civilian paraphernalia and insignia parading through the city. How gloomy was the mood when the tricolor flag* [the French one] *was flying in the Homage fortress instead of the Spanish.*[340]

As agreed in the Treaty of Basel of 1795, the transfer of Santo Domingo to the French was completed five years later. One of the first consequences was the dismantling of the Spanish political apparatus.[341]

At last, Governor García left for Maracaibo, where he arrived with 1,803 people, including political leaders, administrators, military officers, soldiers, families, and, according to the Maracaibo entry record, with 360 slaves.[342]

After three hundred years, the Spanish authorities left the island, leaving behind a population in a very uncertain predicament. What seemed inevitable after the Spanish authorities' departure was the intensification of an already growing national sentiment by the locals that could be identified as specifically Dominican.[343] On one hand, they were strangers to the French language and its economic system, but, on the other hand, they were progressively further removed from Spanish influence.

Toussaint's Hispaniola

By 1801, Toussaint was in control of the whole island. One of his first moves was to require the population to go back to their everyday tasks. He also invited those who had left the island to return. Shockingly, he allowed them to bring along those people of *"whichever color"* they took as their property.[344]

In March 1801, Toussaint consecrated this vision in a constitution that aimed to institutionalize his political authority permanently. The constitution was drafted by a multiracial delegation of men from both colonies; five Dominicans signed it. Among other significant aspects, the document asserted the abolition of slavery. It also named Toussaint governor of the island *"for the rest of his glorious life."* Interestingly the "Carta Magna" declared that Saint Domingue was a French colony, and as such, *"all men* [on the island] *are born, live and die free and French."*[345]

Toussaint's economic vision was to turn the former Spanish colony's economy from a system based on subsistence agriculture and livestock into an intensive farming organization as in Saint Domingue.[346] It was a very ambitious plan. For it to work, he needed an intense labor force resembling suspiciously that of the slave system, so much so that the alleged abolition of slavery he proclaimed proved to be very hard to implement in practice. Some scholars claim that there is no written evidence that Toussaint abolished slavery in Santo Domingo. In fact, as we have seen, he allowed the Dominican owners to return to their country with their slaves and upheld his promise to maintain local institutions and traditions to convince the Dominicans to stay in Santo Domingo.[347]

A dilemma: Intense production system or abolition of slavery

Toussaint wanted the workers to stay on their respective plantations, be treated fairly, and receive a quarter of the profits. But, alas, he also required them to work on these plantations and to remain subordinate and obedient.[348] It was a thin line, and some in Santo Domingo complained and accused the new leader of inducing all Spaniards, regardless of social class and color, into forced labor.[349]

Toussaint, in turn, blamed the inhabitants of the East for being lazy. He did not understand that in Santo Domingo for almost three centuries, in a land dedicated to raising livestock and subsistence agriculture, the pace of labor was not as cruel and demanding as Saint Domingue's intensive export-oriented and slave-based mode of production.

Toussaint wanted to import Saint Domingue's model to Santo Domingo but without slaves, and that would be one of his failures.[350]

Not all of Toussaint's measures were missteps. He favored the growth of the economy in different ways. To combat the poverty in Santo Domingo, he eliminated export taxes except for a 6% levy for sugar, coffees, cotton, cocoa, and tobacco leaving through the former Spanish ports; [351] and he renovated main roads. He included the peoples of Santo Domingo in the island's political life, for example, involving them in the drafting of the constitution. Toussaint even went against his people as he let white settlers emigrate back to their former plantations.[352] To sum it up, the General tended to favor wealthy groups (whether in the east or the west) more than those working in the fields.[353]

Toussaint the Catholic

Toussaint was, without a doubt, a republican and a revolutionary, and also a devout Catholic. Although in open opposition to the French Revolution's secular sentiments, he imposed Catholicism as the official and only religion of the colony and actively repressed other manifestations of faith, especially those associated with the African roots of the population.[354]

His interest in religion went further, as he assumed control of the institutional church in Santo Domingo, overseeing priests' appointments and creating some new parishes.[355]

The exodus from Santo Domingo

Unsurprisingly, Toussaint's measures didn't appeal to all. Many, in the eastern part, were leaving the island. The number of people fleeing the country was such that, after five years of unification, Toussaint prohibited anyone from leaving Santo Domingo except for government officials and military units.[356]

Although we don't know exactly how many people left the colony, an 1803 registry of entries to Cuba counted 16,000 Dominicans. A total estimate of 100,000 people emigrated to Cuba, Puerto Rico and Venezuela.[357]

Among those migrants were Mr. Juan José Duarte Rodríguez (a prosperous peninsular merchant from Vejer de la Frontera, Cádiz, Spain) and his wife, Manuela Díez Jiménez (a native of El Seibo, daughter of the Spanish colonist Antonio Díez Baíllo and of the Creole Rufina Jiménez Benítez). In 1813 the couple became parents of their fourth son Juan Pablo, future Dominican national hero and one of the most important characters in the country's history.

8.

Napoleon Changes Toussaint's Plans

History is always full of surprises. Toussaint could have achieved a durable unification of the island, or on the contrary, he could have to deal with internal conflicts and rebellions. Maybe he could have reached an agreement with the mother country, France, and Spain would have forgotten its first colony forever. We will never know, because the international panorama and that of the Caribbean island was about to change dramatically and soon, due to the adventures, misadventures, and ambition of one man: Napoleon Bonaparte.

Napoleon Bonaparte was born in Corsica (Italy) in 1769. He embraced the democratic and egalitarian ideals of the French Revolution, but his special military skills eventually made him the leader of Revolutionary France. Napoleon had an impressive military record, and no one in France could oppose him. In November 1799 (he was 30 years old), he organized a coup against the French revolutionary institutions, initiating The Consulate period. One of his first measures was to amend the four-year-old constitution. He kept some liberal principles concerning property issues, but he tended to forget about liberty, equality, and fraternity. On matters pertaining to the colonies, he no longer considered French law applicable to all French territories, and slavery became lawful in Saint Domingue again, though not in France.[358]

Napoleon wanted to conquer Europe, and he needed the colonies' resources. Saint Domingue's residents had to go back to forced labor. It was, therefore, necessary to restore slavery and overthrow the leaders of the slave revolution. Napoleon also wanted to obtain the Louisiana Territory (present-day United States, but then a Spanish territory) using Hispaniola as a springboard. To control Hispaniola was thus vital for Bonaparte's expansionist plans. There was only one person in his way: Toussaint Louverture.

The tension between France and Toussaint was such that, in August 1800, the French Minister of the Navy colluded with Spanish officials in Santo Domingo to discuss the sovereignty of the colony after Toussaint was defeated. To do this, the French promised to supply the Spanish army with ammunition.[359]

After glorious and victorious battles in Europe, Napoleon was finally going after Toussaint.[360] Big mistake.

War in Hispaniola: France against the French ex-slaves (1802-1804)

It was Napoleon and his fellow countryman, not the locals or the Spaniards, who halted Toussaint's plans for the development of the island. The French Commander sent a gigantic expedition with 58,000 people led by his brother-in-law, Victoire Leclerc and his wife Pauline, Bonaparte's favorite sister, and their four-year-old son, Dermide. Among the crew, we find Toussaint's son Isaac and his stepson Placide, students at a Paris boarding school. The goal of having the two brothers was to ease the tension in the conflict. Leclerc traveled with mulatto generals deported by Toussaint, exiled planters, and dozens of opportunists hoping to make a fortune in Saint-Domingue. Among the group, there were also the troops' wives and children. Besides sailors and civilians, there were no less than 20,000 experienced soldiers. Later, as the conflict advanced, another 23,000 would cross the Atlantic during the following eighteen months. Most of them would never return,[361] as the plan to defeat the "black revolutionary" was about to fail.

Here is an essential point about Napoleon's plan: the fight against Toussaint to recover Hispaniola had two different goals, one for each part of the island.

Bonaparte wanted a productive colony, and he needed slaves. He requested Santo Domingo's support, where the issue of slavery was not effectively regulated. In a secret instruction of January 1801, Napoleon outlines his plan for the colonies:

> *to remind the inhabitants of the Spanish part, as well as the current administrators… that this country, [Santo Domingo], is henceforth French.* [But at the same time declared that] *the intention of the Government is never to reunite the two parts of the island under one single government. Paris,* he continued, *will govern the French part with and by blacks, and it will govern the Spanish part according to the norms of the country.*[362]

What does he mean? In October 1801, he was more explicit: *"If the political goal of the expedition in the French part of Saint Domingue should be to disarm the blacks and make them cultivators, but free, we should in the Spanish part, disarm them as well, but place them back to slavery."*[363] Smart move. He knew that slavery could not be restored in the French part, but if Santo Domingo was under a different legal status, he had a chance.

For this to work, Napoleon needed Spanish support. So, he acted accordingly. By decree, Toussaint's occupation of Santo Domingo was declared null and void. All ecclesiastical, civil, and military authorities were to remain under Spanish control until the French government had a clear plan for the colony's administration.[364]

Toussaint's death and the beginning of Haitian independentist sentiment

The biggest problem of course was Toussaint. General Kerverseau expressed it very clearly in a letter to Napoleon: no nation as great as France *"should receive laws from a black rebel from one of its colonies."* Napoleon's fateful mistake was to believe that it was preferable to defeat the *"black rebel"* instead of negotiating and collaborating with him. As the French began the attack, a two-year war started that resulted in the independence of Haiti in 1804.

What's noteworthy is that before Napoleon's arrival, there is no hard evidence that Toussaint had any intention of declaring Saint Domingue's independence from France. As we recalled, the 1801 constitution declared Saint Domingue a French colony as long as he was the governor for life. Only when Napoleon's army attacked the island, the ex-slave's struggle became a fight for independence from France.

The first French vessels commanded by General Charles Leclerc, anchored in Samaná Bay in February 1802.[365] A year and three months later, a total of 58,000 people would disembark with the mission to crush the revolution in Saint Domingue.[366] By then, the French colony had more than half a million ex-slaves and about 40,000 white citizens.

Four months after Leclerc's arrival, Toussaint was captured and sent to exile in France with his family. He died in the solitude of a prison cell in 1803.[367] That was the unheroic end of one of the most prominent figures in Hispaniola's history.

Toussaint's exile and death, however, did not mean the end of the struggle. The rebel forces chose Jean Jacques Dessalines as the slaves' new leader.[368]

The slaves' revolution in Saint Domingue began demanding improvement of their living conditions, then developed into a struggle for emancipation. In the end, the fight was for the colony's political independence.

The defeat of Napoleon's troops

For almost two years, the French tried to subdue Saint Domingue's inhabitants, but the locals had an invincible ally: Yellow Fever.

In six weeks, yellow fever would wipe out half of the French garrisons stationed in Santo Domingo.[369] By the end of 1802, around 50,000 French soldiers lost their lives, many to the disease, and only 24,000 survived. Two to three thousand men were dying every month! Six months later, there were only seven thousand left.[370] By November of 1803, barely a thousand survivors surrendered to the rebels.[371]

As the conflict progressed and as their losses increased, the French tried to recruit troops from the "Spanish" army. The recruitment was compulsory, and the conditions for the new soldiers were harsh. In October 1803, on the eve of France's defeat, a Dr. Pedro Francisco de Prado warned his fellow Dominicans of a new threat to the city of Santo Domingo. It was not the *"ominous cloud of blacks,"* but the *"oppressive yoke"* of the French military presence.[372] His worst fears would, eventually and surprisingly, come true.

Sale of the Louisiana Territories (1803)

In history, it is not very useful to dwell too much on the "what-ifs...", but we could make an exception in this case. If Toussaint's army had not defeated the French, the Napoleonic troops could advance from the Caribbean and take control of Louisiana. That would have changed the geography of today's United States significantly.

The Louisiana Territory covered an area of around 828 million square miles. It was around a quarter of present-day United States. It was comprised of two parts, the vast and unexplored Northern Territory and the Orleans Territory, a small and densely populated region in the southern part, in what is now the State of Louisiana. It was like a slice of France in the New World and home to about 50,000 people, mostly French. Starting from 1762, it was under the direction of a Spanish administration. In 1800, Louisiana became French again based on a treaty with Spain, but France did not have effective control yet. The war with Toussaint forced Napoleon to send 20,000 soldiers from New Orleans to Saint Domingue, leaving the territory defenseless. Eventually, the French Emperor accepted the offer of President Thomas Jefferson to buy the region of French Louisiana to the United States for fifteen million dollars in April 1803.[373]

There is no evidence that those in the Orleans Territory were offended as they became Americans. A witness claimed, though, that some wept when the American flag replaced the French flag. The French did not appreciate that their new governor was appointed rather than elected and were outraged when the US government tried to make English the official language, discouraging the use of French. But eight years later, the inhabitants of the Orleans Territory wrote a constitution and asked to become the eighteenth state of the Union.[374]

Independence of Saint Domingue: Haiti is born (1804)

On January 1, 1804, Jean Jacques Dessalines, Alexandre Petión and Henri Christophe declared the Republic of Haiti's independence. Against all odds (especially Napoleon's), the ex-slaves won the war.

During and after the war in the new country of Haiti, the new leaders, Dessalines and Christophe, had killed all existing whites, confiscated their properties, and handed these properties over to the generals. It was an act of systematic and cruel revenge against whites, including women and children. Between 3,000 and 4,000 people died in the massacre. Whites were forever prohibited from owning property in Haiti.[375]

Independence was the result of the only slave revolution that managed to defeat their masters. The revolution's success was a severe blow to other colonial powers who feared that, following the example of Haiti, the peoples they oppressed could also rise. Perhaps that is why, in 1807 in England, a curious publication was made public: "The Slave Bible." This particular version of the Bible modified the traditional texts and omitted the parts that could inspire the slaves to revolt. For example, the account of the Exodus story from Egypt and the liberation of Israel's people led by Moses is not to be found in the "Slave Bible." The passages that emphasized equality, such as Galatians 3:28, "There is neither Jew nor Greek, there is neither slave nor free, there is neither male nor female; for you are all one in Christ Jesus." were eliminated.[376]

Undoubtedly, Haiti's independence was a catalyst and a model for the future struggle for Dominican independence.

9.

French Invasion of Santo Domingo

Let us keep a crucial fact in mind: The French planned to take the whole island of Hispaniola, but while they failed to occupy Saint Domingue, they did manage to seize the Spanish side.

An influential sector of Dominican society welcomed the French. Santo Domingo's owners had never approved the social revolution of Saint Domingue's slaves. Therefore, they had no qualms in backing up Napoleon's plan for the return of slavery and gave their support to the French troops. On February 25, 1802, General Kerverseau and his army took control of Santo Domingo.[377]

The French army had the support of Santo Domingo's Creole population since they rejected Toussaint's anti-slave measures regarding ownership and land use. Many were deprived of their slaves and felt insulted to be forced into farming.

After Haiti declared independence, Hispaniola was again divided but with new actors and flags on each side. The west was the new Republic of Haiti, and the east was now France. It was a fragile situation because the Dominican support of the French was limited to a minor sector of Dominican society. The Dominican discontent with the government of General Kerverseau would soon begin.[378]

French Santo Domingo. Ferrand's time

Napoleon had given General Kerverseau the mission to subjugate and eliminate thousands of "maroons" in Santo Domingo.[379] Napoleon was not hesitating. But the general only had four hundred men, and his position was weak. Kerversau would have had to surrender Santo Domingo in the event of a possible attack from Haiti. But General Louis Ferrand, stationed at Monte Cristi with six hundred men, came to the rescue. Ferrand was not willing to give in so quickly. After 18 days of marching, he arrived in Santo Domingo. On the same day Haiti proclaimed its independence, he carried out a coup against his fellow countrymen, and Kerversau had to leave for Europe.[380] It was a change in military leadership, but Santo Domingo remained French.

Some measures to please the inhabitants of Santo Domingo

Ferrand pleaded to French citizens to live in Santo Domingo. Many did heed the General, including some Spanish families. As a result, Samaná's French population grew significantly, with its coffee plantations and an ambitious urbanization plan.[381] Ferrand also ordered Spanish customs and traditions to be respected, and there was a certain degree of collaboration between the population and the French authorities.

The French promoted trade between Santo Domingo and other countries, except, of course, with neighboring Haiti, with whom Dominican residents were forbidden to make any commercial deals. Another example of how politics can work against the population's interests.

Restoration of slavery in Santo Domingo (1804)

The interest of Ferrand and the plantation owners of Santo Domingo was to reinstitute slavery and once again subjugate thousands of freed people.[382] Slavery, with all its crimes and horrors, was back in Santo Domingo.[383]

Ferrand could count on many former Saint Domingue citizens exiled in Santo Domingo, survivors of the massacres against the whites during the revolution. Their horrible memories and stories would surely motivate Ferrand and his senior officials to embark on racist violence against blacks.[384]

But Ferrand took good care of distinguishing between the *"French blacks,"* associated with Haiti, who he considered especially subversive, and the *"Spanish blacks"* believed to be less dangerous.[385]

Furthermore, Ferrand declared that all *"French black and colored slaves who had been granted their liberty by either of the freed leaders did not have a valid claim to freedom and thus must be considered slaves,"* whereas the Spanish slaves liberated by the King of Spain for their services in the army were to remain free.[386]

During Santo Domingo's French period, new laws were promulgated to the detriment of blacks, limiting the provisions to obtain freedom, controlling those of African origin entering France, forcing blacks to have an identity card, and prohibiting intermarriage.[387] It also included curfews, race-based prohibitions from emigration, measures against vagrants, and even discrimination in the care and treatment of blacks.[388]

Another discriminatory measure from Ferrand's government that affected the area's fragile stability was the prohibition of any trade with neighboring Haiti, particularly cattle sales, which hurt a large part of the Dominican population. In fact, the main leader of the uprising that was soon to take place, Juan Sánchez Ramírez, was a wealthy owner of mahogany, who owned land in Cotuí and Higüey.[389]

There were all sorts of restrictions on the mobility of non-whites, geared to enslave those who could not prove their free status.[390] Reinstating slavery in Santo Domingo for Ferrand was a mixture of opportunism and violent antipathy to the new nation of Haiti.[391]

Ferrand unleashes chaos

Ferrand's discrimination of blacks also reached Haiti where his affronts towards them lead to a radical outcome. In January 1805, Ferrand authorized those living near the Haitian border to move into the neighboring country and seize any Haitian under fourteen as prisoners or property. Girls under twelve and boys under ten were "assigned" or sold to Dominican plantations. Ferrand entrusted his commander Joseph Ruiz and other subordinates to write official certificates stating the owner of those apprehended. In addition, Ferrand ordered the shooting of any Haitian man over fourteen in Santo Domingo's territory. There are still notarized documents that confirm that Haiti became a target for human smugglers across its borders.[392]

French Santo Domingo (Ferrand) vs. Haiti (Dessalines)

From Haiti's perspective, the threat was real, and after three months, they initiated a radical offensive: to invade Santo Domingo.

Dessalines would justify the invasion of Santo Domingo (that by then was French), by accusing the Spaniards of collaborating with the *liberticidal* (freedom killers) purpose of the French. He called on his fellow citizens *"to live or die as free men."*[393] For him, Ferrand's decree was evidence that France's goal was both to recapture Haiti and to restore slavery.[394] In February 1805, Henry Christophe left Cap-Haïtien with the Haitian army towards Santo Domingo. As he passed through Santiago, Dessalines and his men joined him, assembling more than twenty thousand soldiers.[395]

The Haitian army advancing through towns and villages was welcomed by many as a hope for the liberation of the people from French oppression. The only opposition they encountered was at the Santo Domingo outpost defended by 8,000 Frenchmen who were surrounded by an army of 21,000 Haitians.[396] Remember that the conflict was taking place in Santo Domingo, but it was between Haiti and France.

The siege lasted three weeks, and during that period, the besieged had to survive by eating anything they could, including mice. Then an unexpected event halted the action. On March 26, the ships of a French squad appeared on Santo Domingo's city skyline. Two frigates from the fleet continued their way towards the west, and the Haitian troops assumed that they were going to attack Haiti. Given the imminent danger, they decided to lift the siege and return to defend their own land. The truth is that the frigates did not go beyond Azua.[397]

Dessalines took out his frustration and anger by executing a vindictive and cruel maneuver, second only to Ferrand himself. He set fire to Monte Plata, Cotuí, La Vega, Santiago, and San José de las Matas.[398]

Not only that, Dessalines took a thousand prisoners, including men, women, and children, to Haiti. The Haitian military referred to the captives as "the Spaniards," although technically, they were French. They were kidnapped from their homes, forced to travel hundreds of kilometers, and assigned to government-run plantations in the north. The final, sad and cruel irony: the rebels who fought in the first successful slave revolution were now taking people, probably mulattoes and blacks, from Santo Domingo to work for their plantations.[399]

Dessalines already showed his lust for power in 1804, upon learning that Napoleon was to be crowned emperor. The Haitian leader rushed the arrangements for his own coronation and became Jacques I, emperor of Haiti, in October 1804 (two months before Napoleon). The peasants and slaves, who had fought and won a long revolution against oppression, found themselves under an absolute ruler and a slightly modified version of the two-hundred-year-old Black Code. The military officers were outraged at the whims of the former dictator and now emperor. The situation remained tense until October 1806, when a general uprising broke out. Dessalines was lynched by his own officers at the outskirts of Port-au-Prince. The first dictator of Haiti lasted less than two years.[400] The country was politically divided into several states and faced with internal strife.[401]

10.

Slavery and Blackness in Santo Domingo

As all these events unfolded, Santo Domingo was caught in contradictory views. While many hoped for the liberation from French occupation, they still preferred to be under France rather than to become part of Haiti's new Republic. To understand this, we must consider Santo Domingo's social and racial self-perception. They would not consider themselves as blacks like those in Haiti, but neither as whites as the French.

The social and racial make-up in Santo Domingo was mostly people of color: free mulattoes who would consider themselves primarily Spaniards, before French or Haitians, together with poor whites. Through generations, poverty made the different groups socially equal to the point that, over the years, the racial problem in Santo Domingo ceased to be relevant.

In the old Saint Domingue, the black slave population had grown dramatically and differentiated from the white settlers. In Santo Domingo the situation was different: Spanish authorities, pressured by the circumstances, had put aside the legal scruples created by the colonial legislation regarding people of color and accommodated immigrants from the western part, as long as their miscegenation could be properly explained.[402]

In Santo Domingo, an impoverished and confounded society, the critical issue regarding race was not to be totally black or too black to acquire a social category close to white people. To be sure, that was not a racial statement but a socio-economic goal. The term used was *"white of the land"* which meant Dominican or Creole Spanish from Santo Domingo as a way to differentiate themselves from the slaves, the *"real black."* The point was not to be recognized as black but as *"white of the land."*[403] So, even as mulatto, they did not want even remotely to be considered black. This disdain of the mulatto for the Negro was as universal as slavery itself. The mulatto wished to be white, or at least to be considered as such.[404] That was, of course, a social aspiration. The reality that was conveniently ignored was that any mulatto had slave ancestry.

To attain social recognition for the mulattoes was not a whim or a historical claim. There was a genuine concern and fear of being considered slaves. Still, there were about seven thousand unemancipated people at that time, according to a contemporary census.[405]

One of the few means of social recognition that slaves had was Catholic brotherhoods. These brotherhoods had members of various social statuses and conditions and offered them social, material, and spiritual support. Some slaves found in these groups a certain degree of autonomy. In 1806, sixty-one blacks belonging to the rural properties were members of these brotherhoods in Santiago. The authorities were not very satisfied with these groups: *"these blacks have always lived in a state of independence…which has never permitted officials to collect any goods from them"* they complained.[406]

11.

Santo Domingo Feels Spanish Again

After a decade of wars and high instability, Santo Domingo's population dropped drastically from 100,000 to 50,000. About 8,000 people lived in the capital, half of which were registered as French and the other half as Spanish.[407]

As we have seen, the question of allegiance was still somewhat tangled. There was some support for the French, especially by plantation owners. Among the general population, there was a certain tendency to move away from the Haitian "blackness," which, we insist, did not mean skin color or race but its connection with slavery. The fragile support for the French soon began to crumble and was to become outright hostility.

At the beginning of the 19th century, after a convoluted and complicated history, the Dominican national identity was already set. Dominicans did not feel Haitian; they did not share their language, culture, and unique history; they did not feel French, since nothing other than foreign treatises linked the Spanish to the French colony. And they did not feel very Spanish either, as the "motherland" had abandoned them years before.

But the self-proclaimed French Emperor, Napoleon Bonaparte, would awaken a new Spanish spirit in Santo Domingo. Napoleon wanted to control Europe, and he sent his army to various parts of the continent. In 1808, one of these armies invaded Spain, ousting King Carlos IV and installing his brother José Bonaparte on the Spanish throne.[408] A war of reconquest began in Spain, which had its replica in Santo Domingo, where the "Spaniards" were also to reconquer their lands from the French's hands.

When the news about the conquest of Spain by the French reached Santo Domingo, the Dominicans felt decisively more Spanish than French.[409] They felt doubly humiliated by the French, who invaded not only the colony but also the Iberian Peninsula.

The "Spanish" recover Santo Domingo. Battle of Palo Hincado (1808)

The rebellion in Spain began on May 2, 1802, and the colonies heard of it thereafter.

In Santo Domingo, the owners and leaders were the first to react, as they were directly affected by Ferrand's trade restrictions. Besides, they shared a strong monarchical tradition and could not tolerate that the legitimate Spanish king could be sent into exile, deposed, and replaced by Napoleon's brother.

Among the Dominican leaders, it is worth highlighting Juan Sánchez Ramírez, a cattleman with extensive properties, who led the fight against French rule in Santo Domingo and hoped to restore Spanish sovereignty in the land.

As Sánchez Ramírez learned that a recently established Governing Board in Spain had declared war on France, he set about touring the entire colony, inciting its inhabitants to take up arms against the

French. He also maintained an intense correspondence with Toribio Montes, the Spanish governor in Puerto Rico, who promised him all kinds of help. In August, Montes also declared war on France in the colony.[410]

Spanish authorities in Puerto Rico, however, had their own suspicions about Santo Domingo. Montes ordered General Juan Sánchez Ramírez not to admit any black or mulatto from the French side (Haitians, that is) into the Spanish army. Sánchez, turning a deaf ear to such instructions, allied with Haitian President Christophe, who sent him 300 men as auxiliary troops to fight the French.[411]

The anti-French uprising grew in the south, led by the Azuan local Ciriaco Ramírez, helped by Haitians and the English. The movement had the unwavering support of the president of Haiti, who provided the Dominican rebels, among others, with 600 rifles, 800 spears, 800 sabers and funds.[412]

But other than Haitian help, the *renconquista* war was mainly financed with Spanish money from Puerto Rico. Some of it was acquired through a San Juan merchant lender, a Don Reus Cassals. According to the records, the loan was partly returned to Mr. Cassals in slaves.[413]

The advance of the Hispano-Dominican force was unstoppable. By November 1808, six hundred rebels, including two hundred black and mulatto, took Azua against a French regiment of 250 men.[414]

Progressively the French were retreating towards the capital. The decisive battle was fought in Sabana de Palo Hincado, on November 7, of 1808. The Dominicans defeated Ferrand's army.

The dramatic end of Ferrand (1808)

The French army was defeated, and Ferrand tried to run away, but the Dominicans went after him. At one point, after ordering his companions to leave him, Ferrand exclaimed: *"I am the victim of my overconfidence!"* He grabbed the gun from one of his assistants so quickly that no one was able to react in time, *"he primed his pistols, and, at the moment when it was least expected, he destroyed his head* [il se cassa la tête].*"*[415] His head was paraded around as a war trophy in the cities of Higüey and El Seibo by Pedro Santana, father of the future first president of the Dominican Republic some years later.[416]

The defeat of France (1809)

After the defeat at Palo Hincado, with Ferrand gone, the surviving French troops gathered in the capital, where they had been subjected to a painful siege since March of 1809 by Dominicans, with the maritime assistance of three English frigates. The friendly French ships could not supply arms, ammunition, reinforcements, medicine, or food to their soldiers besieged in the city. Spanish governor Montes provided the 300 men from Puerto Rico sent to join the forces of Sánchez Ramírez. It was, of course, in exchange for mahogany.[417] This prolonged siege put French troops on edge, forcing them to eat horses, parrots, dogs, donkeys, cats, mice, and guáyiga flour in order to survive. The siege became unbearable, so they surrendered to the English on July 11, after eight months of siege.[418] The French were not about to face public and historical disgrace by submitting to the Spanish, much less to the Haitians.

So even if the Dominican movement of *reconquista* successfully drove out the French, Sánchez Ramírez was forced to negotiate the colony's control with the English. They demanded four hundred thousand pesos for the expenses incurred during the blockade. After the Dominicans agreed to the terms, in August 1809, Sánchez Ramírez obtained absolute control of Santo Domingo.[419]

Some factors besides the dreaded yellow fever, explain the French defeat. One, the deep anti-French sentiment after the Napoleonic invasion of Spain in 1808; two, the lack of French reinforcements in the area, since France had several open military fronts; three, the weakness of its leaders, as well as Ferrand's self-proclaimed over-confidence; and, four, the support of troops and arms from Spanish Puerto Rico, English Jamaica, and Haiti.[420]

Thus ended six years of French control over Santo Domingo called the French Period that had begun with the Napoleonic expedition's arrival on January 29, 1802.

The population after the reconquest

The siege of the city of Santo Domingo triggered massive evacuations of French citizens living in the capital. Three thousand three hundred people fled the city. That was almost half of its population.[421]

In 1809 the Spanish government in Cuba ordered the expulsion of the French from the island, forcing thousands to emigrate to New Orleans and other areas, ending 200 years of French presence in Hispaniola. By the beginning of the 19th century, Santo Domingo had 80,000 inhabitants,[422] an average of 1.6 inhabitants per square kilometer with two main cities, the capital and Santiago.

12.

La España Boba (Meek Spain)

The war against France, as we explained above, had two heroes: Don Juan Sánchez Ramírez from Cibao and Don Ciriaco Ramírez, from Azua. And alas, the two champions didn't get along at all. Let's see what happened.

Santo Domingo was once again Spanish territory. The Treaty of Basel, Toussaint's rule, and Ferrand's tumultuous years were events from the past. Finally, people could hope for some time of stability. But the Spanish government did not seize the moment, and, instead of showing interest in the disenfranchised inhabitants of Santo Domingo, it demonstrated a complete disregard for the colony's affairs, which led to its increasing poverty. It was what is known as the period of *La España Boba*.

Spain was at war with the South American colonies, and, once again, it did not pay much attention to its distant and small colony. Indeed, Spanish officials in Spain virtually ignored Santo Domingo in its last days as a colony. From 1809 to 1821 (twelve years), the Spanish government sent the colony's maintenance funds only on two occasions. It was *"a policy of manifest indifference."*[423]

Santo Domingo's dilemma: Spain or independence. The Board of Bondillo (1808)

Faced with the neglect the mother country had shown to its first colony, delegates from various cities of Santo Domingo met in Bondillo, near Manoguayabo (today in the municipality of Santo Domingo Oeste), on December 13, 1808, to decide the political future of Santo Domingo.

Two main positions were at stake: the first one represented by Juan Sánchez Ramírez, and the landowners who wished Santo Domingo to be a Spanish colony again. The other one, championed by Ciriaco Ramírez, who advocated for a proclamation of independence.

The accounts differ, depending on political allegiance, but apparently, Juan Sánchez Ramírez managed to distract Ciriaco Ramírez during the Junta to his own advantage. The Junta became a group of Sánchez' unconditional followers and made several resolutions ignoring Mr. Ciriaco Ramírez and his supporters. Juan Sánchez Ramírez maintained a direct link with the prominent Santana family since his father was one of Santana's field assistants.[424]

The Junta officially annulled the Treaty of Basel, and more importantly and contentiously, declared Santo Domingo a Spanish colony, recognized Fernando VII as king and appointed Juan Sánchez Ramírez as the colony's Governor.[425]

The cattlemen imposed their will, as they had more delegates and more economic, social, and political influence.[426]

Sánchez Ramírez sent an envoy to Spain with the news that Santo Domingo had returned to the mother country's bosom, but Spain did not seem too excited. Spanish officials sent a bureaucrat to reorganize the new public administration and formalize the appointment of Sánchez Ramírez as governor.[427]

Sánchez Ramírez, from pro-Spanish owner to hero of the homeland (1808-1811)

Without a doubt, the rise of Sánchez Ramírez was a significant achievement, but, as you can see, it was a step back towards monarchy. Ramírez looked to Spain more than to Santo Domingo. Furthermore, he restored slavery in Santo Domingo.[428]

Ramírez's nationalism was anti-French, pro-Spanish, and monarchical compared to Ciriaco's sovereign, republican, and independent political ideals.[429] The two national ideas would mark the history and the political drama of Santo Domingo and the future Dominican Republic.

The independentist republican movement soon attempted to overthrow Sánchez's government, but the uprisings were crushed. Several rebels were executed, some shot, others hanged and decapitated and left for six hours with an inscription in large letters on their chests: "*This is how justice punishes the traitors of the country.*"[430] This is how Sánchez Ramírez treated his opponents.

Ciriaco Ramírez was arrested, tried, and jailed. He died in Ceuta, a Spanish territory in North Africa, accused by Sánchez Ramírez of conspiring against his colonial government.[431]

Poverty in Santo Domingo

The opposition to Sánchez Ramírez was political, but it was also a consequence of the country's extreme poverty. Ramírez tried to restore the Dominican economy, but the War of Reconquest left the territory in ruins. The population declined from 125,000 inhabitants in 1789 to less than 70,000 by 1809. Agriculture and livestock were practically extinct, and the economy was stagnant. During that period, Santo Domingo lost almost all educated elite and the colonial entrepreneurs who had been responsible for its economic renaissance during the second half of the 18th century.[432]

As a result of this crisis, several conspiracies took place between 1810 and 1812, stimulated by the separatist movements in Caracas and other parts of America.

Juan Sánchez Ramírez became ill and died on February 11, 1811, at age 50. At his death, the Dominicans declared him a Father of the Country; not in vain had he been a hero in the war against the French invasion, although, as we have seen, his pro-Spanish vision may leave some of his decisions to be questioned. Be that as it may, his ashes are located in the National Pantheon.[433]

Upon his death, the government of the colony was provisionally in the hands of Colonel Manuel Caballero. José Núñez de Cáceres became lieutenant governor and political mayor.

Núñez de Cáceres and the independent future of Santo Domingo

Núñez de Cáceres was appointed Lieutenant Governor, General Counsel, and Government Service Judge Advocate General's Corps of the Province of Santo Domingo. His tenacious desire to improve the disastrous economic situation of the colony often clashed with Spanish authorities.

Once the anti-French sentiment was forgotten, many representative groups of society (the military, the merchants, the artisans, etc.), were supporting the separation from Spain.[434] The extent and the conviction of this ideal was still to be tested.

Spain's political power in Santo Domingo was less than nominal, and key local figures were clearly independentists. There were several possibilities ahead for the East side of the island, but independence seemed unavoidable. Or maybe not.

PART THREE
THREE DECLARATIONS OF INDEPENDENCE IN SEARCH OF AN IDENTITY
(1821-1865)

1.

First Independence (1821)

After the Spanish-appointed President Sánchez Ramírez died in 1812, Colonel Manuel Caballero and José Núñez de Cáceres became the new rulers in Santo Domingo. Tension arose between pro-Spanish Ramírez's followers and independentists headed by Núñez de Cáceres.

The situation was uncertain, so France cannily instigated pro-Spanish sectors of Dominican society to form a possible alliance that would help the Gauls take the entire island. This French threat kept the Haitian government in a permanent state of alert, as it feared for its own security and national integrity.[435] For Haiti, a new French invasion meant the possible return to slavery.

But by 1820, amid a severe economic crisis, pamphlets were circulating in Santo Domingo inciting rebellion against Spain. Military officers, bureaucrats, and merchants from the Spanish colony were ready to follow in the footsteps of the rest of Latin America's independence movements.[436]

Jean Pierre Boyer, the new leader of Haiti

In Haiti, that same year, an army man, Jean Pierre Boyer was declared president for life. Boyer was a mulatto, of African and

European descent, educated in France. Before his rise to power, Boyer served under Alexandre Sabès Pétion and Henry Christophe, who, back in 1806, killed the father of Haitian independence, Jean-Jacques Dessalines. Pétion, with Boyer's support, engaged in a civil war against Christophe to control the entire country.[437] When both leaders passed away, Boyer rose to power and managed to unify the country.

Boyer maintained a large army and a highly corrupt civil service, always ready to strike out against the weakest element, the rural population. Inequality between black peasants and urban mulattoes grew significantly during Boyer's presidency.

Almost 20 years after the slave revolution, Haiti's citizens were once again being oppressed, this time, by their leaders' corruption. [438]

Boyer sets his eyes on Santo Domingo

The same year that Boyer came to power, a French fleet arrived in Martinique. There was a rumor that the fleet was heading to Santo Domingo, the most vulnerable coast of Hispaniola, and from there, would take over the whole island.[439] The rumor was false, but the possibility of a French attack was quite real. Boyer worried and realized that to defend the entire island he had to control Santo Domingo. Besides, on the Spanish side he could find much needed new resources.

There was still another factor that made Santo Domingo appetizing for the Haitian leader. He had a large number of idle, high-ranking military officers that could become a source of discontent and a permanent threat of conspiracy. Dominating Santo Domingo, Boyer could expand the national territory and create new positions for these inactive officers.[440]

Consequently, Boyer had a vested interest in creating instability to weaken the Spanish influence to ease his path to Santo Domingo. To do so, he would gladly encourage any movement against Spain in favor of Santo Domingo's independence.[441] To that effect he instructed his agents posted in Spanish territory to stir up the Dominican mulatto population into asking Haiti to take the eastern part of the island.[442]

Independent at last

While the Republic of Haiti was on the alert on the Spanish side, in 1821, José Núñez de Cáceres, with the support of important members of Santo Domingo's political and military elite, and that of the official in charge of the Public Treasury, organized a successful coup against Spanish control.[443] Only a few supported the Spanish governor in office, Pascual Real, who, when he arrived in Santo Domingo earlier that same year, had already been suspicious of the leading officials of the colony, including José Núñez de Cáceres. Pascual did not have enough troops and decided not to confront the instigators. Instead, he devoted himself to consolidating the government's position, trying to buy the favor of important military men. But he was too late, they had also joined the movement led by José Núñez de Cáceres.[444]

In the dark of the night, on Friday, November 30, 1821, the Dominican independentist troops, led by Haitian-born Pablo Ali (head of the *Batallón de Morenos*),[445] along with Núñez de Cáceres, took the military fort of Santo Domingo by surprise. Six hours later, peaceably, they officially proclaimed the *Estado Independiente de Haití Español* (Independent State of Spanish Haiti).[446]

At last, Santo Domingo was independent, with a revealing name and the flag of *La Gran Colombia* (Great Colombia), the current Colombian flag.

Núñez de Cáceres and the Gran Colombia

What Núñez de Cáceres envisioned for the new Republic was to be part of *La Gran Colombia*, a political project promoted by Simón Bolívar, whose full name was Simón José Antonio de la Santísima Trinidad Bolívar Ponte y Palacio Blanco. The Venezuelan leader hoped to integrate several South American nations into a large, federated region. Cáceres sent Dr. José María Pineda to meet Great Colombia's Vice President Francisco de Paula Santander to explore possibilities for belonging to the federation.

Santander informed Bolívar, campaigning in Ecuador, about the visit. The *Libertador* wrote back expressing his opinion in a letter from Popayán dated February 9, 1822:

> *My dear General: Yesterday, I received the pleasant communications about Santo Domingo and Veragua... My opinion is that we should not abandon those who support us because it will not be fair to undermine the good faith of those who believe we are strong and generous. I am convinced that the best thing in politics is to be noble and magnanimous. That island [of Hispaniola] can bring us some advantage in some political negotiations. It should bring us no harm if we speak frankly to them without recklessly making any commitment.*[447]

It seems that Bolívar considered the new state merely as a political advantage in the event of possible negotiations. The liberator did not seem very excited. Pineda's mission was such a failure that he remained in Venezuela and never went back to Santo Domingo.[448]

Boyer in Santo Domingo

Núñez de Cáceres did not find any firm support, neither internationally nor in his own country. At home, his decision not to abolish slavery (he himself was a slave owner) made this first independence attempt unpopular among the general population. Cáceres' political project was bound to fail.[449]

The events in Santo Domingo were a cause of concern in Haiti. Dominican independence from Spain could mean the definitive end of slavery, but the uncertainty of Cáceres' project left many doubts.

Cáceres had no army, and neither the white owners nor Bolivar supported him in his fight against Spain and for the Dominican cause. He did not have many options.

The last plausible alternative to independence was unification with Haiti. It was by no means a far-fetched scenario. Pablo Alí had already changed alliances and joined the Haitian side. In Montecristi and Dajabón, the Haitian flag was waving even before Caceres' independence proclamation; Santiago soon followed suit, and the recently constituted Central Provincial Board requested unification with Haiti.[450]

After all, for many the anti-Spanish sentiment was inversely proportionate to their sympathy for Haiti. Cáceres himself welcomed the unification with Haiti, whose government promised land and the liberation of the slaves.[451]

The Haitian army took advantage of this impasse and entered the Spanish part of the island in 1822. Boyer had the support of cities such as Santiago and Puerto Plata. Many residents in Cotuí, La Vega, Macorís, Azua, San Juan, and Neiba also showed their support.[452]

The Haitian invasion was an effective nonviolent military operation. Boyer made sure to send a notification/threat to Cáceres: Let the Haitian army enter Santo Domingo peacefully or else face the consequences.[453]

Boyer entered the *Estado Independiente de Haití Español* with 10,000 soldiers. On February 9, 1822, he took Santo Domingo. The first Dominican independence lasted merely three months.

In its beginnings, Haiti's domination did not have much opposition.[454] The Dominican politician and diplomat Manuel Joaquín Delmonte wrote: *"Let us all toast to the day that the knot that binds us gets tighter."* [455] A traveler reported how *"Black Dominicans forged the tightest of bonds with arriving Haitian soldiers and administrators."*[456]

Two years after the invasion, Boyer invited black emigrants from the United States, offering them a new home that would increase the workforce to help rebuild Haiti[457] and build the country's international image. Hundreds of them settled in Samaná.[458] That particular settlement produced a multilingual community where residents spoke Spanish, English, and Kreyol[459] and for about ten years was a Protestant refuge on a predominantly Catholic island. They also settled in Puerto Plata, with multilingual schools, churches, and aid societies. The US migrants came from South Carolina and Georgia and arrived from the Florida Keys, thus registered as Floridians.[460]

Problems for Boyer in Santo Domingo

But Boyer had a challenge ahead: the citizens of Santo Domingo already had a sense of national identity. His authority was in a delicate balance. That became evident as he took some unpopular measures for the inhabitants of Santo Domingo. First, he reorganized the military and forced all able men in Santo Domingo between the ages of 16 and 25 to enroll in the Haitian army regiments Numbers 31 and 32.[461] Let's remember that these were Dominican men forced to enroll in the ranks of the Haitian military. The numbers of the regiments will become significant, as they will come up twenty years later in a crucial event in Dominican history.

Another unfortunate decision of the new leader, and incidentally impossible to implement, was the imposition of the French language for all acts of civil and judicial life.

Economically, Boyer made the same mistakes as Toussaint. On the one hand, he wanted to confiscate the lands and properties from the Church and the former Spanish government and cede them or sell them to recently freed slaves.[462] On the other hand, he planned to end the communal system: the use and exploitation of common lands which was a prevalent practice in the Dominican part.

This community ownership method was an unregulated system, ideal for the large extension of land and the small population in which land was shared, and no title deeds were necessary. Much of this land was used for livestock and timber. In theory, the French system seemed more just and modern since it guaranteed legal ownership for each family, but the *comunero* system was more practical for an uninhabited territory like Santo Domingo.[463] Santo Domingo was not used to the idea of labor-intense production as practiced in Haiti since the days of Toussaint.[464] Boyer was unsuccessful, and in fact, the communal land system remained active in the Dominican Republic well into the 20th century.[465]

Boyer was unpopular not only in Santo Domingo but also in Haiti. He could not establish a policy of plantations, since most Haitians already owned small fields, and few were willing to work on other people's lands.[466]

France recognizes Haiti (1825)

In 1825 Boyer scored a resounding political success: France recognized Haiti as a sovereign country, twenty years after the unilateral declaration of independence. Haiti had 351,000 inhabitants. The recognition did not include the Spanish part of the island with only 71,000 people.[467]

The achievement, however, did not come without a price.

France demanded from Haiti a 50% reduction in fees for French imports and a compensation of 150 million francs, the equivalent of about $21 billion in today's dollars, to be paid in five installments.[468]

For the French, the sum would serve as compensation for property lost, both in land and in slaves. Ironically, with this settlement, Haiti's government ended up "paying" for the former slaves who fought for their freedom twenty years before.

One last consideration regarding this "negotiation": lest the Haitian government hesitate, France threatened to leave Haiti diplomatically isolated and block its ports. As a matter of fact, eleven warships were already situated off the Haitian shores and had been instructed to bombard the city if Boyer refused to accept the terms.[469]

One hundred and fifty million francs were equal to the total all Haitian public income for ten years. Not surprisingly, when it came time for the first payment, Haiti had to ask for a loan. France had no problem with that, as long as a French bank provided it. Perfect business, as the loan was to be paid with interest. For Haiti, the debt was an impossible financial burden, and, although reduced on several occasions, was not finally paid off until 1947. It took 122 years to pay for their independence[470] and without a doubt, it has affected Haiti's history to date.

Haitian-Dominican conspiracy against Boyer (1827)

The French recognition did not help Boyer much. By 1827 a group of officers of his own army, displeased by the growing French presence, began a conspiracy against him.[471]

The situation in Haiti was volatile, with increasing conflicts between a Haitian ruling elite and the impoverished black population, who

FIRST INDEPENDENCE (1821)

were not interested in invading foreign countries. In 1837, a group of the military tried, unsuccessfully, to assassinate their commander in chief.

In Santo Domingo, Boyer had a loyal strongman at his service: General Jerôme Maximilien Borgella, with total control and authority and the support of influential Dominicans.[472] Yes, some Dominicans supported the Haitian army, including a famous Dominican personality, Tomás Bobadilla, and other Dominican civil servants,[473] who continued to work for Haiti. In 1827 Borgella's control was such that Boyer believed no extra troops were needed in Dominican territory and ordered the 31st and 32nd regiments (with mainly Dominican men) to move to Haiti.

But one of Boyer and Borgella's goals was to turn Santo Domingo into a natural extension of Haitian territory. In 1830, he prohibited the use of the Spanish language in official documents, tried to force the use of the French language in primary education, and removed all Spanish shields and symbols from public places.

It was an impossible aspiration that only accelerated Dominican opposition to Boyer. Dominican independence had been forged for years and attained in 1822. The national sentiment had been developed as a mestizo society, with strong Catholic roots and Spanish as the vernacular language: Dominican identity was distinctive both from Spain and Haiti, long before 1822.

The joint effort to oust Boyer both in Santo Domingo and in Haiti would lead to the Dominican independence movement that would culminate in 1844.

The origin of La Trinitaria

In Santo Domingo in December 1834, (twelve years after Haitian unification and ten before independence), a seemingly inconsequential event lit the spark of a conspiracy that would ultimately be definitive. A certain Dominican captain, Javier Miura, died of natural causes, and Santo Domingo's Governor General Carrié, instead of appointing his logical successor, Wenceslao de la Concha, appointed his son, Samí Carrié. Now Samí had a lower rank than that of Captain de la Concha. A 15-year-old friend of the captain, José María Serra, was deeply disheartened because Wenceslao, in order of rank, was the expected replacement. This injustice encouraged Serra to take a very peculiar action described here in his own words:

> *I spent those days writing in disguised handwriting against the Government without specifying any cause but calling for revolution. During the night I spread the pamphlets throughout the city. In the morning had an alarming effect, and much happiness on my part. The autograph was: El Dominicano Español.*[474]

This anonymous method of protest made an impact in Santo Domingo. Stimulated by the riots in Haiti, the conspiracy attempts, and using this new anti-government propaganda, a group of young traders and sons of wealthy-class merchants from Santo Domingo created a secret society to organize the Dominican resistance against Boyer, and to eventually secede from the Republic of Haiti.[475]

La Trinitaria

At first, the movement was merely publishing inciting propaganda against the regime. However, when Juan Pablo Duarte, an educated man and philosophy professor, joined the group, it became an organization dedicated to stirring up the Dominican population with clandestine pamphlets reaching San Cristobal, Baní, and Azua.[476]

The name *La Trinitaria* comes from the way the movement was organized, based on triads. One member could connect only with two other men who would only know their mentor. In turn, these two would connect with two more people following the same rules. So, each person would only know the identity of two other people from the organization. If a member would be arrested or become a traitor, he could only implicate two groupmates. La Trinitaria, in this way, formed a conspiratorial network that would penetrate every corner of the city, especially among the Dominicans enrolled in the armed forces and among the youth capable of fighting.[477]

The first nine Trinitarians were: Juan Pablo Duarte, Juan Isidro Pérez, Juan Nepomuceno Ravelo, Félix María Ruíz, Benito González, Jacinto de la Concha, Pedro Pina, Felipe Alfau, and José María Serra. Not all of these *founding fathers* would leave us happy and glorious memories. As we will see in due time, after the third and final independence, Juan Pablo Duarte returned to the Dominican Republic from his exile in Venezuela in 1864. Soon after, he was sent back to Venezuela and died in Caracas in oblivion and scarcity. Félix María Ruíz remained in exile until 1890. By the time he was allowed to return, he could not do so due to health problems. He died in Venezuela. José María Serra would also die in exile (Puerto Rico, 1888). Tomás de la Concha (Jacinto's brother) was shot by order of Santana. Juan Nepomuceno Ravelo and Felipe Alfau joined the annexationist (anti-independence) movements for France and Spain respectively.[478]

Opposition to Boyer in Haiti

While La Trinitaria began its propaganda attacks in Santo Domingo, in Haiti, Boyer's opponents organized the Society for the Rights of Man and Citizen. This society was led by H. Dumesle to fight for Haiti's liberation and to overthrow President Boyer. The Society launched a manifesto in Les Cayes, attacking Boyer and the Parliament and calling for taking over the gerontocracy (the government of a few elders). They hoped to change the Constitution and to organize a provisional government.[479] There were no measures taken against these conspirators, because the government they envisioned included prominent civil and military figures.[480]

The Dominican and Haitian opposition against Boyer's government operated jointly. The link between them was Ramón Mella, a friend of Santo Domingo's Representative M. Benoit, and Alcius Ponthieux, a former Haitian congressman. He was also close to general Borgella, a family friend of the Mella's, from the time he was a commander in Santo Domingo.[481]

The fight for Dominican independence begins in Haiti

January 27, 1843 marked the beginning of Haiti's rebellion against Boyer. Borgella, Boyer's right hand man, did nothing to stop it, since he was part of the uprising and had the support of a significant part of the army. The situation was tense, and, feeling the pressure, on March 13, 1843, Boyer and his family went into exile aboard an English ship. He had ruled Haiti for 25 years.[482]

The success of the Haitian opposition against Boyer was good news for La Trinitaria and for many of Santo Domingo's inhabitants. The power vacuum created by the Haitian rebels gave the final incentive to the rebellion in Santo Domingo.

In the spring of 1843, some Trinitarians, assisted by the Haitian opposition leaders Ponthieux and General Etienne Desgrotte, attempted to retake power in Santo Domingo. Although unsuccessful,[483] it is interesting to note the two Haitian leaders among those fighting for Dominican independence -another historical irony.

It seemed only a matter of time before the Dominicans took control of the country. There was a problem, though: not everyone agreed on the shape of Santo Domingo's future.

Different visions for the Dominican Republic

Within the independence movement, there were several groups. One group consisted of a generation of inexperienced politicians and young liberals -new businessmen- like most of La Trinitaria's members. Sovereignists, they wanted total independence and no international affiliation. They followed the liberal tradition of French liberal movements.

The other group consisted of the traditional and conservative local elites that had been in power for fifty years.[484] This group sought help and protection from a foreign power. Some were pro-Spanish, mainly from Santo Domingo and Puerto Plata, like Father Gaspar Hernández, a key figure in Dominican independence. Fr. Hernández was born in Peru but went to Santo Domingo as a priest and educator. He became a great opponent of the Haitian occupation. He taught Juan Pablo Duarte, and it was in his class where he gathered the first young men for La Trinitaria. Hernández went into exile in 1843 for opposing Haiti's government.[485]

Other politicians sought the end of Haitian rule with French help. Two of its leaders were a wealthy owner from Azua, Buenaventura Báez, who would play a prominent role in Dominican history and Manuel Joaquín Delmonte, the lawyer who, at the beginning of Boyer's occupation, toasted to the new ties between Haiti and Santo Domingo.[486]

Still, another few wanted English support, like Mr. Pimentel from the city of Las Matas de Farfán, where England had an influential presence not long before.

These different views were often conflicting. Buenaventura Báez, while still an Azua official, tried to sabotage his political rivals. In Azua, the francophiles were proud of their local flag, red and white vertical stripes with a French tricolor in the upper left corner. The most fervent defenders of a French annexation were from Azua.[487] The

French were open to a Dominican annexation as long as this would not jeopardize Haiti's payments.[488]

Duarte ditches the rebels in Haiti

Confusion reigned on the island. Boyer's fall opened different political options for Santo Domingo, and at the same time, weakened relations between the Haitian rebels and Dominican independentists.

Haitians wanted a liberal reform for the unified country, maintaining unity on the island, while Duarte's collaboration with the rebels was a strategic move to overthrow Boyer as a necessary step to independence.[489]

Mobilization of the Haitian Army

The power vacuum in Haiti did not stop the army from being confronted with conspiracy attempts in Santo Domingo. In July 1843, the new President, Charles Rivière-Hérard, mobilized his troops into Dominican territory. To his surprise, he had to use an interpreter since the moment he set foot in the border town of Dajabón.[490] He did not speak Spanish, and very few spoke Creole. While it is true that proximity leads to certain linguistic fluidity, only a couple of decades of unification were not time enough to assimilate a language.

Hérard arrived in the city of Santo Domingo on July 12, 1843, technically still in his own country. Upon his arrival, Spanish residents had their doors closed, while those of French origin had their doors wide open.[491]

Hérard ordered the arrest of those involved in separatist activities, including Pablo Duarte who, on August 2, 1843, fled into exile to Saint Thomas (present-day United States Virgin Islands). Duarte's exile was a severe setback for the independence movement, but soon, the mulatto Francisco Sánchez became the new leader.[492]

Hérard returned to Haiti taking many prisoners and leaving Mr. Desgrotte as Haiti's military leader in Santo Domingo. He was the same man who three months earlier seized the Ozama fortress from the Haitians.[493] Perhaps it was another case in which military discipline overpowered personal political ideals. Hérard also took with him the 31st and 32nd battalions who were considered to be too permissive with the Dominicans.[494]

The race for independence

While some struggled to achieve independence, others, like Báez, worked on securing foreign support. He contacted the French consul in Santo Domingo to place the Spanish part under French protection in exchange for the entire Samaná Bay.[495] The French agreed, and began to plan to overthrow Hérard on April 25, 1844.

The sovereigntists were also plotting a coup to take Santo Domingo later in the year, but alarmed by the news of an imminent French attack, they advanced their plan to February 20.[496]

Very stressful moments indeed. If not for the anticipation of the French moves, perhaps today Hispaniola would be under the French. April 25 would become a national day, and Báez would be the country's hero.

The pronouncement was planned for February 20, but it did not happen until February 27. The insurgents needed the people's backing, especially the support of those who had economic power, including the large landowners and cattle ranchers of the Cibao region, such as Ramón and Pedro Santana, brothers and prominent characters in Dominican history.

The tragic beginnings of young Pedro Santana

Pedro Santana's early biography leaves us with a tragic passage. His father was an indigenous Mexican, and his mother from the Canary Islands. They were landowners in the border area between Santo Domingo and Saint Domingue. In 1805 Santana and his family moved to Seibo, where they lived for two years.

Pedro Santana was engaged to María del Carmen Ruíz. Returning from a pilgrimage to the Sanctuary of *Nuestra Señora de la Altagracia* in Higüey, Mrs. Ruíz's horse acted up; Mrs. Ruiz lost control, and fell with such bad luck that she hit a rock and died on the spot. The death of his fiancée plunged Santana into a deep depression. He only recovered when he fell in love with the mother of her future sister-in-law. You read that correctly: his half-brother introduced him to his fiancée and her family, including, of course, her mother, a widow much older than Pedro. Thus, his sister-in-law also became his stepdaughter. The marriage was not a very happy one, but it gave Pedro much influence in the southeast region of the island.[497]

2.

Official Independence (1844)

On February 27, 1844, Duarte and his group of sovereigntists declared the Dominican Republic's independence without significant disruptions. That same day, the first Dominican flag, designed by Juan Pablo Duarte himself, flew from the mast of the fortress of Ozama.

An interesting detail worth mentioning apropos the operation's success: one month before Independence, the Haitian battalions defending the fortress of Ozama were replaced by the 31st and 32nd battalions. You will surely remember them: the units made up mostly of Dominicans transferred to Haiti a year earlier.[498] As it turned out, the Haitian forces defending the Ozama Fortress on that historical day, were actually Dominican.[499]

As the uprising progressed, some Haitian residents in Santo Domingo showed their support for the movement. In contrast, a few Dominican residents, mainly conservative families, fled to Saint Thomas to avoid cooperating with any particular group.[500] Others sought refuge in the French consulate or departed on any available ship.[501]

The day after the declaration of Independence, the Haitian troops stationed in the capital, led by Desgrotte, (the same officer escorting

Núñez de Cáceres during the first independence of 1821), signed the capitulation and surrender of power.[502]

In Haiti, the peasants in the south, embroiled in a revolt for democracy, watched Hérard's failure at the Dominicans' hands with contentment. Sarcastically they sang some verses at the General's expense: *"The Spaniards chased him; he ran like a dog after fresh carrion!"* [503]

Considering the common cause of Haitian and Dominican rebels, it should not be a surprise that the first opposition to the newly launched independence was not from Haiti, but from pro-French Dominicans, led by Báez. Their goal was for France to take control of the Dominican Republic.

The Francophile opposition was such that La Trinitaria had to seek help from the pro-Haitian and pro-Boyer party of Santo Domingo to form the Governing Board. Let's be clear about this; Boyer was the man that initiated the twenty-year Haitian period in the Dominican Republic, and the man that Dominicans fought against for their independence. History couldn't be more ironic.

The new government had two leaders from the Boyer period who had significant social influence: Tomás de Bobadilla and José Joaquín Puello. Bobadilla had enormous prestige among the upper class of the Capital, and Puello among the colored population.[504]

The Central Government Board

Four days after the declaration of independence, on March 3, 1844, the *Junta Central Gubernativa* (J.C.G.) was established as a provisional governing body of the recently created Dominican Republic. The J.C.G. organized and directed the first political and military actions that consolidated national independence. The first members were Tomás Bobadilla, Francisco del Rosario Sánchez, José Joaquín Puello,

Remigio del Castillo, Wenceslao de la Concha, Mariano Echavarría, Pedro de Castro y Castro and Matías Ramón Mella.

The Board's president was Tomás de Bobadilla. The leadership of the national movement was in the hands of the same person who, for 20 years, helped maintain Haitian domination in the country.[505] Conflicts soon arose, as the Junta had two ideologically opposed camps: the sovereign liberals and the conservatives, linked to protectionist plans with other countries.

Black and mulatto Dominicans feared that separation from Haiti could bring back slavery. The Junta emphatically proclaimed in its first decree, on March 1, 1844: *"slavery has disappeared forever from the territory of the Dominican Republic and whoever promulgates otherwise will be considered a criminal, prosecuted and punished if applicable."*[506]

Another measure promptly taken by the Junta was to order and organize Juan Pablo Duarte's return from his exile and to appoint him the new military commander of the Department of Santo Domingo. Duarte returned on March 14, was assigned as commander on March 16 and by March 19 was leading one of the most crucial battles to take place against Haitian forces.

The first battle in "El Número." Santana the National Hero (March 19, 1844)

On March 10, 11 days after independence, Haitian President Hérard placed his army on the warpath. General Pedro Santana was preparing for the defense of Azua with 3,000 men faithful to the independence cause, probably including members of the old Spanish army.

Santana defended Azua's post while waiting for the invading army. But, to everyone's surprise, especially to the Haitian army, then closing in with 10,000 men,[507] Santana abandoned the city, and its inhabitants withdrew to Baní. General Antonio Duvergé, following Santana's orders, moved with the troops about two miles East of Azua, to a mountainous site known as El Número.[508] Duvergé's men managed to cut off the Haitian incursion. The battle was on March 19, and it is known as one of the most outstanding victories in Dominican national history. Had Duvergé's army been defeated, nothing would have prevented the invading army from reaching the capital. Santana was the national hero of the moment.

Conflict between Santana and Duarte

The Haitian troops failed to go beyond El Número and withdrew to a deserted Azua. Duarte traveled to Baní to compel Santana to recover the city, but Santana would not hear of it. Juan Pablo Duarte, a 31-year-old merchant, was giving orders to Santana, a 43-year-old veteran military general. Santana refused to follow Duarte's instructions and continued with his plan, ultimately ending in resounding success. The Haitian army was idly stationed in Azua while Hérard tried unsuccessfully to call his navy into action, which consisted of a few old ships. Before long, inactivity, leisure, and lack of resources affected the Haitian troops' morale. As days went by, they started to defect in significant numbers as Hérard's prestige was diminishing. The situation was so untenable that Hérard decided to leave Azua and return to Haiti. Before doing so, he made sure to burn the city. In their retreat, Hérard's troops were pursued by Dominican guerrillas. Hérard, for his part, knowing what was waiting for him at home, escaped into exile before reaching Port-au-Prince.[509]

Meanwhile, because of the dispute between him and Duarte, Santana asked *La Junta* to accelerate the efforts to obtain France's military and political support. The francophiles wanted to push the plan for a protectorate of France in exchange for the Samaná Bay and Peninsula.[510]

Battle of Santiago (March 30, 1844)

Before the El Número battle, Hérard's army had another front open in Santiago. There, the situation became somewhat puzzling. Haitian General Jean-Louis Pierrot suffered a disastrous defeat in Santiago de los Caballeros, with 715 Haitian casualties and only one Dominican casualty. It was March 30. Pierrot asked for a truce to carry off the fallen in combat and negotiate an agreement between the two sides. But the General was the victim of a historical hoax. The Dominicans delivered an official statement to Pierrot explaining that Hérard had died in Azua: appalled and distressed about his future, Pierrot abandoned Santiago.

The letter was fake. Perhaps somebody forged the stamp or the signature, who knows. But Hérard was still alive and well at that time. Not only was he alive, but he already knew about Pierrot's defection. For Hérard this was good news, as the situation in Azua was desperate. He asked Pierrot to help him defend Azua. But Pierrot had other plans. Maybe out of fear or out of shame, he returned to Haiti where he joined a Boyerist group to conspire on May 2, through a coup d'état, and proclaimed General Guerrier president of Haiti.[511] In two months, Pierrot shifted from loyal General to Hérard to deserter and later conspirator.

While the military battles were unfolding, the Dominican Government Junta was still active. By a May 6 decree, the Junta declared that every Dominican who had been absent from the country since March 9, 1844, would have his assets confiscated by the State, and would lose his civil and political rights, if he had not returned by August. That's a three-month notice, not much time to ensure the decree would have been made known to those affected by this drastic measure.

Juan Pablo Duarte and the first coup in the Dominican Republic

The Junta's position was unstable. For Duarte and the other liberals and sovereigntists, there was a real danger that the conservative pro-French factions could welcome a foreign intervention.

La Trinitaria members did not want to take risks, and they organized a military plot against the *Junta*. The attempt failed, but on June 1, three months after the declaration of independence, the conservative *Junta* requested France's political and military protection, allegedly to defend the country from Haiti.

After a week, on June 9, 1844, the Liberals again tried to take control of the Junta. This time, led by Juan Pablo Duarte, they succeeded, realizing the first coup in the new Dominican Republic. The new Junta ousted President Tomás de Bobadilla, and other conservative members. Rosario Sánchez was appointed the new president, and General Duarte became Santo Domingo's military commander, the most important post in the country.[512]

During these tumultuous times in the capital, General Santana was still with his army in Baní, while Duarte traveled to the northern region of Cibao to undo any potential deals about becoming a French protectorate. Once there, he was unilaterally declared president of the Republic.[513] The struggle for the Junta's control was far from over.

A new coup to the Junta, Santana's turn

A little over a month after Duarte took office, on July 12, Santana entered Santo Domingo with his army to reestablish the order lost with the June 9 coup. The Junta was once again under the leadership of the conservative party. Two days later, the new Junta drafted the country's first Constitution. It would become the first of 32 to date, making the

Dominican Republic the country with the most enacted constitutions in the world.[514]

The new Constitution declared Santana the new president (Chairman). Meanwhile, Duarte, oblivious to what was happening in the Junta, continued to enjoy "his presidency" in Cibao. Mella, from Cibao, sent a note to the Junta, in Santo Domingo, to inform them about Duarte's presidency. When Santana received the news from Cibao, and in no mood to deal with rivals, he dismissed Mella, declared all Trinitarian members traitors, and sent them into exile. In case somebody else was having second thoughts about the measure, 628 army officers signed a manifesto showing their support for Santana.[515]

Santana was resolute. The Trinitarians' persecution was unwavering, to the point that, one year after the proclamation of independence, María Trinidad Sánchez, Francisco del Rosario Sánchez's aunt, was executed for conspiring against the Santana government.[516]

The Constitution of 1844

On November 6, 1844, in San Cristóbal Province, after nine months of power struggles, 31 Dominicans approved the Constitution. This Constitution recognized the country as a Republic, both democratic and secular. It was based on human rights, equality before the law, and the right of association. It established the three independent powers and organized the electoral processes to elect the president of the Republic, whose period of government would last for four years.[517]

The constitution also determined the final design of the Dominican flag. Its history summarized the history of the island: red and blue are a reminder of the Haitian flag, borrowed, in turn, from the French. Haitians had removed the white band from the French flag and made the blue and red colors horizontal (the present-day Haitian flag). On occasion of the 1821 independence, lawmakers altered Haiti's flag, adding a white cross in the middle, leaving the flag divided into four quadrants, the two upper ones blue and the two lower ones white. On the November 1844's flag, the right quadrants were flipped upside down, resulting in the current Dominican flag. The process is shown in the image on the back cover of this book.

Flags are one of the most powerful national symbols, and it is remarkable how a piece of colored cloth can be a cause of pride and joy and of offense and insult. For instance, it is a crime to burn the national flag in Spain but not in the United States. In Denmark, there is no problem in burning and insulting the Danish flag for the sake of freedom of expression. But burning foreign flags is not allowed to avoid international conflicts.[518] In the Dominican Republic, it's not a crime to burn the national flag, but only as stated in the Constitution, when it has deteriorated, become broken, discolored, or is in poor condition. Only then it can be incinerated, observing proper solemnity and decorum (Article 11, Law 360). However, it is forbidden to cut it into pieces, destroy it, throw it away, or otherwise dispose of it (Article 12, Law 360).[519]

Article 210

Congress approved a democratic and modern constitution, but Santana was not pleased with it and added this Article 210: *"The president can organize the army and navy and mobilize the national guard during the current war, while peace is not signed."* The "current war" was of course the war against Haiti.

In case some would hesitate to sign, Santana sent a battalion of soldiers to surround the site of the Constituent Assembly. Sure enough, Article 210 was approved unanimously with one notable exception: Buenaventura Báez. It was a premonition of the rivalry between these two conservative leaders that would last for years to come.[520]

Article 210 is highly significant, because, from that moment on, Santana needed to be at war with Haiti to guarantee his absolute power.

Liberals, conservatives, and the conflict of race

For the elite sectors, landowners, and conservative politicians, the conflict with Haiti was convenient because it allowed Santana to be in a permanent "state of war." Appealing to article 210, he could maintain absolute power as president. But there was more to it. Lingering in the background, the conflict with Haiti was also about race. Since the arrival of slaves in Hispaniola, race was a recurring and evident theme for European colonial powers. That was also true in the process of Dominican independence.

The Dominican elite in the capital were dubbed "white Spaniards" whom many residents considered almost a foreign group. On occasions, the *Junta* conducted white-only sessions and some would brag before foreign authorities about how the whites led the separation.[521]

Santana, a mestizo himself, supported the military forces and prominent whites, lobbying abroad for white recognition, annexation, and white immigration. Santana's collaboration with these white elites displeased and concerned military officials of color in the capital,[522] including Trinitarian General Puello. Understandably, blacks and mulattoes would consider any reference to race as a threat to the reestablishment of slavery, be it as part of the Greater Colombia or as a French protectorate.[523]

The tension between the conservative government and black residents was such that in the summer of 1845, to ease General Puello's protests and appease the city's unrest, Santana agreed for Puello to remain in command of the military. The decision caused the resignation of some racist members of the *Junta*.[524] It was a short-lived victory for Puello. A few years later, on Pedro Santana's orders, he and his brother Gabino, were executed.

Different perceptions about race in the Dominican Republic

As we can see, the differences between liberals and conservatives were not merely political. The racial perception of the new country was a recurring theme on the island. The Liberals' ideal was to achieve national unity beyond racial distinctions: a multiracial society with a predominantly mulatto population. On the other hand, for conservatives, race was still a divisive factor and an element to fuel hostility against Haiti in order to justify international protection.

The conflict was out in the open. On one occasion, Duarte recommended to the Board an amendment to the constitution: *"The unity of race* [he suggested] *is one of the fundamental principles of our political adhesion."* Duarte was alarmed and surprised that the Board firmly rejected the proposal.[525]

Santana took some anti-Haitian measures, on occasions reaching absurdity. There was an attempt to "deport" *merengue*, which was considered a *"horrible and loathsome"* dance.[526] It seemed that the African rhythm bothered the General and the Dominican upper classes. The merengue's origin is unclear, but today it is considered the national dance, both in the Dominican Republic and Haiti.[527]

Pierrot's attempted invasion

The new Dominican nation had more than internal problems. The threats Santana feared were real. Haiti still wanted to regain its lost territory. Pierrot, the General who left Santiago humiliated, became the new Haitian president. It was as if the trap they set for him years before, with the fake letter, had to be avenged.

In May 1845, Pierrot attempted another foray into the Dominican Republic. This time the Dominican resistance was better prepared, and the Haitian army did not get past Matas de Farfán. At the end of that same year, Pierrot tried an attack by sea but failed again, as the ships grounded in Puerto Plata harbor and all the sailors were taken prisoner. Pierrot wanted to try again, but this time his army removed him from office on February 27, 1846.[528] General Riché replaced him. The new leader had no similar ambitions of expansion.[529]

With the situation quieter in Haiti, and despite continuous Dominican victories, Santana, Bobadilla and Baez still insisted on the Haitian threat and on asking for protection from a foreign power.

After decades of collaboration with the Santana administration, it's worth mentioning that Bobadilla would eventually change sides, following his son in opposing foreign intervention.[530]

Santana against the Liberals

By the end of 1846 in the Dominican Republic, Santana had an autocratic and consolidated administration.[531] He appointed loyal officials in his government, expropriated Church lands, and allotted them to his supporters.[532] He even had an archbishop, Monsignor Tomas de Portes, threaten Santana's opponents with excommunication.[533]

It was a period of persecution against the most critical members of the opposition, like the General mentioned above, José Joaquín Puello and his brother Gabino.[534]

The curious and tragic case of the Puello brothers

José Joaquín Puello was born in Santo Domingo and, during Boyer's occupation, became a colonel in the Haitian army. He exercised his authority with equity and justice, winning the affection of blacks and mulatos alike. Possibly out of affinity with the ideals of the Liberals, he joined the Trinitarians.

Surprisingly, however, once independence was achieved, Puello allied with Santana when he entered Santo Domingo city.

Later, and we are anticipating events here, Puello would be assigned to the southern border where, together with General Antonio Duvergé, he defeated the Haitian army in 1845. Santana appointed him Minister of the Interior and Police. However, he remained faithful to the Trinitarian cause raising suspicions from the conservatives and the French consul Saint-Denys, who tried to expel him from the country. In a report to his government, the consul called Puello an enemy of the whites and hostile to France. Santana's ambition had no limits. Despite having favored Puello with the Interior and Police portfolio, Santana saw him as a possible presidential candidate due to his reputation among blacks and mulattoes. Santana waited for the right moment to get rid of him.

The opportunity came as lawmakers discussed the issue of facilitating white immigration. Puello believed that blacks were to have the same facilities as whites to enter the country, causing great scandal among conservatives. Shortly afterward, he was accused of supporting a conspiracy to overthrow the government and of ingratitude towards the white race. Santana had him arrested. A court of 25 people tried him in absentia and without the right of appeal. On December 23, 1847, he was shot along with his brother Gabino.[535]

Santana resigns

A country does not survive on repression and military victories alone. The Dominican Republic was in a deep economic crisis. Santana was good in dealing with invasions, military strategies, forming allies and fabricating enemies, but perhaps not so skilled in matters pertaining to devaluations, imports, or trade balances. Furthermore, the president had some detractors within the army itself. Pressed with this unpopular situation, in 1848, Santana resigned. General Manuel Jiménez, Minister of War and former member of La Trinitaria, replaced him.[536] General Jiménez was elected constitutional president for the 1848-1852 period. He did not last a year. In 1849 Santana would rise to power again. We will see how.

Soulouque, the flamboyant new leader in Haiti (1847)

During President Jiménez's tenure, in Haiti, events would unfold in a most unique way. A 65-year-old unknown, Faustine Soulouque, was elected as the new president. Soulouque was born to a Mandingo mother (an ethnic group from West Africa) and an unknown father. The Haitian Senate had been faced with a presidential vacancy, and after 6 hours of deliberation it was unable to choose between the two leading candidates. The Interior Minister suggested Soulouque, being the third contender, to resolve the impasse since he had obtained a vote in each of the previous voting rounds (hopefully not his own). The plan worked, and on March 1, 1847, Faustine became Haiti's new president. The election was a surprise for many, especially for him. The story is told that as the government delegation approached him to announce his new position, he thought he was the victim of a well-thought-out prank.[537]

If someone hoped that Soulouque would be a transitional politician and easy to control, they would be very wrong. The man led the country for 22 years!

The new President had an exceptional problem: France recognized the Dominican Republic as an independent state. That was a political boost for Dominicans but a blow for Haiti, which lost any hopes of a political reunification and the chance to recover a good source of income through taxes. After 20 years, Haiti still had to pay half of its debt to France.

To make matters worse, an unsubstantiated rumor claimed that France would occupy Samaná Bay in exchange for this recognition. From Haiti's perspective, having the French so close was always a threat.[538]

In March 1849, fifteen thousand men began a new attempt to invade the Dominican Republic. The stage was similar to the March 19 battle of 1844. Even some of its main characters were the same. Soulouque's men reached San Juan de la Maguana on their way to Azua, which was already emptied of troops. The Dominican battalion, led by Antonio Duvérgé, moved to El Número hills. This time though, they had to retreat further East.

The battle took place at Las Carreras. The Dominican army's commander was none other than Pedro Santana. The disputed hero's presence was effective again. After being in Azua for over two weeks, Soulouque retreated.[539]

End of Jiménez' presidency. Buenaventura Báez, first elected president (1849)

Santana's army was victorious, and that was a menace for whoever held power. Boosted by this victory, Santana, who had no support only a year before, entered the capital with his army to seize Manuel Jiménez's position. A short but violent civil war broke out on May 17, 1849, and Jiménez was finally deposed.[540] He died of cholera in Haiti five years later.

Santana called elections for July 5. Santiago Espaillat was elected president, but he did not accept the honor as he did not want to become another one of Santana's puppets. The second in line was Buenaventura Báez. After five years of independence and almost 400 years of colonization, the Dominican Republic had its first democratically elected president. It was a significant feat, no doubt, but the electoral process could hardly be compared to our current democratic system.

Voting was indirect. Those allowed to vote elected the members of each district's electoral college. They, in turn, were free to select their executive and legislative representatives. The first election with a direct vote was held in 1858. Only men were allowed to vote, and they had to meet one of these conditions:

- Be a real estate owner, public employee, or officer of the army of land or sea,
- Be a man registered in any industry or profession,
- Be a professor of any liberal science or art,
- Be a tenant, for at least six years, of a rural business.

The universal male vote was instituted in the constitutional reform of 1865. The constitutional reform of 1924 excluded the right to vote for the military, a provision still in force to date.[541]

Women were not allowed to vote until 1942 (the US passed the 19th amendment in 1919). The paradox is that universal suffrage in the Dominican Republic became official during Rafael Leónidas Trujillo's dictatorship, who used it to legitimize his regime in that year's elections.[542]

In any case, when Báez came to power, 48-year-old Santana decided, oddly enough, to retire to his farm in Seibo for the second time. He would be back.

Báez was a conservative, but Santana's staunch rival. One of the new president's first measures was to pardon several politicians exiled by Santana and to incorporate officials critical of Santana into the army.[543]

In 1853, Báez finished his four-year term. It was again, Santana's turn. This time, Pedro Santana issued a decree expelling Báez in perpetuity. Báez left from Azua for Curaçao [544] but he, too, would be back.

The 1854 Constitution

Santana was having problems in his own government and had strong opposition from Congress for the totalitarian power he exercised and for the extent of the authority granted to him by the constitution. In fact, Santana was thus forced to convene a Constituent Assembly to draft yet another Constitution.

The 1854 Constitution was liberal and democratic, and the president did not have absolute powers. It only lasted from February 25 until December. Under threats, Congress had to change it and redraft it to make it more authoritarian and to keep political control in the hands of a few.[545]

The Dominican Republic moves closer to the United States

The economic situation in the country was quite desperate, and Santana was looking for foreign help. Spain was not an option, because since the Treaty of Basel in 1795, it had not shown much interest in Dominican affairs. Santana showed a new-found interest in the United States and negotiated a Treaty of Friendship, Commerce, and Navigation with them.[546]

American annexation and the case of Mr. and Mrs. Cazneau (1853-1854)[547]

The United States sent Mrs. Cazneau as a special envoy to inquire about the situation of the Dominican Republic. She was the daughter of a congressman and, at the age of 26, divorced; she notably became the lover of Aaron Burr, 76, who had been vice president of the United States and who had killed the very famous Alexander Hamilton during a duel.

During her mission, she worked with five American foreign ministers and three Dominican presidents. Her goal was clear: to annex the

Dominican Republic to the United States, acquire Samaná Bay, and found colonies of freed United States slaves in Santo Domingo.

A few years earlier, in 1845, Jeanne McManus (her maiden name) was sent by the United States' president to Mexico. She was to speculate and acquire Mexican land for the United States. In Texas, she met another speculator, a Spanish-speaking French Catholic by the name of William L. Cazneau, whom she married. He was sent to the Dominican Republic in 1853, by the United States as a secret agent and commissioner, diplomatic missions which Mrs. Cazneau helped initiate. The couple saw an opportunity to make their fortune in the Dominican Republic through land speculation.

During the three governments of Pedro Santana, the four of Buenaventura Báez and the two of José María Cabral, the couple tried to acquire the Samaná Peninsula for the United States and to annex Santo Domingo. To that effect, they rubbed shoulders with five American presidents. They bought a good house in the San Carlos neighborhood, where they welcomed presidents and important guests and bribed Dominican officials to carry out their business. They brought freed slaves from the United States to settle in several projected colonies. They failed. Many of these freed slaves died, and the survivors asked the US government to send them back to their country. Apparently, President Báez and the American business couple did not get along very well. William sneered about Báez: *"he cordially hates North Americans and everything that is American, and his heart is purely French."*

There were tensions between Mr. Cazneau and Dominican officials over the way Cazneau treated the black Dominican Consul. A New York Times reporter explained how the man treated the consul *"like any black man."* It was a prejudiced comment to be sure, but it clearly reflects Mr. Cazneau's disregard and bigotry even towards black government officials.

Spain is interested again in the Dominican Republic (1855)

The US interest in the Dominican Republic worried Spain, since American influence in the Samaná Peninsula could undermine Spanish maritime control in the Antilles. On February 18, 1855, Spain and the Dominican Republic signed a treaty of recognition, peace, friendship, commerce, navigation, and extradition.[548]

Late that same year, the Spanish consul in Santo Domingo, Antonio Segovia, joined Baez in opposing Santana's collusion with the United States. Segovia began to issue Spanish IDs (*matriculas*) to Santana's opponents. The strategy became so widespread that the city of Santo Domingo had a large population of Spanish citizens.[549] Some were so delighted that even a troupe sang: "*I don't fear Santana or Alfao, I only fear Segovia because I am enrolled* (matriculao)."

Lots of things were happening in the eleven-year-old country.

Haiti's Response to America's Plans (1855)

Besides Spain, Haiti was also concerned about a possible transfer of the Dominican Republic to the United States, as slavery was still legal in the US. The US abolished slavery in 1865, twenty-one years after the Dominican Republic had done so.

For Haiti, a treaty between the Dominican Republic and the United States, allowing the latter to take control of Samaná Bay and Peninsula, was unacceptable.[550] Although seventy-three years old, Soulouque was ready for war and organized his army to invade the Dominican Republic yet again.

As usual, Santana would wait for the enemy in Azua, where he set up his headquarters. This time the battle was on December 22 and was one of the fiercest in the Dominican-Haitian conflict. It happened near Las Matas, in Sabana de Santomé, and took 695 lives before the Haitian army retreated. Dominican guerrillas went in pursuit of Haitian soldiers as they looked for safety even in the treetops.[551]

However, the bloodiest battle took place a month later as Soulouque's men attempted an invasion from the northern front, through Sabana Larga, on January 24, 1856. The combat lasted nine hours, from seven in the morning to four in the afternoon, machetes in hand. The Haitian army was defeated, suffering around a thousand casualties, their bodies scattered along the 180 miles separating Sabana Larga from Dajabón.[552]

Santana is retiring, again

Despite yet another victory, many of Santana's followers abandoned him. Deeply depressed, once again, he retired to his estate in El Seibo.[553] Báez returned from exile with Spanish support. Acting President Regla Mota, with no funds, had to dismiss his soldiers and had to leave office. Báez took power on October 6, 1856, unchallenged. He adhered to the 1854 Constitution, as Santana did, which gave him absolute power. It was time for revenge. He unleashed an unrelenting political persecution, sent Santana into exile, compelled Santana's followers to resign from the Senate, and appointed his own people to government positions.[554]

Desiderio Valverde a new president, in Cibao. The 1857 Revolution

The conflict, of course, was not only between Santana and Báez. The liberals opposed them both.

The economic situation was disastrous, and Báez made it even worse. In 1857 he deceived the Cibaeños by buying their tobacco harvest with money he knew was already worthless.[555]

This abuse was the last straw. In July 1857, in Santiago, a group of armed men, together with merchants and intellectuals, began an opposition movement and unilaterally constituted a provisional government. They named Desiderio Valverde as the new and, for them, legitimate president of the country.[556] Baez wouldn't stay quiet for long.

Liberals ask for help to fight Báez

A civil war was in the making between Baez and Valverde's supporters. Báez was strong in the capital, and Valverde's *Cibaeño* government did not have enough men to overthrow him. He needed help; and then the unthinkable happened. The *Cibaeños* requested help from an unexpected man: General Pedro Santana. Jaw-dropping. Valverde allowed the General to return from exile on August 25, 1857.[557] Liberals and conservatives joined forces to dethrone Báez. Not a promising omen.

In a month, Santana recruited his old army and soon he was in charge of the situation. The war lasted almost a year and was extremely bloody.[558] Eventually Santana triumphed for Valverde.

The impossible alliance between liberals and conservatives. Moca Constitution (1858)

Once in power, the Cibao government declared a new constitution in Moca on February 19, 1858 (the Moca Constitution). The document reflected liberal principles such as freedom of expression, transit, and assembly. It championed a civil government over military rule, was popular instead of oligarchic, and backed elected and responsible representatives. The president could not be re-elected, and the armed forces were to obey civil authorities. Santiago became the new capital of the Republic. One of the most radical clauses of the Constitution was the *jus soli* provision, the right to citizenship by birth. Whoever was born in Dominican territory was automatically a Dominican national. This clause resisted all the constitutional changes in the intricate Dominican history, until it was rescinded in 2004.[559]

Santana, again the strong man

Santana for his part, was surrounding Báez and his men in the capital.[560] It was time for Báez to negotiate his surrender. For being such staunch enemies, the conditions for Báez's submission were surprisingly favorable. He was free to leave and take with him all the money he managed to steal from the state coffers during his presidency. As if this were not enough, he was allowed to take the gold and tobacco misappropriated from the cibaeños the previous year. There is more: Báez was also allowed to borrow state ships to travel abroad. Of course, he never returned them.[561]

Predictably, Santana did not abide by the liberal 1858 Constitution. As soon as he entered Santo Domingo, he made sure to undo all the Cibaeños' efforts so as to return to the political status quo of 1856. The Cibaeños, of course, did not accept Santana's betrayal, but without a proper army, they had no other options. By the end of 1858, and benefiting from the Cibao liberal movement, Santana regained control of the whole country again.

Last threat from the Government of Haiti (1859)

By 1859, Haiti was in turmoil. Interestingly, anytime Santana took power, the Dominican Republic entered into some sort of conflict with the neighboring country. This time, the French consul in Port-au-Prince visited Santana on behalf of the self-proclaimed Emperor, Soulouque. The "transitional puppet" had been president of Haiti for ten years and was 77 years old. Soulouque wanted to reach an agreement with Santana to form a federation between the Dominican Republic and Haiti, in an attempt to avoid the United States from annexing the Dominican Republic. Failing to agree to this "offer," Haiti would be forced to take the eastern part.[562]

Soulouque's threats never materialized. There were no more battles in El Número, or Las Carreras or Santiago. The eccentric Haitian president had an enemy at home: the Haitian officers were tired of so many years of tyranny and plotted a conspiracy led by General Geffrard. He defeated and exiled Soulouque in January 1860.[563] Geffrard had a military past linked to Soulouque and was a declared anti-Dominican, mostly known for defeating the Dominican army in 1849 during Soulouque's first invasion in Tábara, Azua.[564] But again, personal alliances and convictions can easily change.

Dominicans with Haiti against Soulouque

In his struggle to oust Soulouque, Geffrard had an unlikely ally: the Dominican people. The Dominican-Haitian collaboration was such that a Spanish officer stated: *"The Dominicans recently made a revolution… to instate General Fabre Nicolas Geffrard in power."*[565]

The Dominican support for Geffrard included the country's liberal political sectors. Francisco del Rosario Sánchez, the national hero of 1844, allied with Geffrard, forcing Soulouque to flee into exile.[566]

One of the Haitian president's new measures was to reduce his army in half and to announce the end of military incursion into the Dominican Republic.[567] The pledge has held true through today. After 145 years, however, occasionally, the fear of a Haitian invasion resurfaces in some Dominican narratives.

In 2004, Haiti celebrated 200 years of independence. This means that all the attempts to invade the Dominican Republic were during the first 55 years of Haitian independence. In the following 145 years, there have been no invasion attempts by either side. Think about it. The last threat was about 160 years ago. Back then, there were no electric light bulbs, no radios, no toilet paper (designed by Joseph Gayetty in 1857), and no pens. People used feathers to write, preferably from left wings,[568] as its curvature adapted better to the right hand's anatomy.

Haiti in the time of Geffrard

After Soulouque's resounding defeat, Geffrard sought a peace and trade treaty between Haiti and the Dominican Republic, and he rejected his predecessor's policies.[569]

Besides adopting measures for a peaceful relationship with the Dominican Republic, or perhaps because of it, cotton production in Haiti increased from 700,000 pounds per year in 1860 to double that in 1862.[570]

There was strong economic expansion, and the plantations, both private and state-owned, needed foreign labor.[571] Haiti invited some 2,000 citizens of color from the United States to work in the fields, but the program was not very successful, as many returned to their country due to harsh working conditions and poverty, among other reasons.[572]

3.

The Annexation Period

By the mid-1800's the Dominican Republic was mainly rural and its citizens were living in poverty, but with considerable autonomy. Eight thousand people lived in the capital and another twelve thousand in other urban centers. Some 200,000 lived scattered throughout vast rural areas, with an estimated 7.4 inhabitants per square mile (not many compared to 169 inhabitants per square mile in Puerto Rico around the same time).[573] The situation was dire but stable until Santana managed to stir things up yet again.

Given Spain's renewed interest in her long-forsaken territory, Santana no longer sought support from the United States. Spain was a better candidate to adopt its former colony. Santana needed annexation because of his country's economic fragility. To justify such a move, he first needed the threat of a foreign country, and Haiti would be the best candidate. Despite Geffrard's unequivocal statements about ceasing any attempts to invade the Dominican Republic, Santana exploited the Haitian threat narrative. External threats (real or fabricated) are often an effective way to unite a nation and to divert attention away from domestic struggles.

Races and anti-Haitian speech to justify the annexation

Supporters of annexation would use the race card to undermine Haiti's declared neutrality. The new Spanish consul, Eduardo San Just[574] wrote to Cuba's Captain-General: *"the territory (Columbus' favorite jewel), must be kept in the command of the Raza that today populates them, never passing, in whole or in part, to the hands of foreign 'razas.'"*[575] The "foreign races" here could refer to the United States, or more likely to Haiti. In private, the consul admitted in a rather hypocritical manner that he did not know if Santana's administration could be called government as he was surrounded by *"blacks from Seybo, half-naked."*[576]

Racial prejudice was used not only for mockery and humiliation but also as the perfect excuse to instill fear. A report designed to measure the possibilities of annexation recommended great caution: if they seem like an invading force, the report speculated that *"the emancipated people from both sides of the island, fearing the reestablishment of slavery, would rise up against the government itself and call on the Haitian Empire, thus establishing race war."*[577]

To make the Haitian threat credible enough to justify foreign protection, history had to be re-written. Santana and his followers argued that the 1844 independence was a test of loyalty to Spain and the people's desire to be under Spanish sovereignty. They conveniently forgot the Independence of 1821 and twenty-two years of reasonable stability during the period of unification with Haiti.[578]

The first independence of 1822 from Spain was underrated and delegitimized. Núñez de Cáceres, was even dubbed as an ambitious traitor and a *"miserable black."*[579] Even Santana himself added fuel to the fire declaring -referring to Núñez de Cáceres- that *"only the ambition and resentment of one man separated us from mother country."*[580]

The newfound pro-Spanish sentiment had racist overtones not only towards the Haitians but, for Spanish authorities, also towards Dominicans. The Spaniards questioned the Dominican's ability to overcome the hardships of subsistence labor. A Spanish official in Cuba asserted: *"The majority of Dominicans, who are all of color, demonstrated the laziness typical of proletarians, because one cannot obligate them to work."*[581]

The Spanish Foreign Minister explained to his queen: *"Her Majesty's government could not be indifferent to the fate of the Spanish part of Santo Domingo* [curiously no longer calling it the Dominican Republic] ... *To abandon her to foreign intrigue, expose her to the invasions of an enemy race, would have been a very grave political error, and a total forgetting of honor and even humanity."*[582]

Following the attack on race, Haitian politics became the target of critique, branding the government tyrannical, exclusive, and of a savage constitution.[583]

Probably not since the time of España Boba, or the Treaty of Basel, did Dominicans feel more sympathy for their Haitian neighbors than for the mother-country. We can only wonder if pro-Spanish sentiment were widespread, why negotiations between the two administrations had to be kept secret.[584]

But why the annexation?

Annexation did not have apparent popular support, and Haiti was not really a menace. Why then would Santana campaign for it?

Santana had several issues that would make annexation a beneficial course of action.

He needed urgent help for a country whose economy had plummeted after the Báez fraud. Besides, he had to protect the country from a possible United States coup by groups of adventurers intruding into national territory, as happened in Nicaragua.

The concern was real. In October 1860, a group of Americans planted their flag on Alta Vela island (barely 0.4 square miles in the southernmost point of the Dominican Republic) and claimed it as United States territory, promptly starting guano mining. The Dominican government had to expel them.[585]

Most importantly, Santana thrived any time there was a military conflict with the neighbors. To be in power, Santana needed to be in permanent conflict with Haiti, and Spain could be more inclined to perpetuate the Haitian-Dominican conflict. Santana believed that the Dominican Republic had to be not just a protectorate but a Spanish province.[586]

The annexation with Spain negotiated in secret

Santana's plan was working. The Spaniards were onboard. Next, he had to convince the Dominican elite, appealing to national pride and the perennial enmity against and fear of Haiti. The southern owners and the Cibao Valley merchants were persuaded that annexation would benefit them, mainly from investments and labor control and celebrated the Spaniard's arrival with ceremony and pageantry.[587]

The rest of the Dominicans were kept in ignorance, as the negotiations with the Spanish government were secret.[588] Secrecy was essential. There was no room for leaks or for dissension. Ramón Mella was arrested in January 1861 and then expelled from the country for disagreeing with the annexation.[589] That was no minor matter. Mella was Santana's commander in Puerto Plata.[590]

The newspaper La Discusión, on April 21, 1861, a month after the annexation, revealed Santana's contradictory political strategies: *"There is an extremely important difference between President Santana cheating the liberty and independence of a people for his advantage and the Dominican people themselves asking for annexation."*[591]

Such was the secrecy that, during the celebrations of the national holidays of February 27, 1861, in his speech, Santana omitted any reference to the country's imminent annexation to Spain, set to occur only nineteen days later.[592]

Santana had kept the operation secret at home, but the Spanish government requested some evidence of the people's endorsement of the plan. No problem for the General. He asked for names in 33 cities and three military posts, collecting four thousand signatures supporting annexation. Considering that the Dominican Republic had more than 200,000 inhabitants, the polling exercise could hardly count as a proper referendum. In reality, the approval rate was merely 2%.[593]

Santana was optimistic about the project. In addition to having 4,000 signatures, he assessed that he would need some 2,000 soldiers and officers to carry out the annexation.[594] He got that part wrong. By the end of the conflict that was about to occur, Spain would have sent 41,000 soldiers in addition to the already 20,000 reservists from the Dominican Republic, Cuba, and Puerto Rico.[595]

Opposition and Báez's conspiracies

Some of the earliest opposition to Santana's plan came from Dominicans in exile, specifically from Buenaventura Báez. Báez, like Santana, was conservative, but he was pro-French.

Báez did not cease in his efforts to return to the country. To that effect, Francisco del Rosario Sánchez maintained contact with support groups in Haiti to start an incursion into the Dominican Republic. The alliance between *Baecistas* and Haitian collaborators greatly concerned the Santana government.[596]

These political intrigues developed thanks to the prosperous trading relations between Haiti and the Dominican Republic, which increased with unusual intensity ever since the Haitian declaration of non-aggression.[597] One of the most prominent Dominican businessmen, coincidentally, was General Valentín Ramírez Báez, Buenaventura's cousin. When Valentín was not in business mode, he promoted the efforts to overthrow the Dominican government.[598]

The annexation (1861)

Despite open condemnation and opposition, the annexation became a reality. On March 18, 1861, at Santo Domingo's fortress, Spanish troops lowered the Dominican flag, and the Spanish flag began again to wave over the city. A witness recalled the episode that took place *"in complete silence, it was a really melancholic spectacle: men and women crying; no applause, or even an audible whimper...and no shot guns."*[599]

Santana had put in place a sound propaganda system and published manifestos forged by the government, giving the impression that the whole country welcomed the reincorporation to Spain while renouncing their Dominican sovereignty.[600]

The bases of annexation

Despite confusion and uncertainty, the annexationist plan was unstoppable. Provisions were made that criminal and commercial laws would be, provisionally, those of Spain, but the civil code would be that of the Dominican Republic, allowing traditional customs and practices.[601] Slavery would remain abolished entirely.[602] The Crown declared that slavery was a horrible practice, though it was still necessary in Cuba and Puerto Rico.[603] This distinction would lead to some problems of a migratory nature, as we will see.

The arrival of the Spanish authorities

The Annexation was real. Forty years since the 1821 independence, an eternity since the Treaty of Basel, after twenty-two years of unification with Haiti and seventeen years of independence, Spanish officials and military personnel began to arrive. They soon discovered that the country they came to rule was not as "Spanish" as they assumed it to be. Most of the population was colored, and their customs were much different from those in Spain.[604]

Unsurprisingly, apart from self-serving politicians and ambitious landowners, Santo Domingo received the Spaniards with suspicion. Reportedly Puerto Plata received the troops *"with the utmost coldness and marked disgust. They contemptuously gave them the nickname 'the whites.'"*[605]

The gloominess and indifference were such that the Spanish officers did not usually participate in the cities' day-to-day lives, in public functions or religious ceremonies.[606]

The arrival of the Spanish army

With the annexation, two different countries with their own traditions and practices were bound by political and military treaties. This created constant conflicts between the Spanish army and Dominican society. Unlike politicians and officials who only related to their Dominican counterparts, the army interacted directly with the people. The Spanish troops, moreover, were spread through all the country.

In three weeks, two thousand soldiers from Havana and 800 from Puerto Rico arrived in the capital. About a thousand went to Puerto Plata by boat, and a few hundred moved on to Azua.[607] There was a total of ten thousand soldiers in the first wave (much more than the 2,000 suggested by Santana). It was a significant number and it represented a logistical challenge. There were only accommodations for half a battalion (about a thousand soldiers) in the capital, and many soldiers had to lodge in convents, court cellars, palaces, forts, or in other temporary accommodations.[608]

Besides, the soldiers needed extra supplies from Cuba, Puerto Rico, and Saint Thomas. The officers admitted, *"the troops and even the Commanders and Officers, have suffered hunger and privation without measure."*[609]

Annexation and racial prejudice

Race conflicts were already foreseen by some. As the Spanish troops disembarked on Dominican soil, a naval commander reminded them to observe *"prudent and caring of conduct with the residents, avoiding disputes and winning, at all costs, the affections and admiration of the Dominicans."*[610] The advice was completely ignored.

The advice had a racial overtone. The difference between Spaniards and Dominicans was not only cultural but racial. Not only was Spain mainly racially white, but in the Spanish islands of Cuba and Puerto Rico, blacks were still slaves. For the Spanish soldiers who arrived from those islands (20,000 from Cuba and 4,000 from Puerto Rico),[611] it was shocking to see a society made up almost entirely of free mulattos and blacks.

But the encounter with the locals was not the only challenge for the soldiers. The Spanish troops were not fully aware of the nature of their mission. Recalling his soldiers' arrival, a General wrote:

"The troops embarked with no orders, no proclamation, without any slogan, like filibusters (pirates) sneakily united for some awful escapade. Neither officers nor the soldiers knew if that territory was enemy or friend, if they arrived as masters, allies, or conquistadors..." Tellingly it was reported that "there was no rule of conduct, no policy warning of any of the contingencies that might immediately arise from the sudden interchange of peninsular soldiers and the population of color." Some officials called the territory "the extinguished republic."

The authorities even asked the Seville archivist what the most appropriate name for the island was: Santo Domingo? Hispaniola? or Haiti?[612]

Not a very promising scenario.

Conflict among two allied armies

As incredible as it may seem, the Spanish troops' first conflicts were with their allies, the Dominican soldiers. Some newcomers asserted that the Dominican generals: "*didn't know anything other than to rise up against one another to take power of the governments.*"[613]

But what really seemed confusing and outrageous for the Spanish army was seeing men of color in positions of authority. The Spanish soldiers could not understand how a black or a mulatto could be a general or a colonel. One of them, puzzled, noted: "*A great number of generals and chiefs were men of color.*"[614] A similar point was made by a Spanish minister: "*so the negro and the moreno put on the sash of General, dress in the most distinguished uniform, flaunt the most prized insignia and decoration, and take part in the governance and administration of the island...*" And he continued pointing out the irony: "*...while the wretched of their race groan in servitude in the other Antilles, fourteen and sixteen leagues away.*"[615]

For some of the Spaniards, the matter was very upsetting, and they belittled or simply refused to be in the presence of colored soldiers.[616] So much for being brothers in arms.

Discrimination was persistent, to the point that by the fall of 1861, just a few months into the annexation, the Spanish military demoted most Dominican military by reducing their ranks.[617]

Prejudice was not only directed towards plain soldiers. Over time, prominent officers and Dominican army officials were also victims of racial intolerance. Santana himself, General Juan Suero, and General Gregorio Lora, were scorned in the presence of their own troops for not being white.[618]

Conflicts between the Spanish army and the Dominican people

Spanish soldiers were in a land where people spoke Spanish like they did, but most were black and mulatto.

For the newly arrived, race and color were a constant topic of talk and gossip. The Spaniards would remind Dominicans that in Cuba and Puerto Rico, they would be slaves, and a person of color *"could be... sold for a certain price."* Soldiers also gossiped about how the government would send black Dominicans to work on the coffee and sugar plantations.[619]

Racism wasn't just a prerogative of soldiers. Spanish officials also showed their prejudices. They had no qualms about telling their own allied and annexation champion, General Santana, a mulatto himself, that the white race would be the engine for the colony's progress. They argued that the population had grown but *"luckily the conditions of the country allow that the white race fulfill this important need."* [620]

The Spaniards' arrogance affected Dominican self-perception to the point that those with lighter skin moved away from their fellow countrymen to avoid being assimilated to them or considered inferior.[621]

Racism was neither veiled nor disguised. The Spanish Foreign Minister wrote about the new annexationist project: *"Under the auspices of Spain, in my humble judgment, the white race is destined to occupy this ever-green tropical island, enriching it and animating it with the triumphs of science, industry, and art."*[622]

Prejudice was evident even when disguised with good intentions. In late 1861 a high-ranking officer wrote that Spanish authorities arriving in the colony should be men *"already proven in these countries,"* of good reputation but also *"without or cured of those reservations ... commonly held against people of color, for the repugnance they inspire in us when we arrive from Europe ... to consider them inferior and despicable."*[623]

The annexation brought about not only political and economic tensions but also racial conflicts and prejudices. An observer tried to justify his own prejudice:

> *It is supposed that the current rebellion is a race one, since the rebels who have been seen are black, and those against whom the excesses have been committed are whites, counting among those victims some whites: but the lack of details on the matter impedes me from confirming this.*[624]

Spanish observers and wealthy Dominican merchants encouraged a radical and simplistic interpretation of the conflict: most Dominican rebels were black farmers and a few were mulattoes.[625]

Indeed, white landowners, merchants, and other prominent Dominicans were the ones supporting annexation and opposing the rebellion[626] and they disguised their racism as paternalism, making of the annexation an act of charity and generosity from the mother country towards an impoverished and inferior country[627]

The Dominican Army's opposition to annexation begins

Spanish officials soon restructured the troops and divided the army into three groups: the Spanish forces, the active reserves from the Dominican Republic and other territories, and lastly, the "passive reserves" unallocated and on standby in case of necessity.[628] The Spaniards moved the Dominican officers to the passive reserves, thus demoting them without their being discharged from the army. It was a significant move, since these transferred officials would be spearheading the opposition to the annexation against their theoretical allies.

At least 27 "passive" officers were suspected of participating in the first anti-annexation riots in Puerto Plata in 1863. Some like Jacinto de Lora and Gaspar Polanco, would become leaders of the *Guerra de la Restauración* (Restoration War), followed by many others demoted from the infantry and other ranks.[629]

Again, the issue of slavery

Among most Dominicans, the Spanish presence on the island was unwanted, not only because of manifest racial discrimination but also because of the ever-present danger of enslavement.

The return to slavery was one of the issues that caused the greatest rejection of annexation, even if the annexationists did not plan to introduce it. In fact, the Spanish authorities reported desperately that the false ideas and the abundant rumors of the return of slavery emptied entire towns and rural areas long before the rebellion was widespread. The authorities tried to calm the tension but soon realized that fear of enslavement was generalized, deeply rooted, a cause of anxiety, and of enormous weight in the anti-colonial struggle.[630]

The Spanish governor himself explained it thus:

> [The division of race] *is nowhere more prevalent than in the Santo Domingo Province, in the jurisdictions of San Cristóbal and Ozama, where the old sugar mills were on the Island and where the African race has the largest population. Those who were enslaved are still alive, even if elderly. Their children who knew their parents as slaves have black children of their own, and they cannot but look at the present day with horror.*[631]

The Governor recognized that slavery was not a chapter in a history book but a practice that many lived in their flesh.

The fear of returning to slavery was such that a boy from Baní revealed that the rebels read letters about slavery to the towns-people and said that *"the whites were going to enslave the blacks and seeing that most people in town were leaving, I left, too."*[632]

Many in Azua and Baní burned their sugar plantations and moved to the mountains with their animals.[633]

Although the restoration of slavery was not in the Spanish plan, for blacks and mulattos, it was a very plausible threat.

The Spanish prime minister admitted that even though Spain's public sentiment was against the slave trade, it would be difficult to suppress it without replacing it with another type of labor force.[634]

A Spanish diplomat, Mr. Manuel Cruzat, informally mentioned to the British consul that Spain effectively wanted to reintroduce slavery.

According to him, owners in Cuba and Puerto Rico with escaped slaves in the Dominican Republic had the right to claim their property back. The consul was stunned: *"If Spanish rule is enforced and considering all children of slaves as the property of their masters, there will hardly be a single black or colored person in the country who will be safe from persecution."*[635]

Migration problems from Puerto Rico and Cuba

Slavery was an omnipresent issue, because, while in the Dominican Republic slavery was abolished, in Cuba (just 353 miles away) and Puerto Rico (only 81 miles from Punta Cana), both Spanish territories, there still were slaves. That was a problem for Spain but an opportunity for the slaves in those islands. For them, reaching the Dominican Republic became a possibility to attain freedom. For Spain, that meant that any person of color from Cuba or Puerto Rico could be a potential escaped slave. So, in June 1861, just three months after the annexation, the Spanish Queen extended an order prohibiting the arrival of free people of color to Santo Domingo from the two neighboring islands.[636]

Even Pedro Santana was scandalized by such measure. He argued that the matter was *"of utmost transcendence and offensive to public morality,* [capable of] *causing all manner of distrust. Allowing free people of color to enter the colony would give the men of color of this Province a better guarantee by calming the spirits of the suspicious."* [637]

For some reason, at the end of that same year, Santana changed his mind and admitted that the measure should apply to people of color from Curaçao as well.[638] Eventually, the resolution created so much controversy that the Dominican governor himself temporarily suspended it.[639]

Another delicate situation occurred when wealthy settlers and authorities arrived to the Dominican Republic from Cuba and Puerto Rico with their slaves and domestic servants, who remained in a dubious status.[640]

From slavery to forced labor

Slavery was illegal in the Dominican Republic, but it was still practiced through forced labor.

Spanish officials and white businessmen requested the immigration of whites as supervisors of non-white workers.[641]

Some newspapers of the time supported the plan, convinced that free blacks, African prisoners, Chinese or Irish laborers who had settled in the country, would be an ideal workforce for the colony.[642]

A word apropos the Asian workers: A railroad industrialist hired ten thousand men and women *"from Calcutta, Hong Kong or Cuba"* knowing that they would not collude with black Dominicans and would serve as a racial wall against Haiti.[643]

A case study would help understand the rationale: In a new association of cotton growers, some argued that black workers were the best, since they were adapted to the hot climate. The association recommended that the workers should be under the careful supervision of whites. The laborers would be recruited voluntarily, with contracts of ten to fifteen years, growing cotton and tobacco, and under the same conditions and regulations as the Asians in Cuba. To supervise the work of the Africans, the company planned to have a Spanish head of the family (people of good manners, morality, and intelligence) for every ten workers.[644]

Although on paper, the agreement with Spain embodied the abolition of slavery, there were highly discriminatory and racist attitudes that made Spanish guidelines highly questionable in practice.

THE ANNEXATION PERIOD

These prejudices, of course, were not unique to Spain. In the American abolitionist civil war, prominent figures who fought against slavery, in turn, promoted racially discriminatory policies. At the end of the 19th century, American President Ulysses Grant wanted to reach an agreement to annex the Dominican Republic to his country for 1.5 million dollars, plus an honorarium of 100,000 dollars for the Dominican president at that time, Buenaventura Báez, an enthusiastic supporter of annexation. Grant's motives, however, were problematic. After five years of violence in the former US slave states, in which blacks were victims of repeated racists attacks, the president came to an intriguing conclusion: Southern whites would never live in peace alongside their former black slaves. His solution was even more bizarre: To relocate more than 4 million recently emancipated blacks outside the United States, where they would be safe and free to prosper.[645] Attempting to forcibly deport 4 million black people, so that whites could live in peace, would be nothing short of non-bloody, racial cleansing.

Archbishop Monzón's calamitous report (1862)

The Spanish prejudice was racial, social, and cultural, and it permeated many sectors of Spanish society, including the ecclesiastical.

The newly appointed archbishop of Santo Domingo, Monsignor Bienvenido Monzón, started off his tenure on the wrong foot. As no proper protocol was followed at his arrival, he decided to remain two extra days aboard the frigate on which he had spent a month traveling. He only disembarked after an adequate reception, with pomp and etiquette, was prepared to his liking.[646]

In 1862 the archbishop wrote a report about his new position. He asserted that the Catholic Church in the former Spanish colony was in a deplorable state, as the faithful have been without an archbishop for four years. There were 28 parishes throughout the country, and five were vacant due to a lack of funds.

It may seem a tiny number of parishes, but per capita, there were more parishes than today. Let's do the numbers. If we divide the number of inhabitants back then (about 150,000), [647] by the number of parishes, they had about 5,000 people per parish. Today the Dominican Republic has some 500 parishes[648] and a little more than 5 million Catholics,[649] that is, roughly 10,000 people per parish. Ergo today, the situation is twice as bad as it was 150 years ago.

But let's go back to the Monzón report. Besides the scarcity of parishes, only three, Puerto Plata, Santiago, and San Cristóbal, had official records. Dominican clergy, complained the prelate, had an exaggerated tendency to superstition and were generally illiterate, although they enjoyed significant power over the faithful. Rural priests who neglected their duties demanded large sums of money for their travels and services, and sometimes they were married.[650]

The archbishop noted that ecclesiastical marriage was rare. He understood that the small number of religious marriages had its roots in colonial life itself since the lack of roads and poverty prevented its inhabitants from having the permanent presence and assistance of already too few priests. Cohabitation was common, and most people, including the priests, accepted it without much concern.[651]

The bishop wrote about his experience:

> *Young daughters of the family enjoyed a grand liberty to leave the paternal house—which would in Spain be inconceivable—going about with whom they wanted most and who seemed the most opportune. Single women,* he continued, *were not embarrassed to live maritally with a man,"* [it is assumed that men were not embarrassed either, but that he did not mention], *and the word infanticide had no application in Santo Domingo."*

He disapproved heartily of civil marriage. Polygamy, even incestuous marriages, revealed how *"relaxed and perverted"* the nation was. [652]

Monsignor Monzón wanted to force Dominicans to marry in the Church, limiting the engagement period. Dominican families did not like the suggestion since, for them, their unions already had a value similar to that of a religious marriage. Furthermore, many people would be considered illegitimate after Monzón's suggested regulation.[653]

The archbishop also found unacceptable the presence of Protestants of color from the United States who, in places like Samaná, made up a third of the residents. He noticed how terrible it was that heresies were taught in public school to innocent boys and girls.[654] In 1862, orders even came from Spain to persecute Protestant practices. Luckily the officials in the capital decided to ignore these orders.[655]

Monzón lamented not only the state of the faithful but also the lack of parish records. Still today, in the Dominican Republic, a baptismal certificate is important legal evidence used to corroborate civil documents. A parish can even issue a certificate of "no baptism" to show that a person has not been baptized in that particular church. It remains unclear what the legal function of such a certificate could be. Back then, church archives were no more than a few almost-impossible-to-read books in a few boxes in poor condition.[656]

The bishop had issues with priests who were illiterate and, for the most part, opposed to the Spanish cause.[657]

Although the archbishop's description may have elements of truth, we should keep in mind that a tragic and chaotic narrative about Dominican society's social and moral situation would help justify Spanish intervention. He was not alone in giving a gloomy picture of the country.

THE FASCINATING ORIGIN OF THE DOMINICAN REPUBLIC

Cuba's Captain Francisco Serrano's report

Captain Francisco Serrano spared no one in his report about his visit to the Dominican Republic in 1861.

> (I declare) *without hesitation that I have found the new Spanish province of Santo Domingo completely disorganized, with very few aspects that can serve for its future reorganization. It has no Treasury, no army, no justice system, no administration, no defined legislation, and no institutions instrumental for educated peoples. The land is not cultivated; the forests are still unexploited as the first explorers found them; the population is scarce, and all sources of production depleted; the industry is dead, and commerce almost unknown. Consequently, there is depressing inertia, a complete indifference to the joys and advantages of social life that serves as a stimulus to prosperity and resistance to any improvement. All has to be done, beginning with the most important and most common jobs. Barracks, hospitals, warehouses, fortifications, roads. Everything, giving preference to the most urgent needs as much as the Spanish Treasury can afford.*[658]

Captain Serrano describes a desolate situation with complex causes and a challenging solution, but as in Archbishop Monzón's case, it served to justify the urgent need for the Spanish presence in the country.

Spain tries to fix the situation

The Dominican Republic's dire state justified a series of measures that, regrettably, did not consider the context, or the extent of the people's support. That amounted to Spanish interference with Dominican society's political, social, and religious fabric and caused outrage and unrest in the population.

Some of the measures were almost whimsical. It was forbidden to wear clothes from the opposite sex or from a different social class or category.[659]

Cockfighting was prohibited without a license. Coincidentally, as it turns out, the first roosters that humans domesticated thousands of years ago were not for eggs or for meat but for organized cockfights.[660] There were also restrictions on traditional dances, and some of them required licenses as well. Of particular concern were Dutch dances, Danois, Tango, and Tambulá.[661] Similarly, midwives also needed a 20-peso license. For many, it was a small fortune that they tried to avoid having to pay.[662] There was also a fine for toddlers who took their first steps on the street naked. On this last ordinance, a local official from Neiba intervened on behalf of the residents, claiming that such a practice was just a harmless matter.[663]

Dominican taxes and other abuses

As it becomes apparent, the issue of permits became a levy of sorts. Another way to collect revenue, much more popular, turned out to be the lottery, already in practice at that time for more than 150 years.[664] Today, Dominicans spend 3.6 million pesos every hour (a total of 31 billion pesos a year) in games of chance, not counting some 30,000 illegal lottery posts.[665] With this money, the government could pay all the country's 92,000 public school teachers for a year, including taxes and union dues.[666]

But it was not only the State that needed revenue. The Church also put in place a mechanism to increase its returns. The laity were growing tired of more and more new stipends. The celebration of a religious marriage, previously quite rare and free, was made compulsory and at the cost of 250 pesetas, an exorbitant amount of money at the time.[667]

The measures of the new archbishop divided the ecclesial authorities. While he had the support of some priests, others lamented their new role as tax collectors for sacraments.[668]

All in all, the new colonial subjects paid proportionally more taxes than people in Spain.[669] It is not surprising that in the Dominican Republic, the State's income through taxes doubled from 1860 to 1862. The merchants were the first to feel the impact.[670] These taxation measures were not going to help in an already unstable situation.

The institutional animal theft scheme and other unpopular measures

Some other measures were less relevant financially but significant for the people and did not help to create a good level of understanding between Dominicans and Spaniards. The so-called "baggage system," for instance, allowed the military to commission pack animals and carriages to transport both military personnel and their luggage without guaranteeing their return. Often the animals were abandoned and lost after being used.[671]

Another peculiar tradition imported from Spanish society but not well accepted in the Dominican Republic was the adjudication of nobility titles.[672] Nobility titles were typical of a monarchical society whereby nobles and aristocrats received privileges in virtue of a person's relevant actions or lineage. Today Spain has as many as 2,200 people holding almost 3,000 titles (some hold more than one title). A case in point is the Marquis of Vargas Llosa, granted to the Peruvian Spanish writer Mario Vargas Llosa.[673] In this case, the author has no privileges, and the title was given to him in recognition of his literary career. In an interview, he confessed: "*I was born a commoner, and I am going to die a commoner, from a republican country. You have to take it with humor and be thankful for the affectionate gesture from the King of Spain. It was an enormous surprise. I never imagined that they would make me marquis."*[674] Vargas Llosa is the author of the novel *La Fiesta del Chivo*, a recommended reading about the Dominican Republic and the dictator Leonidas Trujillo.

4.

Opposition to Annexation

International condemnation

The political process of annexation came at a time when most South American countries were embroiled in national struggles for independence. Ironically, the Dominican Republic already achieved its independence decades earlier, and its annexation with Spain did not sit well with the new Latin American countries.

Peru formally opposed the annexation with an official proclamation. In Jamaica, 4,000 signatures were collected explicitly to condemn Spain's intention to reinstate slavery in Dominican territory.[675] The opposition was widespread: Venezuela, Nicaragua, Bolivia, Colombia, and Argentina, all expressed support for the rebels of the Dominican Republic.[676] This support was not only by way of official declarations. A Venezuelan, Manuel Ponce de León, would write the Act of Independence on behalf of the Provisional Government, and another Venezuelan, General Candelario Oquendo, became an important leader of the Dominican rebel movement.[677]

At times the support was more humble but just as meaningful. At Saint Thomas church in the 6.9 sq mile island of Grand Turks, the faithful listened to a sermon on the Dominican struggle and made a special collection *"in aid of those poor distressed Dominicans"* who were living there as refugees.[678]

The Spanish authorities were disappointed and frustrated with this display of solidarity towards the rebels. A Spanish officer complained about the help the rebels were receiving from Nassau and the Turks Islands. *"It is obvious,"* lamented the disheartened official, *"that one of the main causes of the war's duration is precisely the continuous sending of aid, organized in Nassau and the Turks Islands above all else."* He even wrote to the English government to use all direct or indirect means to prevent, or at least limit, the blatant and practically public sending of aid.[679]

Dominican opposition and first victims

Of course, the most vigorous opposition to the annexation was in the Dominican Republic itself. Pedro Santana's attempt to have the population believe in general support of annexation only proved effective for the Spanish army to take over peacefully. But the truth began to be known, and the opposition to Santana became widespread. Some military authorities and Dominican allies were mobilizing through the center of the island, celebrating the new democracy in Haiti and opposing annexation in the Dominican Republic.[680]

Likewise, within the Dominican ecclesiastical clergy, some prominent figures opposed annexation. One of them was Fr. Fernando Antonio Meriño, who had been exiled in Puerto Rico, and some years later, would be elected the country's president.[681]

The movements and people opposed to Santana and the annexation are known as Restauradores (the Restorers), since the goal was to restore independence and sovereignty in the country that was lost in 1861. The restorationist period would be cruel and would eventually end with the Restauration War.

Repression against the "Restauradores"

One of Santana's first victims turned out to be one of his closest brothers in arms, Antonio Duvergé, the hero in the El Número battle. The political visions of each of the two men were too far apart. Duvergé already showed his different political views when he refused to take part in the overthrow of President Jimenez in 1849.[682] In 1853, Santana regained power, and soon Baéz, from exile, organized a conspiracy against him. The conspirators sought help from Antonio Duvergé and Francisco del Rosario Sánchez, also associated with the movement. The plot failed, and Duvergé was executed along with his son on April 11, 1855, before the annexation was even consummated. Santana's repression was relentless. On May 2, 1861, General José Contreras and his followers, mostly people of color and pro-Báez, pro-French conservatives and especially anti-Santana, took up arms against annexation, denouncing Spanish intent to reestablish slavery.[683] Contreras was 35 years old and a veteran of the war of independence.[684] The rebellion was quickly quenched, and its leaders shot at Santana's orders. Even the Spanish officers showed their disagreement over the executions.[685]

In 1860, Francisco del Rosario Sánchez, ill and in exile in Saint Thomas,[686] organized an operation against Santana with Haitian President Geffrard's support.[687] In June 1861, he entered the country through the San Juan Valley, but Santana would not tolerate any threats.[688]

Santana mobilized several thousand Spanish soldiers towards the center of the island to pursue the rebels.[689] Santana caught up with Sanchez near Las Matas, and, despite protests from the Spanish officers themselves, ordered his execution. Sánchez was executed in El Cercado, San Juan de la Maguana, along with nineteen men on July 4, 1861. Some were shot, others were beaten or killed with machetes.[690] Later, in a manipulation already typical of the General, the newspapers reported that Haiti was responsible for the uprisings.[691]

Sánchez died, but his speech, six months earlier, became a premonition about the Dominican spirit in an atypical, radical and cruel war. *"Prove to the world that you are part of the indomitable and guerrilla peoples who live civilization through customs, words, and its idea but who prefer liberty to all the advantages of rights."*[692] Spain could offer security, prosperity, or infrastructure, but nothing was worth it, if it meant sacrificing the Dominican cultural and national heritage.

Pedro Santana collides with the Spanish authorities and falls from grace

One of the first moral victims of the annexation was its leading promoter, General Santana. He wanted more power and authority, but it did not work out as he expected. With the annexation, he ceased to be president and was appointed Captain General of the Province of Santo Domingo.

At the beginning of the annexation, Spanish officials integrated Dominican authorities into the new colonial administration, but it was only in the first months of the occupation.[693] Over time, Santana and his men's power diminished as the Spanish officials and soldiers arrived to take up their posts, despite the Queen's order to keep Dominican officers in the Spanish troops. However, the Spanish captain, Francisco Serrano, disobeyed the orders, since, according to him, these officers were *"inept and of* [black] *race."*[694]

For the Spanish army, General Santana turned out to be a problematic leader who could jeopardize Spanish interests. The Spanish authorities were frustrated, as Santana rarely performed the duties assigned to him by the authorities. Santana had a loyal group and they had overtly ambitious claims, especially regarding their salaries and position. Eventually Santana could no longer be of service to the Spanish army.[695]

Santana eventually resigned and did so with honors and a generous pension, despite colonial economic hardships.[696] He even earned a title of nobility. The Queen of Spain awarded him the title of Grand Cross of the Royal Order of America of Isabel la Católica and the Marquis De Las Carreras, recalling the 1849 battle against Haitian troops. With this agreement, on January 6, 1862, Santana submitted his resignation as Captain-General of Santo Domingo.[697] Officially, he resigned because of rheumatism. Be that as it may, it was a perfect deal for all involved, including himself, since the pension included all the profits from selling supplies to the Spaniards.[698] He was 61 years old; he could have lived a peaceful retirement. But he was a man of action. As he was abandoning the city, he exclaimed: *"Dominicans, embrace your new father!"*[699] He had no intention to disappear. He would return, and soon.

Haiti, annexation, and the Dominican rebels

Of course, Haiti was one of the countries most affected by the annexation process, which installed a slave power such as Spain as their neighbor.

On April 6, 1861, President Geffrard publicly protested against the Spanish occupation. His words are significant:

> *Our brothers of the East have been tricked, the survival of one people is intricately tied to the survival of the other. We declare that we continue to have a feeling of brotherhood and our most sincere sympathies for this* [Dominican] *population.*[700]

He also explained that the Dominicans had been surprised, deceived, and manipulated by Santana.[701] The communiqués arriving from Haiti were well received by the Dominican rebels.

Before his death, Francisco del Rosario Sánchez praised the *"wise and just"* Haitian government and declared: *"I am persuaded that this*

Republic (Haiti), against whom we fought for our nationality, is today just as dedicated as we are so that we might preserve it."[702]

The feeling of solidarity was spreading. The Government of Haiti published Dominican pamphlets to raise awareness about the crimes of the Spanish annexationists. These pamphlets called Haiti to unite in a common cause: *"the interests of the two peoples are compromised... it is time to fight with what weapons remain."*[703] The same idea inspired a Haitian commentator to assert: *"our climate, our geographical and political position vis-à-vis foreign powers, our preservation, our needs and our hopes are the same."*[704]

The connections between the Haitian authorities and the Dominican rebels kept them in a permanent state of alert for a possible military mobilization in support of the Dominican Republic despite Spanish threats.[705]

In retaliation for this military mobilization, the Spanish army placed its naval force in an attack position off Port-au-Prince city. Under this threat, Haiti had 48 hours to salute the Spanish flag, guarantee that there would be no more disturbances in the territory, and pay a 200,000 pesos fine. After five days of negotiations mediated by the consuls of England and France, Geffrard agreed to salute the Spanish troops and pay compensation.[706]

It was a moral victory for the Spanish army over Haiti. Nevertheless, fines and symbolic gestures would not stop the collaboration and support of the Haitian people with their neighbors. This will be apparent soon.

The Government of Haiti stands out

The Haitian authorities had to navigate between popular support for the anti-colonial rebellion, on the one hand, and the threat of Spanish power on the other. The people of Haiti had no such reservations, and in port cities and the center of the island they defied their authorities and collaborated with the Restoration.[707]

Geffrard was compelled to show his cooperation with the Spaniards, who in turn showed their satisfaction: *"The Haitian authorities,"* they said, *"have shown themselves to be completely divorced from the movement and desirous of order."*[708] Geffrard even passed confidential information to Spain about the conspiracy activities of a former Dominican minister, Felipe Alfau, in Paris.[709] Alfau was a member of the original group of Trinitarians.

Geffrard's political realism, however, had its limits. He vigorously rejected the Spanish authorities' demand to land troops in Haiti.[710] Politically, Geffrard would have to pay dearly for his ambiguity.[711]

There was a significant difference between the government's hesitation and the genuine commitment of the Haitian people. In the Provisional Government's official Dominican bulletin, Ulises Francisco Espaillat wrote to Geffrard: *"Your Excellency, your co-citizens are not bothering to hide their sympathies* [towards the Dominican cause]*, your neutrality is against healthy politics, natural rights and even common sense."*[712]

This neutrality was contrary to popular sentiment and contrary to some political sectors in Haiti who wanted more open support to Dominican Restauration.

Espaillat, who would become vice-president and then president of the Dominican Republic and is considered one of the most honest politicians in the country[713] had this to add:

> *Your Excellency's co-citizens are not bothering to hide their sympathies to a cause that has come to be, in a manner of saying, the most natural bond that could possibly exist... Haitians*

and Dominicans are united together by the tightest friendship between two neighboring peoples, who for common political and racial reasons, have been born to be brothers.[714]

Hardships of the Spanish army and officers in the Dominican Republic

The widespread opposition from the Dominican Republic and Haiti meant in practice that, even before the war started, the Spaniards met with an unexpected challenge: a general boycott that made it practically impossible to settle down in the country.

The complaints of the Spanish officials and local authorities were varied. They complained, for example, that the mail took a week to reach the capital from the East and North. One of the most delayed routes for correspondence was from Santo Domingo to Santiago, which took about two weeks.[715]

Some travelers were outraged that *"from Azua to San Juan de la Maguana, more than 20 leagues apart, there are just six miserable huts [bohíos] in three spots, hours apart on the road."*[716]

Another problem that surely made bureaucratic work difficult was the lack of personnel willing to fill public posts, both at the government and local levels. Spanish officials, for example, could not find anyone to act as Minister of Justice. Applications were sent to mayors across the colony in January 1862. Some of them answered six months later, claiming they had not received any notification. In desperation, Santo Domingo's officials sent yet another notification: Any man, baptized, of robust constitution, and 25 years or older, with proven good morals and conduct could apply for the position. The notice had to be read in all public squares. Some responses came. Azua's mayor reported that, indeed, he had read the edict publicly but acknowledged: *"there is absolutely no person who could possibly be a candidate."*[717] The mayor of Puerto Plata also responded, but he lamented that no one applied for the position. After a year of searching, a French citizen living in the capital took the job but later moved to Saint Thomas. Something similar happened with the notary post in Samaná which remained vacant despite being a coveted position in previous years.[718]

The situation was so dire that according to authorities on the ground: *"It is impossible, from all angles to form a worthy idea of the difficulties one fights against in this country for the simplest things."*[719]

5.

The Restoration War

First warnings (1863)

The opposition to the country's political situation began to be open and, at times, violent. On February 9, 1863, 50 people, including workers, peasants, and other Neiba residents, decided to confront the Spanish administration. They did not have a proper plan, and their goal was unclear even among themselves. One of the leaders, Cayetano Velazquez, assured the small group that help would soon arrive from Haiti and that they could, at last, become Haitians. At these words, some shouted in protest: *"Freedom for Dominicans!"* Others, somewhat confused, clamored for a well-known national hero: *"Long live Santana!"* The first rebellion lasted seven hours, until it was put down by the Spanish troops stationed in the area.[720]

Rebellion in the Cibao

A few weeks later, the towns of Sabaneta and Guayubín in Monte Cristi Province also protested. This time the rebellion spread. The group was larger, about 800 people who took over the few Spanish guards in the area. Soon they were joined by more than 2,200 men arriving from Haiti. Among them were Haitian soldiers, residents, and Dominican refugees.[721]

The fight arrived at Santiago. Capitan General Felipe Ribero soon realized that the war could not be won, and he warned the Spanish government about the futility of fighting.[722] Nobody listened. Ribero declared a state of emergency throughout the country and kept his troops on alert, sending reinforcements to Santiago. Commanding the Spanish troops was none other than General Pedro Santana.[723] The disputed hero had returned to the political and military scene. The Spanish forces and loyal Dominican reserves managed to crush the rebellion.[724]

El Grito de Capotillo (The Scream of Capotillo) (1863)

On August 16, 1863, at last, fourteen Dominicans, led by Colonel Santiago Rodríguez Masagó, (alias Chago, son of Don Vicente Rodríguez, a *hatero* from Santiago and Mrs. Josefina Masagó of Haitian descent),[725] crossed the border from Haiti. At Cerro del Capotillo, Dajabón they flew the Dominican flag. The episode is known as the *Grito de Capotillo*. From that moment on, Haiti was an unconditional ally in the Dominican struggle against Spain.[726] Fifteen days later, La Vega, Moca, Puerto Plata, San Francisco de Macorís, and Cotuí were ready to battle for Dominican restoration, along with the Northern troops all set to take Santiago.[727]

Some Dominican soldiers who served on the Spanish side also joined the Restorationists. A prominent case was General Gaspar Polanco, then in reserve, who commanded the insurgent troops. Polanco had a notorious military prestige for having participated in the war of independence in 1844. He was the first man-at-arms in the revolutionary ranks.[728]

The Battle of Santiago (1863)

On September 1, some 6,000 Dominican revolutionaries arrived in Santiago. The Spanish soldiers withdrew towards the San Luis fortress within the city. There were 817 of them, along with many families who took refuge there. As the initial attack was unsuccessful, Gaspar Polanco decided to start a siege.[729]

It seemed as if the city would fall into Dominican hands quickly. After all, six thousand people were no match for eight hundred. There were seven Dominicans for every Spaniard. But the unexpected happened. While the Spanish were defending the fortress, another fresh Spanish contingent arrived from Santiago de Cuba in Puerto Plata at the end of August, joining the other troops. They soon set off for Santiago, 37 miles away, a 13 hour-march. The column of 1,200 soldiers, led by Spanish Colonel Mariano Cappa, reached Fort San Luis in time.[730] Now it was the Dominicans who did not seem to be able to defeat the Spanish. The battle was cruel and bloody. Then Polanco made a decision that would mark the rest of the Restorationist conflict.

Santiago burns

On September 6, 1863, Polanco ordered the burning of the entire city of Santiago. According to some witnesses, "*a terrible fire raged through the streets,*"[731] creating panic and confusion, not only among city dwellers who were left homeless but also among the Spaniards who on September 13 withdrew to Puerto Plata. As they retreated, they were chased by the Dominicans, causing numerous casualties.[732]

During the battle of Santiago, the actions of an unknown young man stood out. A few years later, he would be one of the most important political figures in the country: Gregorio Luperón.[733]

Gregorio Luperón was the son of Nicolasa Duperón, a modest fruit seller who "Spanishized" her last name to Luperón, and Pedro Castellano, a white, middle-class man who never knew or recognized his son Gregorio. Due to his opposition to annexation, Luperón emigrated to Cap-Haïtien, then to New York and Jamaica. He returned to

Dominican land with a false identity through Monte Cristi and took part in the Sabaneta uprising in February 1863. Many consider this armed revolt the real beginning of the Restoration War, before the *El Grito de Capotillo*. The incident was carried out by 135 people and was quelled by a thousand soldiers. It is nonetheless significant, as its initial symbolic action was publicly dragging the Spanish flag through Sabaneta.[734]

Luperón was literate but refused to accept any administrative position offered to him.[735] As a historical curiosity, we should note that his brother, José Gabriel Luperón, fought in the American civil war, where he became a captain.[736] In fact, both wars were about emancipation and the abolition of slavery.

The conflict spread quickly throughout all the Dominican territory.[737] It was a guerrilla war, using disruptive techniques such as blocking roads and access to rivers and avoiding open spaces. Weapons were scarce and fights often involved close combat.[738]

The Dominican Provisional Government. September 1863

On September 14, only twelve days after Santiago was razed and almost wholly destroyed by the fire, the city was declared capital of the *Gobierno Provisional Restaurador* (Provisional Restorative Government).[739] At the head of this new government were several military heroes who participated in the war: General Gaspar Polanco, Pedro Antonio Pimentel, Benito Monción, and José Antonio Salcedo (Pepillo). The latter was elected as the new president, and he included in his cabinet figures such as Francisco Bonó, Máximo Grullón, and Ulises Francisco Espaillat.[740]

6.

Third and Final Independence (1865)

The new Restorative Government drafted the third and final Declaration of Independence. Pedro Santana was declared a traitor and sentenced to death in absentia. About ten thousand people (presumably all men) signed the declaration in Cibao. But for now, it was all a unilateral move.

The country now had two capitals and two distinct territories: The rebel's territory in Cibao, and the loyal or pro-Spanish territory, mainly Santo Domingo (which was still the best defended), Puerto Plata, and Samaná. The rebels were about to take the cities of Azua, El Seibo, Hato Mayor, and Higüey, but the Spanish army managed, albeit precariously, to maintain its dominance.[741]

There is some evidence that Bani and Azua had certain sympathy (or perhaps indifference) to the Spanish presence. In Azua, the all-Dominican, eight-member municipal government condemned the rebels in a municipal act dated September 3, 1863: *"We come to deplore the scandalous and criminal acts that have just taken place in some parts of the Cibao, raising once again rebellion and abusing the generous pardon of our August and generous Queen."* [742] After the establishment of the Provisional Government, things changed. Within three months, Azua ran out of funds and had no resources to care for prisoners, no security, and no means to proceed with pending trials. Soon, food was scarce too, and the city remained practically empty. The rebels in and around the city reportedly burned farms, kept livestock, and blocked access roads.[743]

Rebel strategies

The combat between rebel and annexationists had no battlefield. It was war in every city and every town. There were no uniforms, no military strategies. Sometimes the insurgents would reach towns where fellow Dominicans, moved by political convictions or, probably, from fear of losing their homes or their lives, were fighting for annexation.

In Puerto Plata, the rebel commander gave explicit orders not to shoot their countrymen, even if they were fighting on the Spanish side. A message was sent to them: *"We have come here like brothers, and it is a revolution of principles for which we need nothing more than unity and fraternity among Dominicans."*[744] It was an attempt to fix things amicably. However, the same message warned that if Dominicans at the service of the Spanish government refused to join the cause, they would be treated as traitors and would be punished accordingly.[745]

On other occasions, the rebels used different types of "weapons." In Guayubín, they confiscated the Virgin Mary's image from the church and processed with it, asking for her intercession in their fight. Likewise in Santiago, someone seized the Virgin of the Rosary, carrying her through the streets of the city.[746]

In Hato Mayor there was no major setback, and the rebels proclaimed the restoration of the Dominican Republic at 4 a.m. on October 2, quietly and without bloodshed.[747]

The rebels moved in groups of a few hundred, relying on family ties in the countryside and their knowledge of the territory for their survival. They would eat the cattle and pigs that roamed freely in the mountains. When possible, they would buy plantains, corn, and meat. Other non-perishable goods arrived from Haiti.[748] They used the weapons stolen from Spanish soldiers, but the ammunition supply was a constant problem.[749] The rebels would burn and destroy archives, steal ammunition, and escape as fugitives. They were ready for an all-out war.[750]

There was no formal army and no overarching plan. The men were usually from the same region and would take one town at a time with the help from Haitian allies and locals, especially women.

The role of women in the war

The rebels' strategy and their survival could hardly have been possible without the help of women. The annexationist forces knew this, and some generals tried to convince the rebels that the fight was too harsh, especially for women, children, and girls. They failed to grasp how grave the situation was, since women were involved in the rebellion as much as men. Many women were left alone and still had to continue working in the fields. Women were also essential to guarantee communication between rebels. The information they supplied was of vital importance in order to send armed men to different towns. They would warn the rebels about the arrival of Spanish forces and ponder about the consequences of possible battles. Women facilitated men's mobility and created information networks in a context of violence in which the arrival of supplies was a matter of life or death. [751]

For Spanish officers, Dominican women represented another type of threat. They were considered *"the enemies of Spain,"* not because of their logistical skills, but, according to them, because they caused lack of discipline in the Spanish soldiers by seducing them and demoralizing the troops.[752]

The War of Restoration and the Civil War of the United States

The Restoration war was not only a war for independence but also a war against slavery. Dominicans, most of them brown or black, would fear becoming slaves at the hands of the Spanish. The war became a true people's war that put all the nation's energies into motion to achieve its independence and to restore sovereignty.[753]

The Civil War in the US and the Restauration War in the Dominican Republic were contemporaneous, and both aimed at the abolition of slavery. In an 1864 speech, Ramón Mella proclaimed: "*Dominicans, the day has come when Spain, the only country that insists on keeping slaves, loses its colonies in the Antilles. America belongs to herself.*" Sovereignty and antislavery were part of the same struggle.[754]

The American Civil War prompted the abolition of slavery, declared on January 1, 1863. The United States Army recruited 180,000 African American soldiers and 18,000 for the navy.[755] Eventually, in 1865, the 13th Amendment was ratified, leading to the final liberation of all enslaved African Americans in the United States of America.

The 13th Amendment freed all black slaves within the limits of the United States. But these limits were not the same as they are today. There were other territories where abolition did not apply: the Indian Territories, where five main tribes of Native American Indians lived. It turns out that they, especially the wealthiest families, also had black slaves. In 1860 the citizens of the Cherokee Nation, owned 2,511 slaves (15% of its total population), the Choctaws owned 2,349 slaves (14%), the Creek owned 1,532 slaves (10%), and the Chickasaws owned 975 slaves (18%), a percentage similar to the percentage of slaves as were in Tennessee. These tribes were still sovereign and therefore were not affected by the constitutional amendment. In 2017, the United States District Court in Washington ruled that the descendants of those slaves should have citizenship rights in the Cherokee Nation,[756] in Oklahoma's northeast area.

As Spain was the only imperial slave power left in the area and slavery a real threat in Hispaniola, Haitian-Dominican collaboration was necessary and crucial in the unfolding events.

Haiti's support in the war of Restoration

Haitian support for the restorationist cause was generalized. A Dominican rebel explained it: *"We cannot understand how the Spanish government can believe for one moment that the Haitian people could stay indefinitely indifferent to an issue that, as they accurately perceive, interests them as much as Dominicans."*[757]

Another Dominican author argued: *"We protest the abuses of the Spanish government...impeding Haitian citizens from taking part in the Dominican cause, which is their own cause."*[758] Haitian collaboration was especially intense on the north coast, with boats transporting people and goods from Cap-Haïtien to Montecristi, Puerto Plata, Turks, and Caicos Islands. Many rebels looked to Haiti for help.[759] The cattle trade through San Juan to Hincha and Port au Prince was constant.[760]

The cooperation also extended to the army. Alliances and joint operations were formed in a semi-secret way. Haitian authorities at the border often collaborated with Dominican rebels. General José María Cabral frequently went to Las Caobas to recruit rebels of all flags.[761]

Haiti, furthermore, became a safe haven for rebel leaders who could spend months in hiding in Cap-Haïtien or other cities where the Haitian military offered them supplies.[762]

Haitian authorities were reluctant to hand over rebel leaders to their Spanish counterparts since exile leaders, and Dominican families in general, were well-liked and welcomed among Haitians.[763]

The center of the island became a supply point where Haitian women traded soap, codfish, flour, salt, and oxen to Montecristi, Guayubín, and Hinche for coffee and tobacco.[764]

In the Haitian capital, the population ignored Geffrard's political precautions. Dominicans arrived with cattle and exchanged them for flour and other imperishable products, then returned to Dominican territory.[765]

Spanish officers tried to mobilize anti-Haitian elites with old tactics, promoting deep-rooted fears of a Haitian invasion. They alerted that 8,000 Haitians were ready to disembark in the East of the country. While that same threat worked for Santana ten years before, this time it was wholly ignored.[766]

The Dominican Republic in flames

Among the rebels' strategies, none was more radical and effective than the one Polanco initiated in Santiago: to burn their own towns and villages. By doing so, the Dominicans prevented the Spanish army from taking control. It was a radical measure but left the annexationists without options. There were no positions to take, no goods to grab, no prisoners to take, and no houses in which to stay.

The rebels' first targets were municipal buildings, destroying archives and setting the buildings on fire.[767]

In October 1863, Puerto Plata burned for three days, destroying 1,200 houses. Homeless families moved to other towns or sought refuge in the fort defended by the Spanish, where, at the very least, they could survive. The Spaniards were surprised by the commitment of the rebels[768] as women were taking charge of these families. Out of 253 families sheltered in the fort, only ten people were men.[769] At the end of the year, 62 buildings were burned down, including many essential warehouses.

At the beginning of 1864 the Spanish general La Gándara found Barahona reduced to ashes. A commercial agent tried to explain to him what was going on: *"No matter where the Spaniards go... when the Dominicans see that they are not able to hold a place, they prefer to lay it in ashes rather than suffer the Spaniards to take possession and hold it."*[770]

The rebels' tactic was radical, but it worked. As the Dominican settlements were deserted, the Spaniards were left with no one to fight and no one to run the colony.[771]

The wear and tear of the Spanish army

The guerrilla-type battles that ensued were a constant source of frustration for the Spanish soldiers who became progressively undisciplined. Insubordination to superiors, obscenities, drunken soldiers leaving their posts, relaxation in the supervision of prisoners, robberies, fights, refusal to wear the uniform, and desertion abounded.[772]

Desertions were common not only among soldiers. Prominent generals, Dominicans at the Spanish army's service also abandoned their posts. A considerable number of defections took place at the beginning of the conflict. On one occasion, as many as 500 soldiers escaped from the army. Many of the deserters returned home rather than joining the Dominican ranks.[773]

Defecting was a risky offense. Traitors could face severe punishment or even execution. A young Spanish soldier from Cartagena was absent from the army for a month. He claimed that he got lost looking for food, and had to sleep in abandoned cabins. His interaction with the locals was only out of necessity. His superiors took pity on him, so instead of execution, they sentenced him to ten years in prison.[774]

Tropical diseases joined the Dominican cause

Diseases, especially yellow fever,[775] were also among the Dominican's most powerful allies. As soon as the war began, Spanish soldiers began to fall ill and die in great numbers. Diarrhea, vomiting, and mosquitoes were killing 1,500 soldiers a month. Yellow fever took more Spanish lives than all the casualties in the 107 combats fought in the war.[776]

The situation was so severe that Cuban and Puerto Rican captains could nor replace the men who were dying daily in Santo Domingo.[777]

The last attempt

Spain did not give up just yet and tried a massive military escalation with 20,000 new troops. 3,000 just for the capital.[778]

The annexationists put in place more strict and repressive measures. All printed material was to be scrupulously examined; all travelers were considered suspects, those carrying arms were to be treated as enemies, and those helping the rebels on ships would be treated as pirates.[779]

The rebels were not intimidated even though they were fighting in extreme and painful conditions. Pedro Bonó observed that *"Barely anyone had uniforms...The drummer was in a woman's shirt and no pants... Many others were shirtless...All were barefoot...no saddles, just plantain leaves covered with goat leather...They were mostly armed with machetes and only a few guns."*[780]

Despite these hardships, the rebel movement was already too popular and was advancing headlessly, but steadfastly, like a hurricane.[781] Soon, the revolution would come to an end.

The final fall of Santana (1864)

Perhaps no episode could illustrate the end of the war better than the final fall of one of its main characters, General Santana. On September 12, 1863, the Spanish governor, Felipe Ribero, sent the General to the city of Santiago with a contingent of Spanish and Creole troops. Santana set camp in Guanuma with the explicit mission of preventing the restorationists' passage from Santiago to Santo Domingo.[782] But Santana was not about to receive orders and ended up becoming a problem for his Spanish allies. When Spanish troops lost Santiago, he received orders to retreat to Santo Domingo. Instead, he decided to stay in Guanuma. Eventually, the Spanish military accused him of disobedience and contempt for his superiors, and he was summoned to a military trial in Cuba. A few days before his departure, on June 24, 1864, he was found dead at his home in Santo Domingo under mysterious circumstances pointing to a possible suicide. He was 63 years old. Santana's death did not cause much grief among the island's inhabitants. At his death, shouts could be heard: *"Down with Spain! Down with the Big Ass."*[783] With equal enthusiasm, an anonymous poet wrote the following epitaph:

Epitaph of Santana

Here lies a donkey colt
Not another despot like him
He didn't understand his destiny
And died like a pig
Not having done any good.[784]

The beginning of the end

By 1864 the outcome of the war was already assumed by all. So much so that the members of the Dominican Provisional Government wrote to the Spanish queen:

> *The fight between the Dominican people and Your Majesty's army would be totally useless for Spain; because believe it, Your Majesty, we could all perish, and the whole country could end up destroyed by war and the burning of the towns and cities, but Spanish authorities governing us again, never....They clearly show that the Dominican prefers homelessness, with all of its horrors, for himself, his wife and children, and even death, more than depending on those who oppress him, insult him and assassinate him without trial.*[785]

The testimony of a Spanish soldier recognizes the inevitable outcome:

> *Dominicans are just and virtuous ... they don't need us; they have enough people, they are just trying to save us from torment. Countrymen, flee those proud and unnatural [Spanish] Commanders who are just trying to reduce us to ashes.*[786]

In Spain, the war no longer had much support. The new governor had to initiate diplomatic negotiations with the restored Provisional Government, headed by military leader José Antonio Salcedo, to end the war.

At the end of March 1864, Juan Pablo Duarte returned to the Dominican Republic from Venezuela. He had been out of the country for 20 years and returned to offer his services. Intriguingly, the new Dominican government did not receive the national hero with much enthusiasm. He was sent back to Venezuela to find support for the Dominican cause. Back in Venezuela, Duarte died eleven years later, destitute, abandoned, and forgotten.[787]

The two trends of the Provisional Government

At times, nothing unites people as much as a common enemy to the point that when the enemy disappears, that unity begins to crumble. As it became evident that Spain could not carry out the annexation, divisions appeared within the Dominican Provisional Government, not unlike what happened after the 1844 independence.

The Provisional Government was made up of two groups. The conservatives aimed to recover national sovereignty, but without engaging in making significant social changes. They did not position themselves on slavery, nor the role of Spain in other colonies.[788]

The second group was much closer to the guerrilla movement. Their goals were not only political but also social. For Ramón Mella, the Dominican motto *"God, Homeland and Freedom"* became: *"Homeland, Honor and Humanity."* Gregorio Luperón's version was even more socially radical: *"Independence, Equality and Freedom."*[789]

Salcedo president ... and executed (1864)

One of the dramas that best reflected the tension between these two groups was President Salcedo's conflict with Polanco. Salcedo was a conservative, a landowner born in Madrid to Dominican parents, who had generous income from timber and rents from his land. He was an avowed conservative and a Báez follower.[790]

Salcedo took power as the Provisional Government's first president when Santiago was already in rebel hands. Once he was in power, due to his eccentricities, he was slowly losing support. In August 1864, he dismissed his minister and was left alone as a leader, accompanied only by his personal secretary. He planned to substitute Vice President Luperón with a wealthy general educated in England. Still, Salcedo was very close to Spanish Brigadier General Buceta, who hoped for secret negotiations to get Santiago back. Rumor has it that the president was planning to bring Báez back and was willing to accept Spanish control of Samaná.[791]

Some of the military officers were confused and shocked by these rumors and openly disobeyed Salcedo's orders. On October 10, 1864, Salcedo was taken prisoner by a popular movement headed by Gaspar Polanco, supported by most military leaders. Gregorio Luperón was in charge of the disgraced president and received instructions to escort him to some point on Haiti's border. Once near Puerto Plata, Luperón informed Salcedo that he had written orders to execute the prisoner on that spot. Salcedo, a man of unquestionable courage, made no visible gesture of protest or rejection of what he knew was his tragic fate. He was shot at Maimon Beach. He was 48 years old.

Before his execution, he passed along some instructions for his wife, to a 20-year-old soldier from the firing squad, named Ulises Heureaux, alias Lilís.[792] Eventually, Lilís would become the country's ruler. He would also end up shot to death 35 years later.[793] In turn, one of his murderers, Ramón Cáceres, would become head of state and he too, would end up shot to death in 1911.[794]

Polanco ordered Salcedo's execution despite opposition, not only from Salcedo's supporters, but also from Polanco's own followers. The most radical period of the restorationist struggle had just begun.[795]

Polanco: liberal and radical president

Gaspar Polanco was president for only three months. A rancher from Guayubín, illiterate but capable, he became an efficient and courageous General. These qualities ensured him a successful career to the highest office.[796] In early 1864, his authority was undisputed.[797]

During Polanco's short term, the official government bulletins included extensive references and praises for the French Revolution, criticisms of monarchies, and calls for expanding democratic practices to the entire population. He and his allies were determined not only to win the war of Restoration but also to revolutionize politics.[798]

Polanco's government approved a decree for financing primary schools in all communities, and he organized a campaign for vaccinations throughout the country.[799] Not a bad idea in retrospect, since even today, 150 years later, and according to the World Health Organization, one in five children in the world does not receive essential vaccines, which results in 1.5 million children losing their lives every year due to a lack of vaccines.[800]

The Polanco period was a final push for the successful restorationist struggle in the Dominican Republic. But his radical ideals were to produce irreparable cracks and internal division in the country's political spectrum.

The new Dominican Republic. Confederation with Haiti

Before the war was over, in late 1864, the new leaders were already strategizing different plans for the country. For many, the Dominican Republic's future was intimately linked to Haiti's. Ulises Espaillat himself wrote in the Official Gazette of June 1864, in the middle of the restorationist conflict:

> *A Word to Dominicans, a Word to Haitians.*
>
> *...How can two peoples composed of the same race, the same political interests, ruled by republican institutions, and who have lived together as good friends, look at each other with indifference when one of them is in danger? Is not the downfall of one also the downfall of another? Is the danger of*

this one not the danger of that? In a word, if the Dominican people fall, does that not precipitate the fall of the Haitian Republic? The Haitian people understand that as well as we do. It seems to us that it is past time that both governments understand... and unite to end the foreign domination on the island of Haiti.[801]

That same summer, the Provisional Government proposed to President Geffrard a federation between the two countries: *"Even though the Dominican people have always been very protective of their Independence and their autonomy, and they remain so today, we do not fear establishing, starting now, the basis or a treaty of Federation."*[802] The Minister of Foreign Affairs of Haiti responded to the offer:

The Dominican people are asking Spain again for their independence, and the Haitian people have nothing to ask. Is it true, as you claim, that Haiti will secure her political future through the consolidation of this alliance, lending a hand to the Dominican insurrection? No, a thousand times no. That is also an error! Haiti is, today, a republican government freely governed by a wise, educated, and popularly elected Leader.[803]

Harsh words perhaps uttered out of fear of continuous Spanish interference in the country mixed with the national pride already in vogue at that time. The man excused himself:

There is no one in Haiti who does not continue to feel sympathy for the Dominican people, no one who does not admire their courage and lament their misfortunes. The Government of Haiti shares these popular sentiments, but it cannot forget the duties it must perform and the sacred interest it must protect...and, he concludes, *the Haitian government will continue its strict neutrality and its moderate and impartial conduct.*[804]

Eventually, the two countries' paths will not merge, although, as always, they would continue to be mutually influenced.

The newspaper *La Regeneración* lamented the missed opportunity: *"God has separated son from father, brother from brother, pueblo from other pueblo. But...can we not form an offensive and defensive alliance to conserve the integrity of our common territory to avoid what just happened to us?"* [805] The article suggested the formation of a federation including practical economic elements like trade and exchange of products for the benefit of the two countries, intensifying and deepening diplomatic relations and the possibility to obtain dual citizenship.[806] Luperón himself and his allies yearned for a federation of the four countries of Cuba, Haiti, the Dominican Republic and Puerto Rico.[807]

Dominican sympathies for Haiti were evident. An anecdote: at the end of the conflict, Haiti's government, at the request of the Spanish and Dominican governments, was assigned to act as an intermediary in the negotiation.[808] In one of those meetings, which lasted an entire month, Polanco's men met with Haitian diplomats in Santiago. At one point, the Dominican authorities raised their glasses to toast to the heroes of the Haitian revolution, to President Geffrard and to peace.[809]

Not everyone had such a harmonious vision. The more conservative Dominican factions did not look favorably on any kind of relationship with the neighboring country.

The anti-Haitian legend of the conservatives

From the most conservative positions, the story was very different. National heroes such as Núñez de Cáceres in the past and Polanco in the present were criticized as "pro-Haitians."[810] The newspaper *El Tiempo* wrote about Luperón: *"he was a somewhat mysterious conspirator and contrary to the true Dominican spirit."* When the possibility of annexation would come at the hands of the US, the same argument would be used against those who opposed it: *"The Puerto Plata movement is nothing other than an attempt to destroy national independence in favor of the Haitians."* [811]

Polanco's presidency lasted 90 days. His Dominican opponents were powerful and included landowners and prominent Cibao families who, from the moment Polanco took power, wanted to take back center stage in the political life of the island.[812] They dreamed of a future after the war in which they would enjoy a family network of patronage and authority with the leadership of Buenaventura Báez.[813]

A Military Junta dismissed Polanco for his despotism, and appointed Pedro Antonio Pimentel as the new Dominican president. A martial court sentenced Polanco to death, but he managed to escape into hiding.[814]

By the time this was happening, Spain had already resolved to leave the country for good.

The war is over. Withdrawal of the Spanish troops (1865)

In December of 1864, the war was over; only the Spanish troops and the administration's withdrawal had to be worked out. There were no festivities or celebrations. The country was half dead and without resources. Only the revolutionary fever sustained it.[815]

On March 3, 1865, the Queen of Spain signed the decree reversing the Annexation. On July 10, the Spanish army began to journey back to Cuba, Puerto Rico and Spain. In fifteen days time, there was not a single Spanish soldier left in Santo Domingo on military duty. Out of spite, the Spaniards threw the ammunition and war equipment that did not fit on their departing ships into the sea. Public buildings were purposely destroyed.[816]

Some in Spain lamented the defeat and argued that Spanish authorities had not much interest in maintaining the territory. The Marqués de Lema complained that a fraction of the forty million pesos spent decorating the Puerta del Sol in Madrid would have been enough to appease Santo Domingo:

"Without sufficient resources to suffocate the African insurrection [tellingly that was the name the Marquis gave to the War of Restoration], *Spain's honor had been compromised."* [817]

There were still Dominican Military officers loyal to Spain, hoping to be assigned outside the island. Shockingly, their destinations were determined by their skin color. De la Gándara suggested that whites should go to Cuba while officers of color would have to be transferred to Puerto Rico, Curaçao, Santo Tomás or other destinations in Spanish territory.[818]

After the war, in a tavern in Azua, a Dominican captain who fought with the Spanish army, took solace in the bottle with other fellow soldiers. As several Spanish military officers began to provoke him, the man lost his cool and, turning towards them, blurted out: *"Pendejos!"* [819]

Epilogue

The Dominican Republic after the Restoration

After the War of Restoration, problems arose between the usual groups: Liberals and Conservatives. The Cibao restorative government lasted less than six months, since southern politicians did not trust it. Worth mention was the return of pro-annexationist General Buenaventura Báez, endorsed by General Santiago Rodríguez and by former President Pimentel, both considered national heroes.[820] The dream of sovereignty was short-lived.

Báez, was named *"Great Citizen"* in 1868,[821] and he assumed power without opposition.[822] He, and his officers with him, favored American annexation. They would share with their United States colleagues the view that anti-colonial goals were for the African race to dominate the island.[823]

Only four years after the War of Restoration, Báez, who only a few years before had firmly opposed Spanish annexation, almost managed to annex the Dominican Republic to the United States.[824] This time, the opponents were already armed and were able to mobilize and form new alliances. For the next six years, the Dominican Republic suffered constant political unrest[825] and changes of government. From 1873 to 1879, seventeen different governments were in power, the longest being Báez's one-year term. The rest lasted an average of two months and one week each.[826]

But that's another story. In 1865, after three declarations of independence in 40 years, the Dominican Republic finally established itself as an independent country.

Twenty-five years later, on October 23, 1891, a baby baptized as Rafael Leónidas Trujillo was born in the city of San Cristóbal.

During the 67-year period from President Salcedo's presidency to Trujillo's regime, 40 governments took on the challenge to govern the country. Out of the thirty-four presidents, six of them served for two terms, and only six in total lasted for more than two years. In sharp contrast with these statistics, in the last eighty years, there have only been eight elected presidents in the country.[827]

History as reconciliation or as conflict. The fall of myths

Statistically, History is one of the least favorite subjects for Dominican college students. Only 2% of them study social science and humanities majors that includes history. The most popular degrees are Accounting (12.2%), Education (11.5%), Business Administration (9%), Law (8.9%), and Agricultural Sciences (1.9%). Business and others majors make up just 0.7%, performing even worse than History.[828] But history can easily become a very effective tool for social and political manipulation. National historical narratives can legitimize unjust social, military, migration, and labor policies and stoke national pride while promoting by necessity, intolerance and discrimination.

To determine all the facts and angles of historical events is an unmanageable task, but that does not mean that to study history is an irrelevant task. We should be suspicious about history when "we" are the good guys fighting against "them," the bad guys. History is about people who make their decisions conditioned by their knowledge, ambitions, fears, and visions, and, as we have seen, they are more often than not, full of contradictions.

What history shows us is that power often corrupts, and it can turn well-meaning people into ambitious and mean characters.

Dominican history is not exempt from any of these characteristics. As is true everywhere, this story was composed of alliances, betrayals, contradictions, nationalism, racism, solidarity, doubt and resentment. They are the bricks of history, because they are also the pieces that make up the human being.

A nation requires, almost by necessity, an enemy to glue its people together. That is why most national histories are partial and build upon myths of heroes and villains. They are useful stories to preserve hazy historical facts as permanent open wounds that fester on past grudges and offenses and that resonate in our own personal experiences when we consider those who are not "us."

History, like time itself, is a continuous flow of events and characters connected by infinite links in time and space and we do not learn from it merely by pruning these connections for the sake of some prejudiced agendas. History becomes enriching, beautiful, and fascinating when we are able to discover and uncover without fear and hesitation, the ironies, flaws and contradictions of our national, regional, or local historical figures and the events they shaped. We can learn from them, specially from their mistakes, when we examine "our histories" with a certain degree of skepticism and with a good measure of humor.

Timeline

PART ONE	WORLD EVENTS
Columbus arrives at the Caribbean- 1492	
Columbus' second trip- 1493-1496	
La Isabela is founded- 1494	
Santo Domingo is founded- 1496	1498- Vasco De Gama reaches India surrounding Africa
Columbus' third trip- 1498-1500	
First native slaves sent to Spain- 1499	
Nicolás de Ovando- 1501	1501- First African slaves arrive at the Caribbean
First African slaves transported to Santo Domingo - 1510	1506- Death of Columbus
Montesinos' sermon- 1511	1513- Balboa, the first European to see the Pacific Ocean
Law allowing colonists to marry natives- 1514	
First pirates in the Caribbean- 1522	1522- First voyage across the globe
Increased importation of African slaves- 1540	
William Drake sacks Santo Domingo- 1586	
Osorio's devastations- 1606	1609- Galileo Galilei builds a practical telescope

PART TWO	WORLD EVENTS
	1626- The Dutch found the city of New Amsterdam (New York) 1626- St Peter's Basilica in the Vatican completed 1640- First book printed in the US
Beginning of the French invasion of Hispaniola- 1656	
Spanish recognition of Saint Domingue- 1697	
Santo Domingo from colonial exploitation to autarchy- 1700-1791	1700- Bartolomeo Cristofori invents the piano
Saint Domingue. Massive production and import of slaves- 1700-1791	1760- The Boston Massacre 1765- James Watt invents the steam engine 1776- USA's Declaration of Independence
Slave Revolution begins in Saint Domingue- 1791	1789- French Revolution
Treaty of Basel- 1795	
Toussaint enters Santo Domingo- 1801	1796- First vaccines against smallpox
Napoleon's troops arrive at Saint Domingue- 1802	1802- Ludwig van Beethoven performs his Moonlight Sonata for the first time
Sale of Louisiana Territories- 1803	
Haiti's Declaration of Independence- 1804	
French Period of Santo Domingo- 1802-1809	1808- France invades Spain
La España Boba- 1809-1821	1808-1814- Spanish War of Independence
	1810-1821- Mexican War of Independence

TIMELINE

PART THREE	WORLD EVENTS
First Independence of the Dominican Republic (DR)- 1821	
Haiti invades the DR - 1822	
France recognizes Haiti- 1825	1826- Invention of photography
Beginning of la Trinitaria- 1834	1833- Abolition of slavery in England
Independence of the DR- 1844	1846-1848- US- Mexican war. Mexico loses California
Slavery is abolished in the DR - 1844	
	1848- Wisconsin admitted to the Union
Election of first president in the DR - 1849	
Haiti's attempted invasion- 1859	
	1860- Abraham Lincoln elected president
The DR annexed to Spain- 1861	1861-1865 US Civil War
	1864- Creation of the Red Cross
Restauration war- 1863-1865	
The DR's third, and last, Declaration of Independence- 1865	
	1867- Last transatlantic trip with slaves

Bibliography

- Eller, Anne, *We Dream Together*. Durham NC, Duke University Press, 2016.
- Girard, Phillipe, *Haiti*. New York, Palgrave Macmillan, 2005.
- Inoa, Orlando, *Historia Dominicana*. Santo Domingo, Editorial Letra Gráfica, 2103.
- Moya, Frank, *Manual de historia dominicana*. Santiago, República Dominicana, UCMM. 1980 (5ª ed.).
- Nessler, Graham. *An Islandwide Struggle for Freedom*. Chapel Hill, NC., The University of North Carolina Press, 2016.
- Thomas, Hugh. *La trata de Esclavos*. Barcelona, Editorial Planeta, 1998.
- *El Imperio Español*. Barcelona, Editorial Planeta, 2004 (2ª ed.).

Notes

1 Eller, A. *We Dream Together*. Durham NC, Duke University Press, 2016, p. 236.
2 https://www.worldatlas.com/articles/islands-that-are-shared-by-more-than-one-country.html
3 Importancia de la Ruta de la Seda y Especias, el comercio de China con Europa. https://historiaybiografias.com/ruta_seda/
4 Inoa, Orlando. Historia Dominicana. Santo Domingo, Editorial Letra Gráfica, 2103, p. 18.
5 Christopher Klein, *Leif Eriksson, the Viking explorer who beat Columbus to America*, 2013.
 https://www.history.com/news/the-viking-explorer-who-beat-columbus-to-america
6 Inoa O. *op. cit.,* p. 19.
7 *Ibíd.* p. 20.
8 Thomas, H. *El Imperio Español*. Barcelona, Editorial Planeta, 2004, 2a ed., p. 115.
9 *Íd*.
10 Thomas, H. *op. cit.,* p.116.
11 Inoa O. op. cit. p. 24.
12 Juan Daniel Balcácer, *Sobre Quisqueya y quisqueyanos*, 2017.
 https://listindiario.com/pun- tos-de-vista/2017/09/20/483177/sobre-quisqueya-y-quisqueyanos
13 Inoa O. *op. cit.* p. 27.
14 *Ibíd.*, p. 29.
15 http://www.hoyenlahistoria.com/efemerides/fecha/1492
16 Thomas, H. *op. cit.,* p. 120.
17 Inoa O. *op. cit.* p. 123.
18 Thomas, H. *op. cit.,* p. 156.
19 *Ibíd.* p. 155.
20 *Ibíd.* p. 175.
21 Lilian Tejeda, *¿Quiénes eran, de dónde venían y cuándo llegaron los primeros turistas a RD?* Listín Diario, December 30, 2018. https://listindiario.com/economia/2018/12/30/547533/quienes-eran-de-donde-venian-y-cuando-llegaron-los-primeros-turistas-a-rd
22 Thomas, H. *op. cit., p.* 160.
23 *Ibíd.,* pp. 160-161.
24 Inoa, O. *op. cit.* p. 40.
25 *Ibíd.,* p. 41.
26 *Íd*.
27 Thomas, H. *op. cit., p.* 186.
28 Thomas, H. *op. cit., p.* 168.

29 Ibíd., p. 139.
30 Ing. Agr. Julio González, *El Cultivo de la Piña*, July 26, 2018. https://agrotendencia.tv/agropedia/el-cultivo-de-la-pina/
31 Frank Moya, *Manual de Historia Dominicana*. Santiago, República Dominicana, UCMM, 1980, 5a ed., pp. 7-8.
32 Inoa, O. *op. cit.*, p. 60.
33 Thomas, H. op. cit., p. 187.
34 Thomas, H. *op. cit.*, p. 357.
35 http://www.hoyenlahistoria.com/efemerides/enero/14
36 Girard, P. *Haiti*. New York, Palgrave Macmillan, 2005, p. 20.
37 Thomas, H. *op. cit., p.* 162.
38 *Íd.*
39 Ibíd. p. 163.
40 Ibíd. p. 168.
41 Ibíd. p. 162.
42 Inoa, O. *op. cit.* p. 45.
43 Thomas, H. *op. cit.*, p. 164.
44 Ibíd. p. 169.
45 Inoa, O. *op. cit.* pp. 46-47.
46 Thomas, H. *op. cit., p.* 176.
47 Ibíd, p.177.
48 Inoa, O. *op. cit.* p. 51.
49 *Thomas, H. op. cit., p. 358.*
50 Ed Prior, *How much gold is there in the world?* April 1, 2013. https://www.bbc.com/ news/magazine-21969100 y https://www.bbc.com/mundo/noticias/2013/04/130404_econo-mia_oro_cuanto_hay_mundo_finde_tsb
51 Thomas H. *op. cit.*, p. 185.
52 Thomas, Hugh. *La trata de Esclavos. Barcelona, Editorial Planeta,* 1998, p. 88.
53 Ibíd., p. 111.
54 Inoa, O. *op. cit.* p. 57.
55 Thomas, H. *El Imperio Español,* p. 169.
56 http://www.hoyenlahistoria.com/efemerides/fecha/1493
57 Thomas, H. *op. cit.,* p.187.
58 María Montserrat León Guerrero, Tesis Doctoral. *El segundo viaje colombino,* Universidad de Valladolid, 2000, p. 471. www.cervantesvirtual.com/descargaPdf/el-segundo-viaje-colombino--0/
59 María Monserrat León Guerrero, *op. cit.*, p. 474.
60 Thomas, H. *op. cit., p.* 211.
61 Ibíd, p. 211.
62 *Íd*
63 Thomas, H. *op. cit.*, p. 199.
64 Ibíd. p. 208.
65 Inoa, O. *op. cit.* p. 65 and http://www.hoyenlahistoria.com/efemerides/fecha/1500
66 Inoa, O. *op. cit.* p. 67
67 BBC redacción, *Pedro Álvares Cabral, el inexperto navegante que "descubrió por accidente" Brasil en 1500,* October 2020. https://www.bbc.com/mundo/noticias-54507707
68 Thomas, H. *op. cit.,* p. 225.
69 Cristina Crespo Garay, *Las cartas de viajes de Américo Vespucio, el navegante que da nombre a América*. National Geographic. July 2018. https://www.nationalgeographic.es/histo- ria/2019/07/las-cartas-de-viajes-de-americo-vespucio-el-navegante-que-da-nombre-america

70 Thomas, H. *op. cit.,* p. 226.
71 Thomas, H. *op. cit.,* p. 323.
72 Analía Llorente, *4 curiosidades sobre el mapa en el que aparece el nombre América por primera vez.* BBC Mundo. October 2018.
https://www.bbc.com/mundo/noticias-america-latina-44219307
73 *Íd.*
74 *Íd.*
75 *Íd.*
76 Thomas, H. *op. cit.,* p. 247.
77 https://www.ecured.cu/Santiago_de_los_Caballeros
78 Thomas, H. *op. cit.,* p. 247.
79 *Ibíd.,* p. 242.
80 *Ibíd.,* p. 251.
81 *Ibíd.,* p. 251.
82 *Ibíd.,* p. 252.
83 *Ibíd.,* p. 256.
84 Thomas H. *op .cit.,* p. 299.
85 Thomas, H. *op. cit.,* p. 254.
86 *Ibíd.,* p. 257.
87 *Íd.*
88 *Íd.*
89 https://www.uasd.edu.do/index.php/informacion-general/historia
90 Thomas, H. *op. cit.,* p. 305.
91 http://www.newworldencyclopedia.org/entry/Hernán_Cortés
92 Moya, F. *op. cit.,* pp. 32 y 34.
93 Joaquín Barañao, *Historia Universal Freak,* Chile 2014, Kindle Edition, loc., 4925.
94 Girard P. *op. cit.* pp. 24 y 26.
95 Moya, F. *op. cit.,* p. 26 e Inoa O. *op. cit.* p. 60.
96 Thomas, H. *La trata de Esclavos,* pp. 90-91.
97 Thomas, H. *El Imperio Español,* p. 357.
98 José Gabriel Atiles Bidó. *Panorama histórico de los estudios del arte rupestre en República Dominicana.* http://www.rupestreweb.info/panorama.html
99 Thomas, H. *El Imperio Español, p.* 447.
100 *Ibíd.* p. 357.
101 *Ibíd,* p. 347.
102 *Ibíd,* pp. 347-348
103 Inoa, O. *op. cit.* p. 79.
104 http://www.hoyenlahistoria.com/efemerides/noviembre/25
105 Thomas, H. *op. cit.,* p. 348.
106 *Ibíd,* p. 353.
107 *Ibíd,* p. 349.
108 *Ibíd, p.* 349.
109 *Ibíd.* p. 358.
110 http://www.hoyenlahistoria.com/efemerides/enero/13
111 Thomas, H. *op. cit., p.* 357.
112 *Ibíd.* 440.
113 Moya, F. *op. cit.,* p. 28.
114 Thomas, H. *op. cit., p.* 454.
115 Moya Pons F. *op. cit.,* p. 29.
116 Marcia Mateo, Listín Diario. *Barahona, quiere saber datos del cacique Enriquillo.* August 2009.
https://listindiario.com/zona-de-contacto/2009/08/07/110682
117 Inoa, O. *op. cit.* p. 123.

118 Thomas, H. *op. cit.,* p. 468.
119 *Ibíd.*, p. 450.
120 Thomas, H. *La trata de Esclavos, p.* 95.
121 Thomas, H. *El Imperio Español,* p. 452.
122 Moya, F. *op. cit.,* p. 33.
123 Thomas, H. *La trata de Esclavos*, p. 97.
124 Thomas, H. *El Imperio Español,* p. 469.
125 Thomas, H. *La trata de Esclavos*, p. 97.
126 *Ibíd.*, p. 87.
127 Thomas, H. *El Imperio Español,* p. 303.
128 *Ibíd.*, p. 344.
129 *Íd.*
130 *Ibíd.*, p. 452
131 *Ibíd.* p. 479.
132 Thomas, H. *La trata de Esclavos,* 102.
133 *Ibíd.*, p. 101.
134 *Ibíd.*, p. 266.
135 National Geographic ed., *Esclavos, la trata humana a través del Atlántico.* March 9, 2018. https://www.nationalgeographic.com.es/historia/grandes-reportajes/esclavos_8681/6
136 Thomas, H. *op. cit.,* p. 102
137 *Ibíd.*, pp. 798-799.
138 *Ibíd.*, p. 176.
139 *Ibíd.*, p. 103.
140 *Íd.*
141 *Íd.*
142 *Ibíd.*, p. 104.
143 *Ibíd.*, p. 208.
144 *Ibíd.*, p. 224.
145 *Ibíd.*, p. 190.
146 *Ibíd.*, pp. 798-799.
147 Girard, P. *op. cit.*, p. 26
148 Thomas, H. *El Imperio Español,* p. 495.
149 *Ibíd.*, p. 496
150 Moya, F. *op.cit.,* p.33.
151 Inoa, O. *op. cit.*, p. 122.
152 Moya, F. *op. cit.*, p. 34.
153 *Ibíd.*, p. 40.
154 *Ibid.*, p.35.
155 Moya, F. *op. cit.*, p. 40.
156 Thomas, H. op. cit., p. 341.
157 Inoa, O. *op. cit.*, p. 133.
158 https://www.listofcountriesoftheworld.com/coastline.html
159 Juan Jesús Llodrá González, *El corsario Jean Fleury y el tesoro de Moctezuma*, May 2018. https://revistadehistoria.es/el-corsario-jean-fleury-y-el-tesoro-de-moctezuma/
160 Inoa, O. *op. cit.*, p. 133.
161 Inoa, O. *op. cit.*, p. 133 and Mora F. *op. cit.*, p. 47
162 Inoa, O. *op. cit.*, p. 134.
163 Moya, F. op. cit., p. 45.
164 Gonzalo González Beneyte, *La catedral de Santo Domingo,* Easy Viajar. https://www.easyviajar.com/republica-dominicana/la-catedral-de-santo-domingo-4011
165 Infojardín. http://www.infojardin.net/fichas/plantas-medicinales/cassia-fistula.htm
166 Moya, F. op. cit., p. 47.
167 Inoa, O. *op. cit.*, p. 145.

NOTES

168 Thomas, H. *La trata de Esclavos*, p. 157.
169 Moya, F. *op. cit.*, p. 47.
170 *Ibíd.*, p. 52.
171 Moya, F. *op. cit.*, p. 49.
172 Inoa, O. *op. cit.*, p. 151.
173 *Ibíd.*, p. 149.
174 Dominicana online ed. https://www.dominicanaonline.org/historia/historia-dominicana/
175 Moya, F. *op. cit.*, p. 63.
176 Inoa, O. *op. cit.*, p. 177.
177 *Íd.*
178 *Ibíd.*, p. 175.
179 https://www.senate.gov/reference/Index/Filibuster.htm
180 Moya, F. *Manual de Historia Dominicana*. Santiago, República Dominicana, UCMM, 1980, 5a ed., p. 79.
181 Maggie Koerth, *Most successful pirate was beautiful and tough*, CNN, 2007. http://www.cnn.com/2007/LIVING/worklife/08/27/woman.pirate/index.html
182 Inoa, Orlando, *op. cit.*, p. 182.
183 Moya, F. *op. cit.*, p. 79.
184 *Ibíd.*, p, 77.
185 http://www.hoyenlahistoria.com/efemerides/diciembre/19
186 Moya, F. *op. cit.*, p. 82.
187 Matthew Craig Harrington, "*The Worke Wee May Doe in the World*" *the Western Design and the Anglo-Spanish Struggle for the Caribbean, 1654-1655*. Florida State University Library, 2004. http://diginole.lib.fsu.edu/islandora/object/fsu:182408/datastream/PDF/view
188 Inoa, O. *op. cit.*, p. 188.
189 *Ibíd.*, p. 190.
190 *Ibíd.*, p. 188.
191 Moya, F. *op. cit.*, p. 91.
192 *Ibíd.*, p. 92.
193 Moya, F. *op. cit.*, p. 106.
194 *Ibíd.*, p. 109.
195 La Guía de Gran Canaria ed. *Palabras Canarias*. http://www.laguiadegrancanaria.com/datos/habla_canaria.php
196 Nessler, Graham. *An Islandwide Struggle for Freedom*. Chapel Hill, NC., The University of North Carolina Press, 2016, p. 12.
197 Moya, F. *op. cit.*, p. 94.
198 Thomas, H. *op. cit.*, p. 187.
199 *Ibíd.*, p. 799.
200 Inoa, O. *op. cit.*, p. 236.
201 Nessler, G. *op. cit.*, p. 9.
202 Redacción BBC News Mundo, *La multimillonaria multa que Haití le pagó a Francia por convertirse en el primer país de América Latina en independizarse*, December 2018. https://www.bbc.com/mundo/noticias-46680927
203 Moya, F. *op. cit.*, p. 93.
204 Girard, P. *Haiti*. New York, Palgrave Macmillan, 2005, pp. 23-24.
205 Moya, F. *op. cit.*, p. 128.
206 Nessler, G. *op. cit.*, p.8.
207 *Ibíd.*, p. 2.
208 *Ibíd.*, p. 13.
209 Moya, F. *op. cit.*, p. 111.
210 *Ibíd.*, pp.13-14.
211 Moya, F. *op. cit.*, p. 155.

212 Nessler, G. *op. cit.*, p. 15.
213 Moya, F. *op. cit.*, p. 155.
214 *Ibíd.*, p. 144.
215 Nessler, G. *op. cit.*, pp. 15-16.
216 *Ibíd.*, p. 152.
217 *Ibíd.*, p. 26.
218 *Ibíd.*, pp. 26-27.
219 *Ibíd.*, p. 10.
220 *Ibíd.*, p.9.
221 Captivating History ed., *Haitian Revolution: A Captivating Guide to the Abolition of Slavery*. Kindle Edition, loc. 148.
222 Nessler, G. *op. cit.*, p. 9.
223 Captivating History ed., *op. cit.*, Kindle Edition, loc. 122-124.
224 Girard, P. *op. cit.*, p. 25.
225 Moya, F. *op. cit.*, p. 108.
226 *Ibíd.*, p. 108.
227 Pedro Gil Iturbides, *Los Minas o Los Mina ¿Qué es lo correcto?*, El Nacional, July 2018. https://elnacional.com.do/los-minas-o-los-mina-que-es-lo-correcto/
228 Nessler, G. *op. cit.*, p.10.
229 Thomas, H. *op. cit.*, p. 253.
230 *Íd.*
231 Nessler, G. *op. cit.*, p. 10.
232 Thomas, H. *op. cit.*, p. 276.
233 *Íd.*
234 *Ibíd.*, p. 284.
235 Moya, F. *op. cit.*, p. 153.
236 Nessler, G. *op. cit.*, p.10.
237 *Ibíd.*, p. 12.
238 Guinness World Records ed, *Largest Residential Palace*. http://www.guinnessworldrecords. com/world-records/largest-residential-palace
239 BBC ed, *El reino de la guillotina, el instrumento de terror de la Revolución Francesa, duró más de lo que quizás imaginas*, October 2017. https://www.bbc.com/mundo/noticias-41365444
240 FAO, *Códigos y nombres de países*. http://www.fao.org/countryprofiles/iso3list/es/
241 Moya, F. *op. cit.*, p. 165.
242 *Ibíd.*, p. 165.
243 https://thelouvertureproject.org/index.php?title=Vincent_Ogé
244 Nessler, G. *op. cit.*, p. 31.
245 *Ibíd.*, p. 33.
246 Captivating History ed., *op. cit.*, Kindle Edition, loc. 227.
247 Moya, F. *op. cit.*, p. 167.
248 Nessler, G. *op. cit.*, p. 32.
249 *Íd.*
250 *Ibíd.*, pp. 36-37.
251 Moya, F. *op. cit.*, p. 168.
252 Nessler, G. *op. cit.*, pp. 34-35.
253 *Ibíd.*, p. 35.
254 *Ibíd.*, pp. 35-36.
255 *Ibíd.*, p. 42.
256 Nessler, G. *op. cit.*, p. 36.
257 *Ibíd.*, p. 35.
258 Eller, A. *op. cit.*, p. 45

259 Mabel López, *En Haití se conmemora el día la Altagracia tanto como en República Domi- nicana*, Diario Libre, January 2019.
https://www.diariolibre.com/revista/en-haiti-se-conmemo- ra-el-dia-la-altagracia-tanto-como-en-republica-dominicana-GB11892127
260 Eller, A. *op. cit.*, p. 45.
261 Nessler, G. *op. cit.*, p. 52.
262 Moya, F. *op. cit.*, p., 168.
263 *Ibíd.*, p. 167.
264 Nessler, G. *op. cit.*, p. 37
265 The Louverture Project ed.
http://thelouvertureproject.org/index.php?title=Philibert_ Fran%C3%A7ois_Rouxel_de_ Blanchelande
266 *Íd.*
267 Nessler, G. *op. cit.*, p. 41.
268 *Ibíd.*, p. 52.
269 *Ibíd.*, p. 24.
270 *Ibíd.*, p. 42.
271 *Ibíd.*, p. 53.
272 *Ibíd.*, p. 75.
273 *Ibíd.*, p. 41.
274 *Ibíd.*, p. 19.
275 Girard, P. *op. cit.*, p. 45.
276 Nessler, G. *op. cit.*, p. 50.
277 *Ibíd.*, p. 48.
278 *Ibíd.*, p. 42.
279 *Ibíd.*, p. 46.
280 *Ibíd.*, p. 52.
281 Nessler, G. *op. cit.*, p.56.
282 Moya, F. *op. cit.*, p. 177. y Nessler, G. *op. cit.*, p.56.
283 Nessler, G. *op. cit.*, p. 47.
284 Nessler, G. *op. cit.*, p. 57.
285 *Ibíd.*, p. 2.
286 Inoa O. *op. cit.* p. 286.
287 Nessler, G. *op. cit.*, p. 5.
288 *Ibíd.*, p. 67.
289 *Ibíd., p. 90.*
290 *Ibíd.*, p. 64.
291 *Ibíd.*, p. 72.
292 Moya, F. *op. cit.*, p. 179.
293 Nessler, G. *op. cit.*, p. 66.
294 *Ibíd.*, p. 73.
295 Girard, P. *op. cit.*, p. p 47.
296 Nessler, G. *op. cit.*, p. 78.
297 *Ibíd.*, p. 79.
298 *Ibíd.*, p. 123.
299 *Ibíd.*, p. 124.
300 Moya, F. *op. cit.*, p. 183.
301 *Ibíd.*, p. 128.
302 Nessler, G. *op. cit.*, pp. 73-74.
303 *Ibíd.*, p. 128.
304 *Ibíd.*, p. 76.
305 *Ibíd.*, p. 93.
306 *Ibíd.*, pp. 92-93.

307 *Ibíd.,* p.60.
308 *Ibíd.,* p.96.
309 Moya, F. *op. cit.,* p. 184.
310 *Ibíd.,* pp. 91-92.
311 Nessler, G. *op. cit.,* p. 91.
312 Moya, F. *op. cit.,* p. 186.
313 Nessler, G. *op. cit.,* p. 94.
314 *Ibíd.,* p.95.
315 Moya, F. *op. cit.,* p. 170.
316 Nathan D. Jensen, *General Donatien-Marie-Joseph de Vimeur Rochambeau,* French Empire, August 2016. https://www.frenchempire.net/biographies/rochambeau/
317 Moya, F. *op. cit.,* p. 171.
318 *Íd.*
319 C.L.R. James, *Black Jacobins: Toussaint Louverture and the Santo Domingo Revolution.* Nueva York, Random House Inc., 1963, p. 181.
320 Moya, F. *op. cit.,* p. 171.
321 Nessler, G. *op. cit.,* p. 101.
322 Moya, F. *op. cit.,* p. 183.
323 *Ibíd.,* p. 185.
324 *Ibíd.,* p. 188.
325 Nessler, G. *op. cit.,* p. 107.
326 Moya, F. *op. cit.,* p. 188.
327 Nessler, G. *op. cit.,* pp. 105-106.
328 Moya, F. *op. cit.,* p. 190.
329 Nessler, G. *op. cit.,* p. 108.
330 Nessler, G. *op. cit.,* pp. 102-103.
331 *Ibíd.,* pp. 104-105.
332 *Ibíd.,* p.83.
333 *Ibíd.,* p.19.
334 *Ibíd., p.102.*
335 Girard, P. *op. cit.,* p. 46.
336 Nessler, G. *op. cit.,* p. 99.
337 *Íd.*
338 *Ibíd.,* p. 109.
339 Moya, F. *op. cit.,* p. 192.
340 *Íd.*
341 Nessler, G. *op. cit.,* p. 130.
342 *Íd.*
343 *Ibíd.,* p. 110.
344 Moya, F. *op. cit.,* p. 193.
345 Nessler, G. *op. cit.,* p. 120.
346 Nessler, G. *op. cit.,* p. 114.
347 Inoa O. *op. cit.* p. 252.
348 Moya, F. *op. cit.,* p. 193.
349 Nessler, G. *op. cit.,* p. 122.
350 Moya, F. *op. cit.,* p. 194.
351 *Íd.*
352 *Ibíd.,* p. 195.
353 Nessler, G. *op. cit.,* p. 116.
354 *Ibíd.,* p. 114.
355 *Ibíd.,* p. 116.
356 *Ibíd.,* p. 127.
357 Inoa O. *op. cit.* p. 250.

358 Moya, F. *op. cit.*, p. 195.
359 *Ibíd.*, p.*98*
360 Nessler, G. *op. cit.*, p.102.
361 Girard, P. *op. cit.*, p. 49.
362 Nessler, G. *op. cit.*, p. 111.
363 *Ibíd.*, p. 133.
364 *Íd.*
365 Moya, F. *op. cit.*, p. 195.
366 Inoa O. *op. cit.* p. 254.
367 Nessler, G. *op. cit.*, p. 134.
368 Moya, F. *op. cit.*, p. 174.
369 Nessler, G. *op. cit.*, p. 145.
370 *Íd.*
371 Moya, F. *op. cit.*, p. 198.
372 Nessler, G. *op. cit.*, p. 145.
373 History.com ed., *The French in New Orleans*, May 2017. https://www.history.com/topics/ immigration/the-french-in-new-orleans
374 History.com ed., https://www.history.com/this-day-in-history/the-french-surrender-orleans-to-the-u-s
375 Girard, P. *op. cit.*, pp. 6 y 64.
376 Becky Little, *Why Bibles Given to Slaves Omitted Most of the Old Testament*, History.com, December 2018. https://www.history.com/news/slave-bible-redacted-old-testament
377 Moya, F. *op. cit.*, p. 196.
378 *Ibíd.*, 198.
379 Nessler, G. *op. cit.*, p. 142.
380 Moya, F. *op. cit.*, p. 198.
381 *Ibíd.*, p. 203.
382 Nessler, G. *op. cit.*, p. 138.
383 Moya, F. *op. cit.*, p. 195.
384 Nessler, G. *op. cit.*, p. 149.
385 *Ibíd.*, p. 154.
386 *Ibíd.*, p. 159.
387 *Ibíd.*, p. 154.
388 *Íd.*
389 Moya, F. *op. cit.*, p. 205.
390 Nessler, G. *op. cit.*, p. 155.
391 *Ibíd.*, p. 158.
392 *Íd.*
393 *Ibíd.*, p. 161.
394 *Íd.*
395 *Ibíd.*, p. 159.
396 Moya, F. *op. cit.*, p. 201.
397 *Ibíd.*, p. 202.
398 *Ibíd.*, p. 203.
399 Johnhenry Gonzalez, *Dessalines' 1805 Invasion of the East*. http://islandluminous.fiu.edu/ part03-slide08.html
400 Girard, P. *op. cit.*, p. 65.
401 Moya, F. *op. cit.*, p. 203.
402 *Ibíd.*, p. 196.
403 Silié, Rubén. *Esclavitud y Prejuicio De Color En Santo Domingo*. Boletín De Antropología Americana, no. 20, 1989, pp. 163–170., p. 165.
404 Moya, F. *op. cit.*, p. 197.
405 *Íd.*

406 Nessler, G. *op. cit.*, p. 151.
407 *Ibíd.*, pp. 151-152.
408 Nessler, G. *op. cit.*, p. 185.
409 Moya, F. *op. cit.,* p. 204.
410 *Ibíd.*, p. 205.
411 Nessler, G. *op. cit.*, p. 186.
412 Luis Alfonso Escolano Giménez, *La guerra de la Reconquista en Santo Domingo (1808-1809): una lucha por la continuidad histórica*. Boletín del Archivo General de la Nación Año LXXI, Vol. XXXIV, Núm. 125, p.635. http://www.centotredicesimo.org/wp-content/ uploads/2015/11/Guerra-de-la-reconquista-en-Santo-Domingo-1808-1809-libre.pdf
413 Francisco Berroa Ubiera, *Historia Dominicana; La España Boba*, February 2007. http://historiadoresdominicanos.blogspot.com/2007/02/historia-dominicana-la-espaa-boba.html
414 Nessler, G. *op. cit.*, p. 188.
415 *Ibíd.*, p. 188.
416 Inoa O. *op. cit.* p. 261.
417 Moya, F. *op. cit.,* pp. 205-206.
418 *Ibíd.*, p. 208.
419 *Íd.*
420 Nessler, G. *op. cit.*, pp. 188-189.
421 *Ibíd.*, p. 188.
422 Moya, F. *op. cit.,* p. 211.
423 Eller, A. *op. cit.*, p. 63.
424 Francisco Berroa Ubiera, *op. cit.*
425 Altagracia Castillo, *Batalla de Palo Hincado, cuando los criollos vencieron a los franceses,* El Día, November 2013. https://eldia.com.do/batalla-de-palo-hincado-cuando-los-criollos-vencieron-los-franceses/
426 Provincias Dominicanas ed., La Junta De Bondillo, June 2016. http://www.provincias- dominicanas.org/la-junta-de-bondillo/
427 Inoa O. *op. cit.* p. 264.
428 Johnny Guerrero, *De héroes y traidores*, El Día, February de 2018. https://eldia.com.do/de-heroes-y-traidores/
429 *Juan Sánchez Ramírez, héroe de la batalla de Palo Hincado declarado paladín de la Reconquista*. March 19, 2005. https://hoy.com.do/juan-sanchez-ramirez-heroe-de-la-batalla-de-palo-hincado-declarado-paladin-de-la-reconquista-2/
430 Francisco Berroa Ubiera, *op. cit.*
431 Johnny Guerrero, *op. cit.*
432 Moya Pons, F. *Santo Domingo y la guerra contra Napoleón en España*. April 2012. http://www.revista.raha.es/moyapons2.html
433 Natalí Faxas, *El panteón de la patria, descanso de héroes.* El Caribe, November 2012. https://www.elcaribe.com.do/2012/11/17/sin-categoria/panteon-patria-descanso-herores/
434 Francisco Berroa Ubiera, *op. cit.*
435 Moya, F. *Manual de Historia Dominicana.* Santiago, República Dominicana, UCMM, 1980, 5a ed., p. 217.
436 *Ibíd.*, p. 216
437 https://www.britannica.com/biography/Henry-Christophe
438 https://www.britannica.com/biography/Jean-Pierre-Boyer
439 Moya, F. *op. cit.*, p. 217.
440 Moya, F. *op. cit.*, p. 219.
441 Moya, F. *op. cit.*, p. 220.
442 *Ibíd.*, p. 221.

443 *Ibíd.*, p. 220.
444 Hector Tineo, *Llega a Samaná el nuevo gobernador español Pascual Real*. La Vanguardia del Pueblo. https://vanguardiadelpueblo.do/1821/05/14/llega-samana-el-nuevo-gobernador-espanol-pascual-real/
445 Moya, F. *op. cit.*, p. 220.
446 Ibíd., p. 222.
447 Américo Moreta Castillo. *José Núñez de Cáceres Albor*.
http://dbe.rah.es/biografias/43151/jose-nunez-de-caceres-albor
448 Inoa O. *op. cit.*, p. 268.
449 *Íd.*
450 *Ibíd.*, p. 270.
451 Moya, F. *op. cit.*, p. 222.
452 *Íd.*
453 *Ibíd.*, p. 223.
454 *Ibíd.*, p. 226.
455 Eller, A. *We Dream Together*. Durham NC, Duke University Press, 2016, p. 23.
456 *Íd.*
457 Girard, P. Haiti. New York, Palgrave Macmillan, 2005, p. 69
458 Eller, A. *op. cit.*, pp. 39-40.
459 *Ibíd.*, p. 40.
460 Eller, A. *op. cit.*, p. 39.
461 Inoa, O. *op. cit.*, p. 273
462 Moya, F. *op. cit.*, p. 227.
463 *Ibíd.*, p. 247.
464 Inoa, O. *op. cit.*, pp. 277-278.
465 Eller, A. *op. cit.*, p. 42.
466 Moya, F. *op. cit.*, p. 236.
467 Diario Libre ed. *Demografía dominicana (1795-1844)*, March 2010.
https://www.diariolibre.com/opinion/lecturas/demografa-dominicana-1795-1844-NJDL236812
468 Redacción BBC News Mundo, *La multimillonaria multa...*, *op. cit.*
469 Moya, F. *op. cit.*, p. 239.
470 Redacción BBC News Mundo, *La multimillonaria multa...*, *op. cit.*
471 Moya, F. *op. cit.*, p. 243.
472 *Ibíd.*, p. 244.
473 *Íd.*
474 *Ibíd.*, p. 258.
475 Eller, A. *op. cit.*, p. 24.
476 Moya, F. *op. cit.*, p. 258.
477 Pedro Troncoso Sánchez, *Episodios duartianos*, Colección Duartiana, Vol II, Santo Domingo, 2010, p. 44. https://web.archive.org/web/20110206093111/http://institutoduartiano.org.do/PDFs/episodios_duartianos.pdf
478 Rafael Chaljub Mejía, *El destino final de los trinitarios,* El Día, March 2014. https://eldia.com.do/el-destino-final-de-los-trinitarios/
479 Moya, F. *op. cit.*, p. 260.
480 *Ibíd.*, p. 264.
481 *Íd.*
482 *Ibíd.*, p. 266.
483 Eller, A. *op. cit.*, p. 25.
484 Moya, F. *op. cit.*, p. 268.
485 Héctor Tineo, *Nace Gaspar Hernández*. La Vanguardia del Pueblo. https://vanguardiadelpueblo.do/1798/01/nace-gaspar-hernandez/ hernandez/
486 Moya, F. *op. cit.*, p. 270.

487 Eller, A. *op. cit.*, p. 26.
488 *Íd.*
489 Moya, F. *op. cit.*, p. 270.
490 *Ibíd.*, p. 272.
491 *Ibíd.*, p. 273.
492 *Ibíd.*, p. 274.
493 Inoa, O. *op. cit.*, p. 312.
494 *Íd.*
495 Moya, F. *op. cit.*, p. 276.
496 Ibíd., p. 277.
497 Ramón Lugo Lovatón, *El Carácter de Pedro Santana*, 1953. https://web.archive.org/web/20160304064848/http://bagn.academiahistoria.org.do/boletines/boletin78/ BAGN_1953_No_78-02.pdf
498 Inoa, O. *op. cit.*, p. 316.
499 https://www.ejercito.mil.do/reglamento-de-uniformes-insignias-y-condecoracion-ejercito-de-republica-dominicana/57-historia
500 Eller, A. *op. cit.*, p. 27.
501 Moya, F. *op. cit.*, p. 282.
502 Inoa, O. *op. cit.*, p. 316.
503 Eller, A. *op. cit.*, p. *27*.
504 Moya, F. *op. cit.*, p. 279.
505 *Ibíd.*, p. 280.
506 Inoa, O. *op. cit.*, p. 366.
507 Moya, F. *op. cit.*, p. 283.
508 *Ibíd.*, p. 282.
509 *Ibíd.*, p. 285.
510 *Ibíd.*, p. 295.
511 *Ibíd.*, p. 285.
512 *Ibíd.*, p. 289.
513 *Ibíd.*, p. 291.
514 Cordeiro, Jose Luis, 2008. *Constitutions around the world: A View from Latin America*. IDE Discussion, Institute of Developing Economies, Japan External Trade Organization (JETRO). https://ideas.repec.org/p/jet/dpaper/dpaper164.html
515 Moya, F. *op. cit.*, p. 293.
516 *Ibíd.*, p. 297.
517 El Día ed. *Hace 174 años se aprobó en San Cristóbal la primera Constitución de República Dominicana*. November 2018. https://eldia.com.do/hace-174-anos-se-aprobo-en-san-cristo-bal-la-primera-constitucion-de-republica-dominicana/
518 *History and Debate of Flag Burning.* https://web.archive.org/web/20140730065632/ http://www.debate.org/flag-burning/
519 Elizahenna, *25 de febrero: Día del Natalicio de Ramón Matías Mella*. Plan Lea, Listín Diario. February 2019. https://planlea.listindiario.com/etiqueta/patria/
520 Moya, F. *op. cit.*, p. 295
521 Eller, A. *op. cit.*, p. *27*.
522 *Ibíd.*, p. 28.
523 *Íd.*
524 *Íd.*
525 Eller, A. *op. cit.*, pp.27-28.
526 *Ibíd.*, p. 34.
527 Darío Tejada, *La pasión danzaría*. Academia de Ciencias de la República Dominicana, Santo Domingo 2000. En: Universitat de València. https://www.uv.es/angomez/Historia%20del%20Merengue.htm

528 Eller, A. *op. cit.*, p.30.
529 Moya, F. *op. cit.*, p. 300.
530 Eller, A. *op. cit.*, p.235.
531 *Ibíd.*, p. 29.
532 *Íd.*
533 *Íd.*
534 *Íd.*
535 En Caribe ed., *José Joaquín Puello.* http://www.encaribe.org/es/article/jose-joaquin-puello/1553
536 Moya, F. *op. cit.*, p. 304.
537 Inoa, O. *op. cit.*, p. 336.
538 Moya, F. *op. cit.*, p. 305.
539 Eller, A. *op. cit.*, p. 50.
540 Moya, F. *op. cit.*, p. 307.
541 José Ángel Aquino, *El Derecho al Sufragio*, Acento, May 2016. https://acento.com.do/2016/especiales/8349126-derecho-al-sufragio-2/
542 Descorides De La Rosa, *Mujeres y elecciones: 70 años votando y ninguna mujer ha sido presidenta*. Hoy Digital, mayo de 2012. http://hoy.com.do/mujeres-yelecciones-70-anos-vo-tando-y-ninguna-mujer-ha-sido-presidenta/
543 Moya, F. *op. cit.*, p. 311.
544 *Ibíd.*, p. 312.
545 *Ibíd.*, p. 315.
546 *Ibíd.*, p. 316.
547 Bernardo Vega, *La niña mala*. Acento, January 2018. https://acento.com.do/2018/opinion/8532048-la-nina-mala/
548 Inoa, O. *op. cit.*, p. 345.
549 Moya, F. *op. cit.*, p. 319
550 Moya, F. *op. cit.*, p. 316.
551 *Ibíd.*, p. 317.
552 Inoa, O. *op. cit.*, p. 343.
553 Moya, F. *op. cit.*, p. 319.
554 *Ibíd.*, p. 320.
555 Inoa, O. *op. cit.*, p. 421, y Moya, F. *op. cit.*, p. 325.
556 Inoa, O. *op. cit.*, p. 349.
557 Moya, F. *op. cit.*, p. 327.
558 *Ibíd.*, p. 328.
559 Eller, A. *op. cit.*, p. 230.
560 Moya, F. *op. cit.*, p. 329.
561 *Ibíd.*, p. 330.
562 *Ibíd.*, p. 333.
563 *Íd.*
564 Inoa, O. *op. cit.*, p. 350.
565 Eller, A. *op. cit.*, p. 56.
566 *Íd.*
567 Inoa, O. *op. cit.*, p. 350.
568 Mary Bellis, *A Brief History of Writing*, ThougthCo., September 2018. https://www. thoughtco.com/brief-history-of-writing-4072560
569 Eller, A. *op. cit.*, pp. 67-68.
570 *Ibíd.*, p. 89.
571 *Ibíd.*, p. 90.
572 *Íd.*
573 *Ibíd.*, p. 41.
574 Inoa, O. *op. cit.*, p. 340.

575 Eller, A. *op. cit.*, p. 65.
576 *Íd.*
577 *Ibíd.*, p. 64.
578 *Ibíd.*, pp. 68-69.
579 *Ibíd.*, p. 69.
580 *Ibíd.*, p. 70.
581 *Ibíd.*, p. 72.
582 *Ibíd.*, p. 81.
583 *Ibíd.*, pp. 112.
584 Moya, F. *op. cit.*, p. 334.
585 *Ibíd.*, pp. 339.
586 Inoa, O. *op. cit.*, p. 353.
587 Eller, A. *op. cit.*, p. 93.
588 Moya, F. *op. cit.*, p. 334 y Eller, A. *op. cit.*, p. 55.
589 Moya, F. *op. cit.*, pp. 341-342.
590 Inoa, O. *op. cit.*, p. 355
591 Eller, A. *op. cit.*, p. 78.
592 Inoa, O. *op. cit.*, p. 356.
593 Eller, A. *op. cit.*, p. 73.
594 *Ibíd.*, p. 67.
595 *Ibíd.*, p. 209.
596 Moya, F. *op. cit.*, p. 339.
597 *Íd.*
598 *Ibíd.*, p. 342.
599 Eller, A. *op. cit.*, p. 84.
600 Moya, F. *op. cit.*, p. 343.
601 Eller, A. *op. cit.*, pp. 81-82.
602 *Ibíd.*, p. 74
603 *Ibíd.*, p. 82.
604 Moya, F. op. cit., p. 345.
605 Eller, A. op. cit., p. 118.
606 *Ibíd.*, p.119.
607 *Ibíd.*, p. 94.
608 *Ibíd.*, p. 97.
609 *Íd.*
610 *Ibíd.*, p. 87.
611 *Ibíd.*, p. 94.
612 *Ibíd.*, p. 88.
613 *Ibíd.*, p. 98.
614 *Ibíd.*, p. 98.
615 *Ibíd.*, p. 222.
616 *Ibíd.*, p. 140.
617 *Ibíd.*, p. 100.
618 *Ibíd.*, p. 140.
619 *Ibíd.*, p. 148
620 *Ibíd.*, p. 107.
621 Moya, F. *op. cit.*, p. 345.
622 Eller, A. *op. cit.*, p. 88.
623 *Ibíd.*, p. 115.
624 *Ibíd.*, p. 151.
625 *Ibíd.*, p. 152.
626 *Íd.*
627 *Ibíd.*, p. 88.

628 *Ibíd.*, p. 100.
629 *Ibíd.*, pp. 139-140.
630 *Ibíd.*, p. 146.
631 *Ibíd.*, p. 161.
632 *Ibíd.*, p. 161.
633 *Íd.*
634 *Ibíd.*, p. 85.
635 *Íd.*
636 *Ibíd.*, p. 92.
637 *Ibíd.*, p. 113
638 *Ibíd.*, p. 114.
639 *Íd.*
640 *Íd.*
641 *Ibíd.*, p. 107.
642 *Ibíd.*, p. 106.
643 *Ibíd.*, p. 107.
644 *Ibíd.*, pp. 106-107.
645 Thomas Craughwell, *Deport Blacks to Santo Domingo* en: *Top 10 Mistakes by U.S. Presidents*, January 2009 http://blogs.britannica.com/2009/01/9-deport-blacks-to-santo-domingo-the-10-worst-decisions-by-us-presidents/ and Inoa, O. *op. cit.*, p. 427.
646 Inoa, O. *op. cit.*, p. 389.
647 https://www.diariolibre.com/opinion/lecturas/demografa-dominicana-1795-1844-NJDL236812
648 Viviano de León, *Iglesia Católica en el país cuenta con 600 sacerdotes*. Listín Diario, March 2008. https://listindiario.com/la-republica/2008/3/18/52177/Iglesia-Catolica-en-el%20pais-cuenta-con-600-sacerdotes
649 Manuel Alcántara Sáez, *La religión en la política*. El País, Abril 2018. https://elpais.com/ elpais/2018/04/03/opinion/1522768168_990629.html
650 Eller, A. *op. cit.*, p. 101.
651 Moya, F. *op. cit.*, p. 347.
652 Eller, A. *op. cit.*, p. 102.
653 Moya, F. *op. cit.*, p. 348.
654 Eller, A. *op. cit.*, p. 102.
655 *Ibíd.*, p. 103.
656 *Ibíd.*, p. 95.
657 *Ibíd.*, p. 154.
658 Inoa, O. *op. cit.*, p. 382.
659 Eller, A. *op. cit.*, p. 109.
660 Lawler, Andrew and Adler, Jerry. *How the Chickens conquer the world*. Smithsonian Magazine, 2012. https://www.smithsonianmag.com/history/how-the-chicken-conquered-the-world-87583657/
661 Eller, A. op. cit., p. 109.
662 *Ibíd.*, p. 135.
663 *Ibíd.*, p. 134.
664 *Ibíd.*, p. 104.
665 Esteban Delgado. *Dominicanos gastan RD$3.6 MM cada hora en juegos de azar*. El Dinero, June 2015. https://www.eldinero.com.do/13215/dominicanos-gastan-rd3-6-millones-ca-da-hora-en-juegos-de-azar/
666 Hoy, ed. *Maestros de centros de excelencia ganan hasta 68 mil pesos mensual con incentivos*, March 2017. https://hoy.com.do/maestros-de-centros-de-excelencia-ganan-hasta-68-mil-pesos-mensual-con-incentivos/

MINERD. *Situación del Personal Docente de la República Dominicana 2017* http://www.ministeriodeeducacion.gob.do/transparencia/media/presupuesto/evolucion-contratacion-de-recursos-humanos/sueldos-docentes-en-el-marco-del-presupuesto-2017pdf.pdf
667 Eller, A. op. cit., p. 134.
668 *Ibíd.,* pp. 134-135.
669 *Ibíd.,* p. 94.
670 *Ibíd.,* p. 129.
671 Inoa, O. *op. cit.,* p. 386.
672 Eller, A. *op. cit.,* p. 183.
673 *Boletín Oficial del Estado,* España, February 4 2011. https://www.boe.es/boe/dias/2011/02/04/pdfs/BOE-A-2011-2137.pdf
674 América Economía, ed. *Mario Vargas Llosa y su título de marqués: "nací plebeyo y voy a morir plebeyo",* February 2011. https://www.americaeconomia.com/politica-sociedad/politica/mario-vargas-llosa-y-su-titulo-de-marques-naci plebeyo-y-voy-morir-plebey
675 Eller, A. *op. cit.,* p. 150.
676 *Ibíd.,* p. 210.
677 *Ibíd.,* p. 211.
678 *Íd.*
679 *Ibíd.,* pp. 211-212.
680 *Ibíd.,* p. 57.
681 Moya, F. op. cit., p. 395.
682 Emilia Pereyra, *El trágico final de Duvergé, valiente batallador contra huestes haitianas.* Diario Libre, Abril 2019. https://www.diariolibre.com/revista/cultura/el-tragico-final-de-duverge-valiente-batallador-contra-huestes-haitianas-LF12538333-
683 Moya, F. *op. cit.,* p. 343.
684 Inoa, O. *op. cit.,* p. 379.
685 *Íd.*
686 Moya, F. *op. cit.,* p. 342.
687 Eller, A. *op. cit.,* p. 57 y Inoa, O. *op. cit.,* p. 381.
688 Eller, A. *op. cit.,* p. 117.
689 *Ibíd.,* p. 120.
690 *Íd.*
691 *Ibíd.,* p. 117.
692 *Ibíd.,* p. 187.
693 *Ibíd.,* p. 96.
694 Inoa, O. *op. cit.,* p. 385.
695 Eller, A. *op. cit.,* p. 123.
696 *Ibíd.,* p. 128.
697 Moya, F. *op. cit.,* p. 344.
698 Eller, A. *op. cit.,* p. 124.
699 *Ibíd.,* p. 129.
700 *Ibíd.,* p. 119.
701 *Íd.*
702 *Ibíd.,* p. 120.
703 *Íd.*
704 *Íd.*
705 Moya, F. *op. cit.,* p. 351.
706 Eller, A. *op. cit.,* p. 122.
707 *Ibíd.,* p. 180.
708 *Ibíd.,* p. 195.
709 *Ibíd.,* p. 196.

710 *Íd.*
711 *Ibíd.*, p. 199.
712 *Ibíd.*, p. 201
713 El Nacional ed., *Nace Ulises Francisco Espaillat, político y presidente de la República*, February 2019.
https://elnacional.com.do/nace-ulises-francisco-espaillat-politico-y-presidente-de-la-republica/
714 Eller, A. *op. cit.*, p. 201.
715 *Ibíd.*, p. 126.
716 *Ibíd.*, p. 127.
717 *Ibíd.*, p. 126.
718 *Íd.*
719 *Ibíd.*, p. 127.
720 *Ibíd.*, p. 144.
721 *Ibíd.*, pp. 144-145.
722 Moya, F. op. cit., p. 354.
723 *Ibíd.*, p. 350.
724 Eller, A. op. cit., p. 145.
725 Diario Digital RD. ed. *Santiago Rodríguez: El patriota ignorado*, January 2006.
https://diariodigital.com.do/2006/01/29/santiago-rodriguez-el-patriota-ignorado.html
726 Inoa, O. *op. cit.*, p. 391.
727 Moya, F. *op. cit.*, p. 351.
728 Inoa, O. *op. cit.*, p. 391.
729 *Ibíd.*, p. 393.
730 *Íd.*
731 Eller, A. *op. cit.*, p. 155.
732 Moya, F. *op. cit.*, p. 351.
733 Inoa, O. *op. cit.*, p. 393.
734 Hoy Digital ed. *El árbol de Sabaneta*, July 2006. http://hoy.com.do/carretera-xel-ar- bol-de-sabaneta/
735 Eller, A. *op. cit.*, p. 191.
736 *Íd.*
737 *Ibíd.*, p. 145
738 *Íd.*
739 Moya, F. *op. cit.*, p. 351.
740 Moya, F. *op. cit.*, p. 352.
741 *Íd.*
742 Eller, A. *op. cit.*, p. 165.
743 *Ibíd.*, p. 167.
744 *Ibíd.*, p. 169.
745 *Ibíd.*, p. 171.
746 *Ibíd.*, pp. 157-158.
747 *Ibíd.*, p. 158.
748 *Ibíd.*, p. 188.
749 *Ibíd.*, p. 189.
750 *Ibíd.*, p. 147.
751 *Ibíd.*, pp.147-148.
752 *Ibíd.*, p. 224.
753 Moya, F. *op. cit.*, p. 352.
754 Eller, A. *op. cit.*, p. 186.
755 History.com ed., *Lincoln issues Emancipation Proclamation 1862*. November 2009.
https://www.history.com/this-day-in-history/lincoln-issues-emancipation-proclamation

756 Alaina E. Roberts, *How Native Americans adopted slavery from white settlers.* Aljazeera, December 2018.
https://www.aljazeera.com/indepth/opinion/native-americans-adopted-slavery-white-settlers-181225180750948.html
757 Eller, A. *op. cit.*, p. 180.
758 *Íd.*
759 *Íd.*
760 *Ibíd.*, p. 197.
761 *Ibíd.*, p. 196.
762 *Ibíd.*, p. 155.
763 *Ibíd.*, p. 197.
764 *Ibíd.*, p. 198.
765 *Ibíd.*, p. 199.
766 *Ibíd.*, p. 197.
767 *Ibíd.*, p. 157.
768 *Ibíd.*, pp. 156-157.
769 *Ibíd.*, p.164.
770 *Ibíd.*, p. 171.
771 *Ibíd.*, p. 172.
772 *Íd.*
773 *Ibíd.*, p. 173.
774 *Ibíd.*, p. 220.
775 *Ibíd.*, p. 213.
776 Moya, F. *op. cit.*, p. 353.
777 *Ibíd.*, p. 354.
778 Eller, A. *op. cit.*, p. 178.
779 *Ibíd.*, p. 174.
780 *Ibíd.*, p. 176.
781 *Ibíd.*, p. 179.
782 Inoa, O. *op. cit.*, pp. 395-396.
783 Eller, A. *op. cit.*, p. 182.
784 Rodríguez Demorizi, *Santana y los poetas de su tiempo.* Santo Domingo, Editora del Caribe, Academia Dominicana de la Historia, Vol. XXV, 1969, p. 341.

> Epitafio de Santana
> Aqui yace un pollino
> Despótico cual ninguno
> Que no entendió su destino
> Y murió como un cochino
> No habiendo hecho bien alguno.

785 Eller, A. *op. cit.*, p. 177.
786 *Ibíd.*, p. 220.
787 Inoa, O. *op. cit.*, p. 401.
788 Eller, A. *op. cit.*, p. 179.
789 *Ibíd.*, pp. 183-184.
790 *Ibíd.*, p. 192.
791 *Íd.*
792 EducanDo ed., *José Antonio Salcedo.* https://www.educando.edu.do/articulos/estudiante/jose-antonio-salcedo/
793 La Vanguardia del Pueblo ed., *Matan a balazos al dictador Ulises Lilís Heureaux.* https://vanguardiadelpueblo.do/1899/07/26/matan-balazos-al-dictador-ulises-lilis-heureaux/

794 Hoy Digital ed., *Trágicos finales de tres gobernantes.* May 2009. http://hoy.com.do/tragicos-finales-de-tres-gobernantes/
795 Eller, A. *op. cit.*, p. 193.
796 *Ibíd.*, p. 189.
797 *Ibíd.*, p. 191.
798 *Ibíd.*, p. 193.
799 *Íd.*
800 Javier Bañuelos, *1,5 millones de niños mueren cada año por no estar vacunados.* Cadena Ser, August 2015. https://cadenaser.com/ser/2015/08/18/sociedad/1439902805_519732.html
801 Eller, A. *op. cit.*, p. 200.
802 *Ibíd.*, p. 201.
803 *Ibíd.*, pp. 202-203.
804 *Ibíd.*, p. 203.
805 *Ibíd.*, p. 229.
806 *Íd.*
807 *Ibíd.*, p. 233.
808 *Ibíd.*, p. 203.
809 *Ibíd.*, p. 204.
810 *Ibíd.*, p. 235.
811 *Ibíd.*, p. 236.
812 *Ibíd.*, p. 205.
813 *Ibíd.*, p. 181.
814 Inoa, O. *op. cit.*, p. 402.
815 Eller, A. *op. cit.*, p. 204.
816 Inoa, O. *op. cit.*, p. 404.
817 Eller, A. *op. cit.*, p. 222.
818 *Ibíd.*, pp. 225-226.
819 *Ibíd.*, p. 218.
820 *Ibíd.*, p. 231.
821 Inoa, O. *op. cit.*, p. 423.
822 Eller, A. *op. cit.*, p. 231.
823 *Ibíd.*, p. 235.
824 *Ibíd.*, p. 233.
825 *Íd.*
826 Inoa, O. *op. cit.*, p. 420.
827 Alberto Caminero, *Solo siete fueron electos a presidencia RD en último 80 años.* El Nacional, December 2010. https://elnacional.com.do/solo-siete-fueron-electos-a-presidencia-rd-en-ultimo-80-anos/
828 Oficina Nacional de Estadística, *La población con estudios universitarios en República Dominicana asciende a 1,600,000 personas.* April 2015. https://www.one.gob.do/noticias/2016/04/14/1469/la-poblacion-con-estudios-universitarios-en-republica-dominicana-asciende-a-1,600,000-personas

CPSIA information can be obtained
at www.ICGtesting.com
Printed in the USA
FSHW011749071221
86684FS